DEMOCRATIC SPORTS

SPORT, CULTURE & SOCIETY

DAVID K. WIGGINS, SERIES EDITOR

DEMOCRATIC SPORTS

★ ★ ★ ★ ★ ★

Men's and Women's College Athletics during the Great Depression

BRAD AUSTIN

The University of Arkansas Press
Fayetteville
2015

Manufactured in the United States of America
978-1-55728-758-8 (paper)
978-1-61075-563-4 (e-book)

19 18 17 16 15 5 4 3 2 1

Designed by Liz Lester

♾ The paper used in this publication meets the minimum requirements of the American National Standard for Permanence of Paper for Printed Library Materials Z39.48-1984.

LIBRARY OF CONGRESS CONTROL NUMBER: 2014958341

Parts of chapters two and three originally appeared in the *Journal of Sport History*, and sections of chapters two and four originally appeared in the *Journal of East Tennessee History*. We thank the editorial staff of both publications for granting permission to use the material.

To LaGina, Stella, and Phoebe

CONTENTS

ACKNOWLEDGMENTS

I have accrued many debts over the last decade as I have worked on this project, and while I have tried to express my gratitude to folks over the years, I am very happy now to have the opportunity to acknowledge their contributions more formally. First, I would like to thank my mother and father, Julia and Bill Austin, for always emphasizing the importance of education, for helping me develop a love of learning, and for always supporting me as I've migrated from school to school and from Tennessee to Arkansas, Scotland, Tennessee (again), Ohio, and Massachusetts. I also thank my siblings, Andy and Shelly, for their constant encouragement and support. Additionally, I want to say how much I appreciate the genuine understanding that my in-laws, the Swetnams, have provided as their daughter and I moved far away from them and as I remained, essentially, unemployed throughout the first decade of my tenure as their son-in-law.

I have been fortunate to work with and learn from numerous outstanding scholars and teachers, and I would like to thank them for providing exemplary role models for young students. In particular, I want to recognize the role that Jane Fagg and John Dahlquist played in my intellectual development and in my maturation as a thinker. I'd like to think that neither would be especially surprised that this book saw print, and I am confident that, if they were still living, both would ask rather pointed questions about what took so darn long. Of all of my undergraduate professors, Terrell Tebbetts probably did the most to shape my confidence and style as a writer. I'll leave it up to you, as you read through the rest of this volume, to decide just how much credit he really deserves. Without the help and guidance of these undergraduate professors, I never would have pursued a career in history. Of course, over the years I have sometimes wondered if I *should* thank them for helping me choose this path, but, in the end, I am glad they did.

I am also grateful to my primary advisers at the University of Tennessee, James Cobb, John Finger, and Elizabeth Haiken. They taught me how to be a graduate student, how to read for argument and to write with one, and, especially Cobb, how to push myself to reach whatever potential I possess. I attribute much of my success to the lessons I learned from them.

No one who reads this book will be surprised that it started as a dissertation. I certainly hope that I've improved it in the multiple drafts I've completed since I earned my degree, but the book still seeks to answer the questions I initially asked in graduate school. Simply put, I cannot imagine working with a better dissertation committee than the one I was fortunate enough to assemble. My committee members' talents and areas of expertise overlapped perfectly for this study. More importantly, each member was always willing to talk with me at length about the project. Throughout the process, I never felt like I working alone, and that provided more comfort than they probably understand. K. Austin Kerr was an ideal adviser, someone who always forced me to look at the big picture, who was a penetrating critic of my writing (and whose suggested phrasings still survive in sections of this book), and who was always willing to talk about my progress, often over a lunch he bought. I knew him first as a gentleman and a scholar, and I am now proud to call him my friend.

Mel Adelman served as a co-adviser on the initial project, and sometimes it seemed that his critiques of my chapters were as long as the chapters themselves. They were certainly as thoughtful and better written, and I could not have written this without his wise counsel. Having a true pioneer and leader of the sports history field helping me to ask better questions and look for more complete answers was an absolute blessing.

In seminars and throughout the dissertation-writing process, Susan Hartmann continuously forced me to express my ideas as clearly as possible, to think broadly, and to connect my arguments as tightly as I could. I was constantly impressed by the amount of time she was willing to devote to my project and to my subsequent job search. I remain grateful for her attention to both. Working with her made this a much better project.

I could not have competed this project without the able and eager assistance of university archivists across the country. Although I could never thank all who have helped me, I want to thank, in particular, Bertha Ihnat of Ohio State University, Anne Turkos at the University of Maryland, Ralph Elder of the Center for American History in Austin, and Bill Roberts at the Bancroft Library in Berkeley. Each of these men and women made my research expeditions much easier than I had any right to expect. I would be remiss if I did not devote a little space to thanking my graduate student friends and colleagues who helped keep me sane and on track during my time at the University of Tennessee and Ohio State. I have sincerely appreciated getting to know and learning from Michael Rogers, Stephen Berrey, Jeff Bremer, Matt Masur, Jenn Walton, Mike Fronda, Bill Carraher, Marc Horger, Pam Pennock, Brian Etheridge, Jack Wells, John Tully, Doug Palmer, Mark and Susan Spicka, Greg Wilson, Laura Hilton, and many more. These were the people on whom I tested my ideas and who forced me to rethink and defend my approach innumerable times. For that I am deeply grateful. We also had a whole lot of fun figuring out how to be historians. Good times.

My colleagues at Salem State University deserve special thanks for taking a chance on a relatively young and inexperienced historian and for serving as such exemplary role models. In particular, Dane Morrison, Tad Baker, Donna Seger, and Chris Mauriello mentored me as I developed as a teacher, and they showed me that it is possible to have a productive scholarly life while also caring deeply about students. I have appreciated the generous research support my department and the College of Arts and Sciences have provided me, and I have appreciated even more the moral support that my friends and colleagues provided after I lost this entire manuscript when a thief broke into my car and stole my laptop at a New Hampshire mall in the week before Christmas several years ago. In particular, I've enjoyed griping about setbacks and celebrating successes with Bethany Jay, Michele Louro, Jessica Ziparo, Alex Kyrou, and Jamie Wilson.

No one was more important to the recovery of my manuscript and, consequently, to the publication of this book than one of my undergraduate students, Peter Crowley. Peter was an archetypical Salem State student: a smart fellow who was working his way through school by taking night classes and driving a delivery truck during the day. I got to know him pretty well when he would talk with me after the historiography class we had together. Like many Salem State students, Peter realized that he would not be able to get a career kick-start based on his social capital or family connections, so he asked if

I had any research projects he could help with, just so he would get some relevant experience and because he was genuinely interested in seeing firsthand what historians do. I told him about the stolen computer and told him that I had only a hard copy of the last draft (with my scribbles on every page) and access to a PDF version of my dissertation, a document that was several iterations removed from the then-final draft. Peter agreed to take a shot at recreating my last draft, and, remarkably, he was able to do so. His perseverance and initiative allowed me to move forward much faster than I would have otherwise, and I am thrilled to be able to thank him publicly and officially in print. Thanks, Peter.

Once Peter had worked his magic, I was able to return to the project with renewed enthusiasm and with fresh hopes of getting it ready for publication. My good buddies John Tully and Andrew Darien read the entire manuscript closely and improved it immeasurably with their editorial, stylistic, organizational, and "big picture" suggestions. Outside of the editorial and peer review teams of the University of Arkansas Press, no one has read this more closely and carefully than John and Drew. I'm grateful for their friendship and professionalism, and I want to be clear that if any errors somehow remain in the text, they hold some of the responsibility for them. That's only fair, right?

Sending manuscripts out for peer review can be incredibly nerve-wracking. When this manuscript was under review, I found myself worrying, "What if they don't read it closely?" Of course, I also worried, "What if they read it *too* closely?" In the end, I don't know if I could have hoped for more useful reader reports. The readers obviously spent a lot of time with the manuscript, and their appreciation for my approach and argument gave me great confidence as I completed my final revisions. Just as importantly, their suggestions on how to improve the manuscript were irrefutable. I hope that they'll see how their advice made this a much better book, and I hope they'll forgive me if my prose remains, if only in a few places, "workmanlike."

Larry Malley has been one of the most important champions of sports history scholarship over the past several decades. He has used his editorial eye and influence to nurture numerous landmark works through publication, and I am honored to have him be involved in this project. Having David Wiggins, another giant of the field, involved in this process as the series editor has been tremendously rewarding. I remember the first time I talked with David, when he called me to see if I would write a chapter for a project that became the award-winning *Rivals* (also with the University of Arkansas Press). When he told me about the incredible roster of scholars who was writing for the book, I asked him, "Are you sure you want me involved in this?" I haven't completely gotten over the fact that editors and scholars whom I have respected for years were eager to help bring this project to press, but I sure am grateful that they were. I still owe David Stricklin a beer for making sure that Larry read my proposal, just as I owe Gayle Fischer a couple of drinks for helping make the proposal *worth* reading.

Toward the end of the process, Larry handed the manuscript over to Mike Bieker, who responded to my many, many questions and occasional deadline extension requests with equal parts understanding and humor. I've truly enjoyed working with him and with Tyler Lail-Whitehead throughout the process. They have made an anxiety-ridden process much easier than I ever anticipated. With her careful copyediting and focus on clarity, Karen Johnson made this a much cleaner manuscript.

Finally, I must thank my wife, LaGina, for reminding me daily, through her presence but never her words, that there are much more important things in this world than books and paper. She is my best friend, my most perceptive critic, a trained editor, and the love of my life. I thank her for sharing herself and her talents with me, and I dedicate whatever is good about this project to her and to our two beautiful and rather spirited daughters, Stella and Phoebe.

One more thing: be sure to back up your computer files. You'll thank me if you ever leave a laptop exposed in your backseat at a New Hampshire mall.

INTRODUCTION

In October 1930, the editors of Ohio State University's alumni publication were convinced that the nation's worsening economic problems would not affect their alma mater. They trusted the state legislature to provide for all of the university's needs, and they counted on the support of Ohio's citizens to "give short shrift to any possible cry of 'economy,' 'hard times' and the like."[1] Their optimism was misplaced. Two years later, students were protesting across campus, as budget cuts caused "more far reaching injury than [officials] had feared." Ohio State students objected most vehemently to the restrictions on the school's library. Not only had the cloakroom closed, causing students to leave their books, hats, and jackets lying around on the floor and giving the library the "appearance of an ill-kept warehouse," but the library had cancelled its subscriptions to academic periodicals and cut its hours. The state of the university's finances was so imperiled by 1933 that the university president had to officially declare that the university would, in fact, remain open for the spring term.[2]

If the library was jeopardized, the football team was not. Even though athletic receipts plummeted from almost $420,000 to $129,111 between the academic years 1929–30 and 1932–33, university officials never considered eliminating its most expensive team. For even while faculty layoffs, library restrictions, and declining state funds told one story of Ohio State's fortunes, the football team's continued profitability and increased public profile told another. If the former was a story of crisis and distress, the latter was a story of young men learning how to compete and, supposedly, along the way, teaching others about the virtues of competition. To understand American life and sports during the Great Depression, we need to know both of these stories and how they intersect.[3]

To do this, historians must avoid the easy trap of characterizing the Depression as a uniformly tragic period. Certainly, throughout the 1930s all sorts of catastrophes lurked as possibilities for Americans; but for most, real ruin remained outside their experiences. Even in the worst periods, almost 75 percent of Americans seeking jobs had them, even if many of these workers were underemployed. Ultimately, though threatened, the US economic, social, and political systems did not collapse; instead, their organizers and participants adapted these structures to meet the challenges the decade offered. The same is true for the US sporting system, which, by the 1930s, had college sports as one of its key components.[4]

In his landmark 1971 essay, "American Culture and the Great Depression," Lawrence Levine noted the importance of studying the culture of the 1930s. He wrote, "It is ironic, then, that we still know so little about the culture of a decade that has made such a lasting imprint upon us, and that so much of what we do know is overwhelmingly political and institutional." He continued, pointing out the problems with this approach, writing, "Until relatively recently, we have spoken and written as if the political culture of the 1930s represented all of American culture; as if Franklin Roosevelt and his advisers spoke for the vast majority of Americans; as if one could understand the impact of the Depression upon American consciousness by comprehending the reform impulse of the 1930s." Levine clearly believed that historians should pose new questions, that there was something about studying culture that could shed new light on the period that traditional political and economic history could not. To this end he argued forcefully, "Until we begin to explore more fully than we have the varied cultural dimensions of the Depression decade, we will continue to have more questions than answers."[5] This study follows Levine's suggestion and asks new questions about American culture and society during the 1930s.

Writing after Levine, Warren I. Susman, perhaps the foremost historian of 1930s American culture, argued that Depression-era Americans looked for a common cultural ground where people could unite during the shared crisis. The economic collapse of the Depression was, Susman contended, more of a shock to the middle class than to any other group.[6] Despite this reasonable conclusion, historians have paid a disproportionate amount of attention to the working class and to fringe movements on the political left and right, focusing on those groups that experienced and advocated for the most radical changes.

In his *Culture as History*, Susman echoed Levine and wrote about the 1930s, "The fact remains—and it is a vital one if we are to understand the period and the nature of American culture—that the period, while acknowledging in ways more significantly than ever before the existence of groups outside the dominant ones and even recognizing the radical response as important, is one in which American culture continues to be largely middle-class culture."[7] At the onset of the 1930s, college sports served as an important component of this middle-class culture, and they held a more significant position at its end. The study of US college sports during the Great Depression offers a unique and useful perspective on the institutional, gender, and community dynamics that shook middle-class men and women during the 1930s.

For those who believed in the tandem of progress and prosperity, the Depression-era experience was harrowing and unprecedented. The onset of the Depression introduced tangible fear and uncertainty to the US middle class, and as these Americans tried to insulate themselves from the insecurity attacking their lives and their psyches, they also tried to protect their political and social institutions from attacks. Intercollegiate athletics served as much more than a diversion for the masses. In university administrators' eyes, college sports could help protect and preserve a specific version of the American way of life.

During the 1930s, protectors of intercollegiate athletics faced two different types of challenges. One emerged from a highly publicized and extremely critical Carnegie Foundation for the Advancement of Teaching report on the conduct of college athletics; the other resulted from the Depression itself. Although it was not the only exposé of its kind, the 1929 Carnegie report was easily the most influential and important. Entitled *American College Athletics* and authored primarily by Howard Savage, the Carnegie report argued that intercollegiate athletic programs had abandoned their commitment to principled amateurism, that commercialization and professionalism undermined the purity of the college games, and that the universities needed to work more diligently to prevent, among many other things, the recruitment and compensation of players by alumni groups. This report's public prominence compelled university and athletic administrators to reexamine their institutions' athletic practices and to justify them to an inquiring press corps and the general public. Nor was the 1929 report the end of the matter. Throughout the following decade national magazines frequently published articles exposing the abuse of big-time athletics, especially football, and many faculty members continued to criticize the corruption of the academy that so often seemed to accompany intercollegiate athletics.[8]

The challenges to the existing structure and operation of intercollegiate athletics epitomized by the Carnegie report grew out of a long history of criticism, not out of Depression conditions. Many other problems confronting university officials, however, had direct roots in the turmoil caused by the uncertainty of the Depression years. As US universities spent the 1930s confronted by numerous challenges to the legitimacy of their methods and to the society and institutions they helped uphold, they also faced daunting financial difficulties caused by the massive economic downturn. The economic crisis for public universities and their athletic programs, though severe for the early 1930s, was neither as great nor as permanent as those trying to manage it initially feared. In fact, the public universities and their athletic programs generally emerged from the 1930s relatively intact and often more stable than they had entered the decade.

After enjoying a decade of unprecedented growth in popularity and in construction of facilities, athletic officials in the 1930s struggled to continue operating extensive athletic programs on sharply reduced budgets. They fought on for several reasons. First, they pragmatically and understandably wanted to protect their own jobs. Second, the athletic associations running intercollegiate athletics had assumed substantial debts as they upgraded facilities and paid professional coaches in the 1920s. These debts did not disappear along with the prosperous times; they remained, looming over the athletic associations as surely as did the newly constructed stadiums over the surrounding academic buildings. Third, continuing a "progressive" view of athletics, the athletic officials sincerely believed that intercollegiate athletics could teach students valuable life lessons, lessons valuable not only to the individuals but also to the society as a whole.[9]

University officials modified this third, more ideological justification for the continuation of athletics in response to the changing social context of the 1930s. As numerous scholars have noted, this was a decade of intense political debate, and this debate occurred on university campuses all across the nation. Prompted by political, social, and economic disparities and supported by national movements and communication, many student and faculty groups began lodging very public complaints about the established US social, economic, and political orders and their stated and implied priorities. Although university environments had produced thinkers ready to challenge middle-class society and its institutions before the 1930s, in that decade such left-leaning social critics were more numerous, active, and vocal than ever before. Consequently, they also seemed more threatening to university and community leaders. Their numbers, actions, and rhetoric certainly caught the attention of already skittish campus administrators and government officials. These university leaders responded to the challenges, real and perceived, by attacking the critical students and by crafting new justifications for existing institutions and activities, including the sporting ones.[10]

University and athletic conference officials came to argue in the 1930s that men's intercollegiate athletics, characterized by unforgiving rules and fair competition, could teach the young men playing and watching the contests how to survive and thrive in the modern capitalist world. These universities used their athletic programs as a mechanism to uphold traditional values, as they perceived them, and, at the same time, to promote a new set of consumer values as well. Nationally, despite a wave of criticism of the commercialization and corruption of male college athletics, male university and athletic leaders emphasized the importance of intercollegiate athletics to the transmission of desired masculine traits and habits. Through participation in, or even observation of, intercollegiate athletics, college men could learn how to compete relentlessly, play by a set of fixed rules, be individuals but still work as part of a team, and accept victories with magnanimity and defeats without complaint. These leaders believed that their programs would not only create young men well prepared for life in modern society, but also that these properly trained men would help protect that very society from the many threats of the 1930s. Specifically, athletic leaders hoped that the lessons of competitive athletics would inspire young men to embrace the principles of democratic government and a laissez-faire economy and to resist government interference in their life and society. In a time of social turmoil and an increasingly powerful federal government, athletic leaders stressed the societal significance of their activities.

The Depression-era discussions of the importance of athletics in building character and inculcating "proper" and "democratic" values had explicit gender and racial connotations. Whereas the men's athletic programs stressed the importance of competition and individualism to the survival of a democratic society, most women's programs deemphasized individual acclaim and attention in favor of group activities, with programs at African American colleges being the most notable exceptions. In many ways, most white women's athletic programs were a conscious reaction to the problems many women saw in the operation and orientation of men's college athletics and in women's industrial league athletics. Rejecting these two models of sport for a variety of ideological, pedagogical, and personal reasons, the female physical educators argued that only by denying gifted athletes special opportunities not available to the others, deemphasizing competitions and the importance of victory, and allocating precisely the same amount of time and resources to all college women could women learn their role in the US democratic system.[11]

Throughout the Depression, the actions of female physical education leaders reflected class, gender, racial, and professional anxieties; they believed that drastic steps were necessary to protect college women from the excesses seen in both working-class women's sporting activities, particularly industrial league basketball games that capitalized on the display of young women's active bodies in colorful and rather revealing uniforms, and in men's intercollegiate athletics. The women working within the academy fully recognized the validity of the criticisms of men's intercollegiate sports expressed in *American College Athletics*. They had long wanted to prevent the commercialization, corruption, and impurity of the men's game from contaminating women's athletics.

Women athletic leaders warned repeatedly and vehemently about the corruption that could be caused by overemphasizing competition in women's athletics, especially since most female physical educators during the 1930s agreed with their male counterparts about the nature of competition. In their eyes competition was a masculine drive that was necessary for the continuation of American life as they knew it but that should be moderated very carefully in women. Women, the university educators held, should concentrate on "democratic" cooperation and companionship, not on the competitive fight for glory and personal achievement, and they argued that only properly trained women (themselves) could coordinate such a program.[12]

Although this push for "democratic" women's sports with no special opportunities for elite athletes was a national movement with great strength in the physical education professional societies, during the 1930s a significant challenge to the existing orthodoxy arose as dissenters emerged at several colleges and universities, most importantly at Ohio State University. Women's intercollegiate athletic programs had never completely disappeared during the preceding decades, but they had been dramatically altered. Women's intercollegiate athletics survived the doldrums of the 1920s and the 1930s in new forms that encouraged physical fitness without allowing much direct competition. Nonetheless, despite official organizational edicts, educators and students at some schools continued to agitate for additional competitive outlets for collegiate women throughout the 1930s. In the late 1930s, an Ohio State contingent of female physical educators proposed a new national organization to oversee women's intercollegiate athletics, a women's national collegiate athletic association, and a national women's intercollegiate golf tournament.

These upstarts were often a generation younger than their profession's leaders, the women who had created and defended the profession's standards. As a generation that matured with the right to vote, that had the license to challenge social norms during the 1920s, and that had an ever-increasing number of female role models in public office and the public sphere, these women were more willing than their elders to reconsider the limits of acceptable activities for athletic college women during the 1930s.

Although the specific changes they proposed were remarkably moderate, the professional reaction was not. Analyzing the vitriol unleashed on the Ohio State leaders and their proposals and studying the intramural and intercollegiate activities across the nation increases our knowledge of women's athletics and activities during this period. It also sheds light on the conflicting ideas about what was desirable and permissible for white, middle-class women and collegiate wives-in-training, ideas that circulated within and emerged from the 1930s in the nation's universities.

At this same time, universities accelerated an existing trend by consciously using their athletic teams to establish their brands in the minds of the consuming public. They used their athletic programs to cultivate relationships with powerful individuals and interest groups and to associate themselves with certain popular and powerful belief systems. University officials tried to manipulate the desire for communal ties found across the increasingly impersonal nation by emphasizing the utility of universities' academic programs to the citizens of the states they served. They also used their athletic teams to make the alumni and the general population stay interested in and supportive of public universities during such hard times.

Although the universities' leaders worked to preserve a "traditional" American culture based on old-fashioned "American values," through their actions they helped usher universities into a new age of catering to the consuming public. Universities increased their commercial orientation, marketing themselves to various communities by using athletes as their most visible and effective advertisement. Using radio broadcasts, athletic publicity departments, charismatic male coaches, glossy game programs, and a willing cadre of newspaper publishers and writers, the university officials successfully sold to the general public and their alumni the possibility of being connected to a winning team and, more importantly to a larger, if imagined, community. By doing so, they generated measurable ticket revenue and immeasurable goodwill toward the state university. The success of this town-gown-touchdown connection, more than anything else, ensured the continued survival of men's intercollegiate athletics during the dark days of the Depression.

Much of this book's detail comes from primary sources found in the archives of five representative US public universities: the University of California at Berkeley, the University of Maryland at College Park, the University of Texas at Austin, the University of Tennessee at Knoxville, and the Ohio State University in Columbus. This approach strengthens the work in several ways. First, these universities represent the regions and athletic conferences that supplied the backbone of 1930s big-time college athletics, including the Pacific Coast Conference, the Big Ten Conference, the Southern Conference, the Southeastern Conference, and the Southwestern Conference. Because of their regional diversity, these schools offer valuable sources for any study of the institutions and practices of big-time college athletics during this period. Second, the sample includes institutions of vastly different scales in terms of student population, state support, and athletic spending and revenue, allowing a more complex understanding of how big, or small, big-time athletics could be.

Third, the concentration on public schools also strengthens the book and contributes to its originality. While writing the history of the creation of US college sports and the culture that surrounded the institution, scholars have focused most of their attention on the elite, private, and usually eastern universities that paved the way for others to follow. By the 1930s, however, the nation's large state universities were beginning to assert their dominance over the more established, but athletically fading, traditional powers. Therefore, a sample drawn from the pool of these emerging powers seems appropriate, especially considering the importance of the rhetoric of democracy to athletic officials during the period. Where better to evaluate the goals and lessons of democratic sport than in the institutions created by the people and their representatives, institutions that existed to serve the citizens of particular states? The advantages of studying public universities seemed too great to ignore.

Finally, each of these schools has significant archival holdings relating to their athletic operations, and, as public universities, all allowed easy and full access to their collections. Although no university had *all* of the records relevant to this study, collectively they had enough to permit a comprehensive picture of the athletic programs and philosophies at US public universities to emerge.

By focusing on the actions and attitudes of five representative public universities during what almost all Americans perceived as a time of crisis, this book adds substantively to the sports history literature in one final way. Just as most of the literature on college athletics' formative years focuses on the Northeast and on private institutions, most also end their discussions by the 1920s. This situation caused

Benjamin Rader to write in 1996, "No adequate treatment of the intercollegiate football spectacle exists for the entire 1890–1950 era." Those that do extend into the 1930s usually concentrate on only one institution, often ones unique in their celebration or cancellation of big-time college athletics: the University of Notre Dame and the University of Chicago, respectively.

Since Rader wrote about the gap in the historiography, John Watterson has produced a comprehensive look at college football. Watterson's work, with its breadth and its focus on controversy and spectacle, still leaves room for more detailed and focused discussions of a critical period in US college athletics. Others, most notably, Michael Oriard, have explored how different groups and narrative forms endowed college football with multiple meanings. *Democratic Sports* complements Oriard's work nicely, adding a focused institutional perspective that his work lacks.

Raymond Schmidt's *Shaping College Football: The Transformation of an American Sport, 1919–1930* argues that the 1920s were the critical years for the entrenchment of college football within the American sporting landscape, and *Democratic Sports* modifies that argument in two ways. First, it extends the timeframe by recognizing the growth of football's popularity in the 1920s but contending that the 1930s were the years when football weathered its most significant financial and ideological challenges. Many fads of the 1920s did not survive the 1930s; college sports did.

Secondly, by considering other men's and women's sports alongside football, this work provides new and original insights as well as the most comprehensive examination of the era's college athletics to date. By examining men's and women's sports together, *Democratic Sports* provides the opportunity to compare both the scale and the stated purposes of men's and women's college athletics at a critical juncture. During the 1930s, leaders in both fields were dealing with the practical considerations of how to organize and promote their sporting activities while remaining true to their philosophical commitment to offering democratic sports to their students and their audiences. Exploring how the definition of "democratic" sport was used and fiercely debated during the decade illuminates a great deal about the social and economic worlds these sporting programs were preparing young men and women to enter.

Wary of the unnecessary repetition and lack of cohesion that would have resulted from a pure case-study approach to my questions and the equally unsatisfactory confusion that a strictly chronological approach would have supplied, I have organized the chapters thematically. Chapters 1 and 2 deal most explicitly with the study's themes and questions regarding institutional survival, asking how the universities' leaders acted to protect their schools and their athletic programs from the Depression's effects. More specifically, chapter 1 examines how the nation's public universities suffered through and survived the financial difficulties of the Depression. Chapter 2 offers a more focused analysis of the same essential questions in terms of athletic departments' finances, using all types of financial records to uncover just how bad the 1930s were for men's athletic programs, how long the tough times lasted, and how officials sought to ameliorate and manage the crisis.

Chapters 3, 4, and 5 focus on the importance of gender constructions to the prevailing ideologies of athletics and to the gendered definitions of "democratic" sport. Chapter 3 examines the masculine values and competitive lessons male athletic leaders believed their intercollegiate sports programs should teach the future leaders of US society. Just as importantly, it shows how athletic leaders connected these values and lessons to specific US institutions and belief systems, putting these discussions within the context of the social turmoil of college campuses during the period. Chapter 4 looks closely at the process of establishing and implementing a dominant philosophy of women's sports, explaining how this ideology spread and how completely the individual universities implemented the orthodoxy. Chapter 5 expands this discussion, explaining how and why the challenges to the official expectations for athletic, middle-class college women emerged during the Depression. Chapter 6 brings together the study's other themes in its discussion of the universities' attempts to create real and imagined communities through the commercialization and commodification of athletics.

Finally, I'd like to offer a brief explanation of the choices I've made regarding how to refer to the universities that constitute the bulk of this study. While I certainly recognize that there is more than one public university in each of these states (in fact, I teach at a regional state university), I've chosen for clarity's sake to refer to the flagship campus as *the* university of its state. Accordingly, in this book, the

Knoxville campus refers to the University of Tennessee and the Austin campus is the University of Texas. The University of California refers to the Berkeley campus, and I've tried to be specific when discussing its interactions with the Los Angeles campus.

CHAPTER 1

In the "Trough of a Depression"

The Fate and Finances of Public Universities during the 1930s

> *We expect to see the citizens of Ohio to give short shrift to any possible cry of "economy," "hard times" and the like. If more mothers and fathers than ever before can afford to send their sons and daughters to the Ohio State University, the state itself can afford to balance the account by providing adequate teaching staff and facilities to take care of them.*
>
> —*THE OHIO STATE MONTHLY*, 1930.

Public universities in the United States felt the effects of the Great Depression just as forcefully and as painfully as most other large US institutions, and while their responses reflected the differences created by local economic and political contexts, they also had much in common. The national economic crisis forced large state universities to budget their resources more closely and carefully, to cut their payrolls, to create new oversight boards, to seek new sources of revenue, and to evaluate their commitments to academic and athletic programs. Examining how representative large, public universities grappled with the Great Depression illuminates how universities adapted their structures and the ways they imagined and presented their missions throughout the crisis. Understanding the larger goals and problems of these institutions is essential to understanding how members of the college communities thought about athletics and why many believed athletic programs helped further broad university goals.

Throughout the 1930s, large, public universities had to reconcile their rapidly expanding student populations with shrinking operating budgets. State legislatures simply could not fund higher education at the levels that they had previously and certainly not at the levels the decades' increasing numbers of students seemingly mandated. Instead, during the 1930s state legislatures dramatically cut funding to public universities, while, at the same time, they demanded that the universities not only maintain their existing character but also expand their range of services provided to the general public. The conflict between the universities' missions and the available resources was not lost on the university administrators, who had to make some tough choices of their own. During the worst years of the crisis for most universities, 1931–37, universities slashed salary rates, teaching positions, equipment budgets, and even entire academic departments. Many public university presidents felt so threatened that they were compelled to announce that the universities themselves would remain open. In many ways, this was a real crisis for public higher education, and the beleaguered leaders of universities certainly perceived of it that way.

Like most other American cultural, social, government, and financial institutions, however, the public universities survived the Depression in essentially the same form as they had entered it, and a close examination of the experiences of representative public universities helps explain why and how they did so. These universities felt the pinch of hard times in innumerable ways, yet by managing their resources carefully, building personal and institutional relationships with a wide variety of interested communities, and selling themselves as vital instruments of public welfare, they emerged remarkably unchanged and in many ways strengthened. By the late 1930s, faculty salaries in most places had returned to near their late 1920s levels, as had the levels of state support.

Moreover, during the Depression the universities established important new relationships with the federal government, particularly with New Deal agencies, whose funding helped employ the universities' students and improve their campuses. In the early 1930s, however, the leaders of US institutions, educational or otherwise, could not anticipate this relatively happy ending. The sense of crisis that they felt throughout the Depression influenced the way they thought about all aspects of American and university life, including their views about athletics.[1]

Although university campuses remained overwhelmingly the domain of the white middle and upper classes during the 1920s, more people than ever attended college during this decade. Consequently, more Americans felt the Depression's effect on US universities than would have a mere decade before. In 1920, the US undergraduate population numbered 341,000; by the end of the decade, more than 750,000 Americans were enrolled in college courses. The numbers of courses offered increased proportionately. In 1930 Stanford offered 1,095 classes, 385 more than it had offered ten years before. Similarly, Howard University almost tripled its number of courses, going from 158 to 437 during the 1920s.[2]

Detailed comparisons among representative state universities highlight this pattern and help put the 1930s' continued expansion of student populations into proper perspective. Enrollment at the University of Texas at Austin and at the University of California at Berkeley increased dramatically in the decades before the Depression. In the 1910–11 academic year, the main campus of the University of Texas enrolled 1,729 undergraduate students. By 1920–21, the student population had exploded to 4,056. During the 1920s, Texas's undergraduate program increased another 40 percent, with 5,763 undergraduates in 1929–30. In sum, in the twenty years before the Depression, the Austin campus's total student population grew more than 330 percent. The growth at Berkeley was even greater. In the 1909–10 academic year, 2,953 undergraduates (1,080 of them women) and 425 graduate students attended Berkeley; by 1919–20 there were almost 9,000 undergraduates attending classes. The student population plateaued during the 1920s, however, as California enrolled more than 9,000 undergraduates only once during the decade, and by 1929–30, Berkeley had 8,959 undergraduates.[3]

The University of Tennessee at Knoxville and the Ohio State University at Columbus experienced similar tremendous growth in their respective student populations during the relatively prosperous 1920s. In the 1919–20 academic year, Tennessee's fall enrollment was 1,194; ten years later, over twice as many students, 2,433, studied on "the

Hill." In contrast, building upon an already impressive student population exceeding 7,000 in the early 1920s, Ohio State had grown to more than 14,000 by the end of the decade. The decade of the 1920s was a time of unparalleled growth and optimism for most public universities. This optimism would not last long into the 1930s, even though the pattern of growth would continue relatively unabated.[4]

Students continued to flock to the country's campuses during the 1930s, despite the Depression's real threats to the nation's entire system of public higher education. This growth occurred for a variety of reasons. For example, historian Donald Whisenhunt reasonably attributed the continued growth of Texas's student population to the nation's high unemployment rates and to the relatively low costs of state colleges and universities. Beginning the decade with a student population numbering below 6,000, the University of Texas experienced steady growth, educating a student population exceeding 8,500 by 1936–37. The academic year 1933–34 offered the only slight exception to this trend, when enrollment fell slightly. During the next year, however, enrollment increased by over a thousand to 7,662; and it continued to grow during the rest of the decade, crossing the 10,000-student barrier in 1937–38.[5]

Similarly in California, the Berkeley campus's undergraduate student population increased each year between 1929–30 and 1939–40, totaling a growth of almost 65 percent.[6] At the University of Tennessee, the increase was even more dramatic, as after a minor dip in the 1931–32 academic year, the student numbers doubled for the second consecutive decade, totaling 5,730 in 1939–40.[7]

With the increasing numbers of college and university students came increased taxpayer expectations, if not legislative assistance. These expectations often came in the form of explicit statements about the duties of public institutions, such as this September 1931 message from "poor old Country Boy" to the University of Texas president and registrar:

> There is going the rounds in state circles that you are noted for getting these poor little country boys and girls enrolled [to] get their fees and in a few weeks Bodily kick them out. Just at these depressing times when the people are clamoring for a bare existence and when poor ambitious folks are borrowing money to

> get their loved children in School, you high browed bullies who have been bullying and kicking poor kids out, you had better take a measure of warning and tell your harebrained PHD's and Old Maids and Wee small Mustached Prof's that they had better get comfort to these Ambitious young people and see to it that not quite so many Freshmen are kicked out. Better take warning for if these depressed times keep up you will have a Hell of a time explaining your damned rules.[8]

This correspondent expected cordiality, consideration, and a very high percentage of passing grades given to the students of his state's public university, and he felt entitled to demand those conditions in the most explicit of terms. In an economy with very few jobs, many Americans expected the state universities to occupy the time of young adults for a few years and to prepare them for later success. Although this author was not alone in his expectations or in his perceptions of universities as a privileged places, US university officials during the 1930s painted a much different picture as budgets did not in any way match the expansion of the student population.

Many Americans viewed universities as the domains of privileged and pampered "harebrained PHD's," forcing public university presidents to spend a good deal of their time countering this public misconception and demonstrating both their institutions' poverty and their practical value to the citizens they served. Perhaps no public university had a more difficult case to make than the University of Texas at Austin, and the man most responsible for shaping the public perception of the school during the 1930s was its president, Harry Y. Benedict, the first alumnus of the university to lead the institution. The general population's belief in the university's affluence stemmed from the university's ownership of thousands of acres of mineral-rich land, profitably leased to oil and gas companies after 1924.

The University of Texas at Austin profited from the provisions of the Texas constitution of 1876 that set aside one million acres of public domain land for the use of the state university system. Seven years later, the state legislature allocated another million acres for the same purpose. Located in semi-arid regions of western Texas, the land was impossible to sell, and railroad companies consistently rejected it as worthless. Primarily leased as grazing land, these two million acres generated revenues that funded the construction of almost all of the university's buildings up through 1928 while also helping to offset operating expenses. This income was essential to the functioning and growth of the university because the state constitution prohibited using tax money to construct university buildings.[9]

In 1924 prospectors discovered oil on the university's lands, and the revenue it produced almost immediately began flowing into the university's coffers. Unfortunately for university administrators, the money had restrictions. All money from the new oil and gas royalties went directly into the university's permanent fund, and the university could spend only the income from the fund's investments. In the 1929–30 academic year, four oil fields on university land produced more than forty thousand barrels of oil, generating royalties exceeding $2,000,000, in addition to the lease revenue of $1,800,000. Although this was certainly a substantial source of income, one all other universities in the country would have cherished, it was not as lucrative as its appearance suggested to most Texans. In 1935, President Benedict explained this fact to the University of Texas Ex-Students Association, telling the assembly that "oil is the chief source of University wealth and your lack of knowledge of the University is its chief source of poverty." Benedict continued, contrasting the revenue of the university to that of other institutions, arguing that the alumni and friends of other universities were contributing more to their schools than oil money did to his university. His conclusion was pointed: "active and informed Ex-Students are worth far more than gushing oil wells to American universities."[10]

The leaders of almost all public universities, including the University of Texas, would have been satisfied with simple, sustained support from their state legislatures, but such support was not forthcoming, especially before 1937–38. In a 1935 commencement address, Benedict very publicly summarized his position on state support of education. He told the graduates and their guests, "The amount spent for chewing gum in Texas is about equal to the amount spent for the University, and all education, public, private, and denominational, upper, lower, and in the middle, costs not more than one fifth as much as we are spending for automobiles."[11] One can infer that Benedict wanted the audience to chew on the fact that there were misplaced priorities in his home state.

The frustration Benedict expressed in 1935 had built up over the preceding five years as he struggled with the state legislature to protect the university's national stature along with its faculty members' salaries, autonomy, and morale. It was not an easy task.

Meeting biennially, the state legislature had budgeted precisely the same amount, $1,408,810, for the 1929–30 and the 1930–31 academic years. In a period of national deflation, this stability actually meant a slight ($32,023) increase in purchasing power.

That stability ended very quickly; the next appropriation bill, for the 1931–32 fiscal year, slashed almost $400,000 from the university budget. Even when the budget's size is adjusted for deflation to just more than $1,120,000 in 1929 dollars, the cuts were still substantial. These cuts included a total of $206,696 from the university's teaching budget, which funded tutors, maintenance, equipment, and salaries, and $190,515 from the non-teaching budget. Over the next several years, the situation would only worsen, in Texas and elsewhere.[12]

Much like the Texas officials, the University of California administrators recognized the problems of student growth during a stagnant economy almost immediately. After Robert G. Sproul assumed the university presidency in July 1930, one of his primary missions was to secure sufficient state funding for university operations. Few people could have been better suited for the challenge than Sproul. Like Benedict of Texas, Sproul was his school's first alumnus to become the institution's president, and many hailed Sproul's ascension as the quintessential American success story. As a child, Sproul had supported himself through various odd jobs, and as a California student he had lettered in track while also leading the campus YMCA. A 1913 graduate, Sproul had returned to his alma mater after only a year, working his way through the bureaucratic maze by serving as a cashier, secretary to the regents, and comptroller.[13]

Sproul offered more than institutional experience and loyalty to his beloved university; among his other gifts were an excellent speaking voice, a persuasive style, and a history of deep thought about the importance of a university to a state and a democracy. According to a historian of the university, Verne A. Stadtman, Sproul's educational philosophies "were the products of his personal experience, the examples of his predecessors, . . . the political stance of progressive Republicanism, the morality of the Presbyterian church, and the ethics of his fellow Rotarians."[14] Sproul's commitment to the university, its ideals, and its standards, along with his persuasive abilities, would serve the university well throughout his tenure, especially during the 1930s.

Sproul presented his first biennial report to the governor eighteen months into his tenure as university president. Sproul wrote in December of 1932 that the university's story during the prior two years had "been one of achievement in the face of difficult general conditions" and that the "adequate appropriations" granted by the state legislature had allowed the university to "weather the years of stress without serious impairment to its efforts."[15] Sproul was not as optimistic about the ability of the university to persevere as admirably through the upcoming budget cycle as large cuts loomed. In December 1932, the State Affairs Committee suggested slashing $39,520,000 from the state's education budget, with millions of the cuts coming directly from the University of California. In an effort to help balance the state's books, Sproul and his staff submitted a university budget that was almost 18 percent lower than the previous one. Still, Sproul cautioned the governor that such a reduction would "mean curtailment of some activities important to the present and future welfare of the State." His message was clear: reduce our budget, and you will reduce our usefulness to the citizens of California when they need us the most.[16]

As a former liaison between the university and legislators in Sacramento, Sproul had a finely tuned sense of the limits of the legislature's will and ability to fund the university's programs and growth. His accurate sense during the early years of the 1930s was that the state could afford very little. In the 1929–30 fiscal year, the state of California granted to the UC system almost $8.5 million, including $1.3 million for capital improvements; and in 1930–31, the university received $7.3 million with building funds. In 1931–32 and 1932–33, as Sproul indicated, the university still enjoyed a stable level of support, receiving more than $8 million each year from the state for operations and construction projects. Although Sproul had warned that the university required adequate funding to continue "the never-ending search for the truth that still . . . is the only liberator of the people" and that the "reduction of costs is hailed as a facile panacea," his argument fell on deaf ears. By 1933–34, the bottom dropped out of the university's revenue trough. That year, the state appropriated only $6.1 million to the university system, and although the next several years saw annual increases of between $100,000 and $400,000, the state funding did not again exceed $7 million until 1937–38, after which it continued growing incrementally and slowly. In a period of growing student numbers, president Sproul, like most of his counterparts, believed his university was underfunded and its efforts underappreciated.[17]

Sproul did not hide his frustration, introducing his 1938 report to the governor with his contention that "the administration and faculty ha[d] done their best to meet the impossible situation created by six years of depression and subnormal State appropriations, on the one hand, and by steadily increasing student enrollments and demands for public services, on the other." The conditions of these six years had forced many difficult decisions at Berkeley and at the other six UC campuses, and the lack of state support threatened to continue a process of "internal decay." According to Sproul's calculations, to maintain, not increase, the 1930 level of support for the university and its students, the state should have provided an additional $18 million over the preceding eight years. Sproul recognized that the state "must still practice economy if it is to carry those relief burdens that the physical welfare of the populace demands," but he also insisted that the university's physical and intellectual welfare was similarly threatened by the lack of support. In 1940, the situation had not changed enough to satisfy Sproul, as he labeled the period from 1938 through 1940 as "one of the most difficult in the history of the University." Sproul lamented that the "limited financial relief that the Legislature of 1939 felt justified in granting . . . [was not] sufficient either to overcome the cumulative effect of the depression budgets of the past six years, or to meet the added burden" of an overwhelming influx of new students during the decade.[18]

The Depression hit the people and the largely agricultural economy of Tennessee equally hard. With the onset of general economic instability, augmented by existing drought-induced troubles of the state's farmers, Tennessee businesses began to fail. In 1930, more than 240 Tennessee businesses failed; in 1931, more than 350 did likewise, followed by an additional 578 failures the following year. Meanwhile many Tennessee banks were closing their doors as well, including the Holston Union National Bank, which failed in November 1930 while holding more than $400,000 in university funds. The university would never recover this much-needed money. Adding insult to injury, the university's administrators discovered in that same year that the school's treasurer, a beloved secretary to the board of trustees and someone who had worked at the university for more than forty years, had stolen more than $10,000 from the institution. This was hardly an auspicious beginning to the new decade. By this time, the university could ill afford to surrender its resources to failures of institutions or ethics because the 1931 state legislature would prove far more parsimonious than its predecessor.[19]

As happened across the nation and throughout the economy, the early 1930s brought many difficulties to large institutions, public and private. Unfortunately for the University of Tennessee, state leaders realized that they could no longer spend money they did not have. In several sessions the 1931 general assembly chipped away at the University of Tennessee's appropriation package. The regular session of the legislature knocked off 10.1 percent from the 1929 appropriation of $925,000; and after the state property tax had been repealed, the special session of the legislature removed an additional $124,000 from the school's allotment. This left the 1931 budget a full 23.6 percent lower than the one approved only two years before. At the same time the student newspaper, the *Orange and White*, began running a series of articles by a student about his experiences with "regular bums," comparing that group explicitly with his other main category, "college students," and implying that existing conditions might force the two categories to merge into one. The articles ran under an ominous title, "If This Depression Keeps Up, Read This for Advice."[20]

In the next year, 1932, Tennesseans responded to conditions by electing a new governor who campaigned on a platform of strict economy and harsh spending reductions. University officials recognized the ramifications of these campaign promises as soon as Governor Hill McAlister took office and began confronting a state deficit exceeding $16,000,000 and outstanding bonds worth more than $85,000,000. Despite university officials' pleas, McAlister could not exempt the state universities from his cost-cutting measures.[21]

University officials would have been much happier with the newly reduced appropriations if the school had actually received all the money that the legislature promised. It did not, and the university treasurer refused to let the absence go unnoticed, bombarding the state comptroller with letters calling attention to the missing funds.

These unfailingly polite letters gently reminded the comptroller of the problem, telling him, for example, "The State, as you know, is $514,250.00 in arrears on the University's appropriation." The messages usually concluded with the note that university officials "trust that this letter will remain attached to the report in order that anyone examining it may have a complete understanding of the University's financial situation."[22] In July 1933, acting university president James Hoskins informed the university's trustees that the failure to receive even the limited funds promised to the university had led to "consolidations of departments, elimination of members of the faculty and employees, and reductions of activities that necessarily mean[t] an inadequate operation of the university."[23] Many surviving letters and memos from late 1932 and from 1933 expressed sincere optimism that the university's checks would *probably* not bounce, while others offered suggestions on how the school could raise more money from students if not from the legislature.[24]

Despite concerns about losing its accreditation, the University of Tennessee managed to continue its operations, persevering on annual state support of less than $500,000 from 1933 through 1936. As historian James Montgomery has described, the state's gradually improving financial condition, along with the election of a new governor in 1936, Gordon Browning, brought some much-needed optimism to the university by the latter part of the decade. This initial optimism was compounded when university officials learned that Browning wanted to increase the university's appropriation by over $300,000, to a total of $750,000. As happened at Texas and elsewhere, however, increased legislative interference became part of the university's appropriations packages during the Depression.[25]

Browning took office in 1937 with a mission to refinance the state's almost $130 million debt, up from $97 million at the beginning of the beginning of the decade, and to increase state revenue. By May 1937, Browning had pushed through the state legislature a new revenue bill that raised taxes on more than a hundred kinds of businesses as well as a plan to pay down the debt by consolidating all debts and issuing one type of bond to finance it. From 1937 to 1939, the University of Tennessee "voluntarily" adhered to the restrictions of a new reorganization law that mandated state government offices in Nashville to dispense all state funds for specific and approved purposes only. In other words, state budget officers and bureaucrats had veto power over the state university's expenditures, exercising the power to "impound" appropriated funds until they were certain that the necessary assets were in place. As Montgomery explained, "In practice [impounding] meant the loss of appropriations."[26] The university fought to gain exemption from the statute, but until it did in 1939, it suffered from the many problems associated with unsure revenue streams. University officials constructed budgets based on the promised appropriations but found they had to operate on considerably less.

In 1938, President Hoskins warned the trustees that the university had to get more money somehow or it risked losing its accreditation. The state budget director publicly responded to Hoskins's concerns by doubting if the loss of accreditation would significantly hurt the university since, as one editor quoted him as saying, "[It] never has been anything but a second-rate school."[27] Conveniently for the university, within a few weeks of this increasingly personal and public squabble, and after picking a fight with the political boss of Memphis, Governor Browning lost the most important election in 1930s Tennessee politics, the Democratic primary, to Prentice Cooper.[28]

Cooper, once elected governor, worked to ensure that the university got the funds promised to it and that it could use these funds without impounding or oversight. At the same time, President Hoskins publicly argued that public education was key to saving the South, contending, "The South's failure to meet national standards of health, housing, wealth, and income is almost precisely in proportion to the failure to support public education."[29] Hoskins envisioned state universities as somewhat like civilian "officers' training camp[s]," preparing men and women to act more socially responsibly and to seek useful careers "designed to relieve the economics and social distress burdening the South," not just to fatten their wallets.[30] Despite this and other arguments for the necessity of well-financed state universities, Governor Cooper did not push for the $1,000,000 appropriations that university officials considered essential. He was, however, still a much closer university ally in Nashville than his predecessors, and under his leadership the university would again reach 1929 funding levels in the early 1940s.[31]

The relationship between the University of Maryland and the Maryland state government highlights the enduring importance of personality, personal connections, and good fortune, even during (perhaps *especially* during) tough times. Although the state legislature had approved the 1920 formation of the University of Maryland, accomplished by merging two existing institutions, the university's position had never been secure. In fact, one contentious budget squabble led some legislators to threaten the institution's dissolution. Historian George Callcott observed, "Although it was easy for the general assembly to approve a merger [of the schools], it was something else to take responsibility for it."[32] With the university's Baltimore professional schools and the College Park campus never really under the same administrative control, budgeting seemed predestined to be difficult. It certainly was. The university's president from September 1926 through June 1935, Raymond A. Pearson, possessed neither the ability to inspire enthusiasm nor a vision for creating a hotbed of intellectual activity. Instead, Pearson was more of an operator than an originator, someone worried more about the building of classrooms than what occurred within them. Facing a stingy legislature and governor, Pearson's tenure at the university was neither a happy nor a particularly successful one, and his presidency and personal style offered the perfect contrast to that of his one-time assistant, almost complete opposite, and eventual successor, Harry C. Byrd.[33]

Pearson's arrival in College Park coincided almost exactly with the onset of economic and social hard times. By all accounts Pearson proved unable to expel either the economic or social depression from the campus; in fact, he played a role in perpetuating the general malaise. Callcott reported that by 1927 the combination of farmers struggling with the consequences of overproduction and blaming the university's agricultural agencies for their problems, the continued fiscal restraint practiced by the state government, and Pearson's lack of imagination, unwillingness to fight to protect the university's budget, and inability to inspire others undermined campus morale long before the stock market crashed in New York.[34]

Actually, the state appropriation to the university increased slightly during Pearson's early years, growing from $229,242 in the 1926–27 academic year to $246,047 in 1927–28 and 1928–29 and to $311,947 in 1929–30. These numbers, however, pale in contrast to the increases his predecessor, Albert F. Woods had desired. In pursuit of his vision of making the University of Maryland a world-class university, Woods had pushed for a doubling of the 1926–27 budget and for more than $3,500,000 in extra appropriations to finance a large building campaign, but Pearson agreed to comparatively small general budget increases and a $935,000 building fund. This one-sided compromise set the tone for the rest of the Pearson administration: as enrollment almost doubled under his nine-year watch, there was not a parallel rise in educational spending. In fact, after the university secured $332,047 for the school year 1932–33, the funding level for educational purposes dropped to about $220,000 for the following three years. Whereas in 1927–28 the state provided 44 percent of the cost of education for students at College Park, by 1935–36 that percentage had fallen to 28, while the state's contribution per student during the same period fell from $224.50 to $109.86.[35]

To give Pearson personal responsibility for all of the problems of the University of Maryland during the early years of the Great Depression would be a mistake, however. Most likely, the state legislature could not and would not have granted much more generous spending bills; and as the evidence from Ohio, California, Tennessee, and Texas demonstrates, the struggles at Maryland were not dramatically different than the challenges elsewhere in higher education. The sums certainly differed greatly, but the trends followed the same general path. What eventually cost Pearson the confidence of his faculty and, ultimately, his job was the perception that he was not truly concerned with creating, supporting, and nurturing academic excellence. He was a builder who worked closely with Governor Albert Ritchie, a politician who wanted to compensate the university for operating more inexpensively during lean years while also generating construction jobs.

Together these men gained more than $4,000,000 for construction projects at College Park and Baltimore, but Pearson's collaboration with a spendthrift legislature and governor and his refusal to fight the good fight, as the faculty saw it, cost him the support of the people teaching in the new buildings he helped build. After the *Washington Post* editorialized that since the appointment of Pearson "a gathering cloud of criticism has appeared over College Park and the university's position has lowered appreciably" and that a "snappy R.O.T.C., triple-threat full backs and elaborate landscaping have superseded considerations of classroom and laboratory," and after forty-nine of fifty-five professors indicated in an anonymous survey that they had no confidence in Pearson's leadership, the board of regents demanded and received his resignation.[36]

Harry Clifton Byrd replaced Pearson, first on an interim basis and then as the permanent university president. Much like Sproul at California, Byrd was an institutional legend, a former athlete when the school was still the Agricultural College and someone who had fulfilled almost every role at the institution since then, most notably as successful football coach, vice president—a position created just for him—and the public face of an institution. His reputation as a personable winner served him well throughout his overlapping athletic, administrative, and political careers. If Pearson's personality and lack of enthusiasm had depressed all associated with him, then Byrd's style had the opposite effect. He was the consummate charmer, an incredibly handsome man who did not deny rumors about his romances with undergraduate women and who inspired even H. L. Mencken to praise him. "Curley" Byrd, as almost everyone knew him, was, like Pearson, not an intellectual's intellectual, but Byrd clearly cared about the university. He served the university by using his personal skills and his political connections to secure ever-increasing sums of money from the state and federal governments. During the late 1930s, these connections and his personal magnetism aided the University of Maryland immeasurably.[37]

The power of personality can take a person only so far within an organization; at some point one must produce results. While Byrd had innumerable valuable connections at all levels of government, in many ways the university's return to relative prosperity, over which Byrd presided, was more the result of luck than any plan or action.

During Byrd's tenure, the university received a $1,000,000

bequest; the new governor restored many of the university's budget cuts, and several New Deal programs, particularly the Public Works Administration, began pouring money and concrete into the College Park building and educational programs and creating a sense of institutional momentum. Although any University of Maryland president would have had similar opportunities during these years, the combination of the new financial resources and Byrd's optimism and charisma encouraged observers to give Byrd the credit for the revitalization of the university despite their realization that, in may ways, Byrd was simply more fortunate than Pearson had been.[38]

Almost immediately upon becoming acting president of the university, Byrd announced that the National Youth Administration would provide approximately $50,000 for Maryland students during the 1935–36 school year; and by March 1937, Byrd could report to the board of regents that the university would probably get from the state legislature all that it asked for, assuming the funds were available. In September 1937, Byrd told the regents that he expected a $30,000 budget surplus that the university could use for general maintenance and operation. After intense and personal lobbying of the legislature to convince the members that the university needed one large appropriation, and that such would "be ample for many years to come," Byrd got even more money for the next biennium than he had originally requested.[39]

Conditions looked so good to President Byrd that he wanted to tell a Chapel Hill colleague his good news. Byrd wrote, "Things are going so well I am halfway beginning to look for 'the nigger in the woodpile.' In the last Legislature we got another million and a quarter dollars for a building program, and our annual maintenance appropriation was raised from $738,000 to $2,302,000."[40]

Besides giving a glimpse into the racial vernacular that was common even among educated whites in Maryland (as the controversy over the university's law school integration in 1935 also highlighted), this statement shows Byrd's optimism about the future of the University of Maryland in late 1937. Later appropriations bills would test this optimism, as later reduced appropriations again forced the university's leaders to contemplate salary cuts. After a great deal of negotiations, in which Byrd proposed that the university use Board of Public Works money and increased student fees to offset any legislative cuts, the budget was balanced, even allowing for a few small raises to placate disgruntled faculty members. By the middle of 1940, Byrd could again declare that the "present financial condition of the University" was "satisfactory."[41]

The state legislatures that vexed the university administrators also had to address many more pressing concerns than the diminished status of their largest public universities during the 1930s. In a decade of countless tough choices, state legislators could not keep everyone satisfied, much less pleased. Public university presidents and other administrators could not accomplish this task either. As Tennessee's Hoskins explained, the budgetary cutbacks led to a wide and damaging array of remedies, including the systematic slashing of professors' and administrators' salaries, eliminating full-time faculty positions, cutting equipment budgets, and even consolidating or eliminating entire departments. In many places, talk of closing the universities entirely forced their presidents to announce officially the continuation of the university's operations. The reality of these cuts and this pessimism should not obscure a vital point: in spite of numerous and substantial financial, personnel, and departmental cutbacks, while the responsibilities of the universities increased dramatically during the 1930s, the nation's public universities largely managed to continue meeting their responsibilities.

Public university leaders responded to the financial troubles of the 1930s by cutting the salaries of their professors and by eliminating faculty and administration positions altogether. For example, the Texas legislature adopted a "general salary reduction rule" when preparing the 1933–35 appropriations bill. This bill instituted a sliding scale of university salary cuts, ranging from a 35 percent cut of salaries that had been over $6,500 in 1932 to a 25 percent cut of all salaries under $2,800. The new bill established maximum teaching salaries of $4,200, a sum received by few more than 50 out of 255 professors in the 1931–32 academic year. The new bill, however, also identified certain people by name to be paid more than their peers within the same salary classifications. Many in the university community took extreme exception to this situation. After officially recognizing the necessity of budget reductions and expressing willingness to "share proportionately in the reduction," a group of Texas professors argued that "control of rank, salary, and promotion by the President and Regents is preferable to adjustment of such details—however well meant—by the Legislature." These faculty members also pointed out that the potential for favoritism and political maneuvering would create a "demoralizing situation in the University."[42] If paying professors and instructors much less to teach many more students seemed unfair to faculty members, then having the state legislature identify particular professors as more deserving than their peers seemed even worse.[43]

Along with the presidents of fourteen other Texas state universities, President Benedict took his concerns directly to the governor and to the individual members of the state legislature in January 1937. These presidents pointed out that between 1928–29 and 1934–35, inclusive, the state had cut funding of higher education by 49 percent, while enrollment across the state had increased 22 percent.[44] During this six-year period, the state had reduced the amount it spent per student a full 58 percent. Arguing that "higher education, to be efficient, must receive more liberal appropriations," the united presidents pled for additional funds for the next biennium.[45]

The governor and legislature found some merit in the presidents' arguments. Although they could not restore all salaries to previous levels, they did have the ability and the will to return many of them to 1932–33 standards. In the 1936–37 academic year, the compensation of Texas's instructors, assistant professors, and associate professors returned completely to previous levels. However, the sliding scale remained in place, though modified, for full professors in Austin. Whereas in 1932–33 the salary scale for full professors had ranged from $3,750 to $6,500, the 1936–37 budget limited them to salaries between $3,600 and $5,500. This represented in every case at least 84 percent of the previous salary and in most cases a restoration of more than 90 percent.[46] While, as a result of deflationary pressures, this adjustment constituted a raise in "real" dollars, it is easy to take this point too far. Fixed debt, be it on houses, cars, school buildings, or bonds, remained the same and actually became more difficult to pay off with the lower salaries.

In October 1930, the editors of Ohio State's alumni publication had been happy to predict that the nation's economic problems would never trouble their alma mater. They argued that the university's increased enrollment necessitated parallel, increased appropriations, and they fully expected that the state legislature would provide for all necessities, regardless of the economic conditions. Moreover, the alumni publication's editors counted on the support of Ohio's population, writing, "We expect to see the citizens of Ohio to give short shrift to any possible cry of 'economy,' 'hard times' and the like. If more mothers and fathers than ever before can afford to send their sons and daughters to the Ohio State University, the state itself can afford to balance the account by providing adequate teaching staff and facilities to take care of them."[47] Over the next several years, Ohio State's leaders would have to fight daily with the legislature to make sure that the university could "take care of" the student-citizens in its care, with the university president having to reassure Ohioans that their university would, in fact, remain open for the spring quarter.[48]

By the spring of 1931, Ohio State was already responding to its growing budgetary crisis by reducing the number of its professor and lowering the salaries of those who remained. The dramatic reductions in state funding forced the university to make cuts in all areas of operation, eliminating numerous teaching, clerical, and maintenance positions. Specifically, the administration and trustees had to cut more than one hundred faculty positions, leave vacant positions unfilled, and reduce remaining salaries of more than $3,000 by 5 to 10 percent. President George Rightmire and others immediately recognized the significance of these cuts as both harmful measures and as dangerous precedents. Rightmire reported to the governor that the university needed at least $2,500,000 more per biennium to "accomplish the reasonable purposes and results which may be expected from the institution," arguing that the "University cannot even mark time but must certainly retrograde both with reference to its educational activities with students and also in a material way" under the existing appropriation.[49]

Rightmire was prescient. By December 1931, the university alumni publication cited a multitude of student protests as evidence that the budget cuts were "doing more far reaching injury than [officials] had feared."[50] Ohio State students reacted most visibly to the changes the new economy had brought to the university's main library. Not only had the cloakroom closed, causing students to leave their books, hats, and jackets lying around on the floor and giving the library the "appearance of an ill-kept warehouse," the library had cancelled its subscriptions to academic periodicals.[51] This type of retrenchment inspired the people organizing sixty-eight alumni clubs to celebrate a traditional "Ohio State Day" to shift the theme to "Mobilization Day" in support of the university. Although valuable and appreciated, the alumni's moral support was not enough to ward off further budget cuts and tough decisions.[52]

In 1933 alone, the Ohio State Board of Trustees announced the abolition of 236 university positions, the vast majority of them again coming from the university's teaching staff. The colleges of "agriculture, arts and sciences, commerce and administration, education, and engineering" lost 169 of the 184 sacrificed teaching positions. As a result of three stages of salary cuts, each more intrusive than the last, the university cut over $1,000,000 from a budget of $4,775,928 within four years. In total, the university president lost 32 percent of his salary; deans and department heads lost 22 percent, and other salaried employees lost between 10 and 19 percent of their income.[53]

The university community responded to the Depression conditions by commissioning the Committee on Courses, Activities, and Programs in the summer of 1932. Unofficially known as the Klein Committee, after its chairperson Dr. Arthur J. Klein, this body recommended sweeping changes in Ohio State's structure in order to ensure the school's survival and continued viability. One commentator responded to the Klein Committee's report with the grim and altogether accurate summary that "the bitter medicine stage has been supplanted by amputation."[54] The report recommended that the university discontinue completely 337 courses and offer 69 others only in alternate years. Moreover, the committee suggested combining thirty-three classes and reducing the frequency of thirty more. At the same time, the committee emphasized the importance of keeping class sizes as small as possible to provide the best possible education despite the difficult circumstances.[55]

Although sweeping in nature, the Klein Committee's proposed cuts proved insufficient; financial realities mandated an even more severe curtailment of university offerings and programs than the Klein Committee recommended, while class sizes continued to grow. President Rightmire reported to the board of trustees in 1934 that the

Ohio State students noting the 1932 presidential election results. *Courtesy of The Ohio State University Archives.*

university's teaching staff was faltering under the strain of providing more classes to more students with fewer materials and assistants. He noted that, despite diminishing resources, "people do not expect less of the University under these conditions; indeed the urge to expand University Activities into new fields is constantly being pressed."[56]

In 1936, Rightmire was in another battle with the legislature and Ohio governor Martin L. Davey. With the football team a preseason favorite to contend for conference and national titles, Rightmire figured that he had the leverage he needed to pressure the government for more funding for the university. Rightmire threatened to cancel the season if the state would not support its flagship university adequately, but Davey called his bluff, responding, "We recognize the fact that football has become the supreme purpose of higher education. We have certainly done our part, because we have most of the football squad on the state payroll." After this public rebuke, Rightmire decided that the university would be able to field a football team after all.[57]

After spending most of the decade in the "trough of a depression," the university's economic outlook brightened by the end of the decade.[58] Although aided only slightly by state appropriations, Ohio State's total available income increased from $8,372,799 in the 1937–38 academic year to $10,230,341 in 1939–40. One historian of the university argued that by early 1938, when Governor Davey signed an additional appropriations bill giving the university $429,000 in supplemental funds and President Rightmire announced his retirement, the "University was definitely over the Depression breakers." Rightmire left the university in June 1938, knowing that Ohio State was, in his words, "nearer normal financing than at any time since the Depression had set in."[59]

Maryland followed this same national pattern of retrenchment and survival. In 1931, when the governor demanded that the University of Maryland return 15 percent of its budget to the state treasury, the money came from the salary and equipment pools; and in 1933 the cycle repeated itself. Meanwhile, many state officials continued looking for other ways to cut back on the university's appropriations. A 1933 report, entitled "Committee Appointed by the President of the Senate of Maryland to Investigate the Affairs of the University of Maryland," stated that "salaries of deans, professors, assistant professors, and many other employees . . . are now on too high a basis and should be scaled down to present-day conditions." The report also rejected the idea that the University of Maryland should pay its faculty and staff at the same rate as other land-grant institutions because the state government in Maryland also helped support other institutions, whereas in some other states that was not the case.[60]

Maryland faculty salaries declined between 7.5 percent and 15.0 percent between the 1930–31 and 1935–36 academic years, and university officials never developed a plan for a systematic restoration of salaries. During these years, the teaching load increased to almost twice the previous levels, and classes met in "conditions far from desirable—some class rooms being in the basements of old buildings." Since their president showed no inclination to support them in their scholarly or teaching efforts, a good percentage of the teaching staff fled the university.[61] According to one disgruntled former professor, the attrition was tremendous: more than twenty faculty members and administrators, including deans and department chairs, left the university under Pearson's administration, even as enrollment almost doubled.[62]

At the University of California, the attrition rate was not quite as severe, although the difficulty in finding and funding enough full-time professors to carry out the university's mission was comparable. While attendance at all University of California campuses increased almost 50 percent between 1929 and 1938, overall state support dropped below 1929 levels in 1933; and in 1938 the state's support per student was barely more than 70 percent of what it had been only nine years earlier. In a refrain common to all university presidents during the Depression, the faculty and staff of the University of California were told to do more in terms of statewide service and instruction with lesser amounts of state funding.[63]

All members of the university community felt the effects of these "subnormal" budgets, and President Sproul went out of his way to emphasize the continued devotion of the faculty and students to the university in his reports to the governor. In 1932, Sproul revealed that the university's faculty members and administrators had voluntarily allowed the university to withhold $300,000 from their paychecks and return the funds to the state treasury to help alleviate the general budget deficit. In his 1934 report, Sproul discussed the faculty salary situation in a section entitled "Steadfast Loyalty of the Faculty." In 1933, he had pointed out to university alumni that California's average faculty salaries were far lower than those at Berkeley's peer institutions (including the University of Michigan, Princeton University, and Stanford University); and in 1934, he told the governor that most faculty members had received a 10 percent salary reduction and that many had received a 20 percent cut. He warned that "this necessary action in the face of rising prices and the fact that very few other State departments or activities have made any reductions whatever in salaries, is bound, if not corrected, to bring eventual heavy losses in the ranks of the able and highminded men whom we are most anxious to retain."[64]

Sproul had not exaggerated the hardships endured by the university's faculty and staff. In 1929, the average California full professor made $5,459; and at the lowest point during the 1930s, the average salary for full professors was $4,902, in 1935. After 1936, the average full professor salary never receded below $5,100; and by 1941, the average was back up to $5,423, an almost full restoration of pre-Depression salaries. The same general trends occurred with the average salaries for assistant and associate professors and for instructors. Although the salaries for people holding these positions did not reach their nadir until 1937, the total decline in each case was less than 10 percent, and by 1941 salaries had either surpassed or come within $30 of 1929 levels.[65]

Like public universities everywhere, the Berkeley campus also responded to the twin pressures of accommodating thousands of new students and maintaining existing (and very high) standards by trimming the ranks of its professors, assistant professors, and associate professors and by adding large numbers of instructors and lecturers. During the academic year 1929–30, the Berkeley campus had 176 professors, 101 associate professors, 102 assistant professors, 36 instructors, and 60 lecturers. Although the number of assistant professors declined to 89 by 1931–32, the other categories remained relatively stable. By 1934–35, however, the forced reliance on instructors was becoming evident, as their total had almost doubled to 67. Writing in 1938, President Sproul argued that the university's continued reliance upon instructors was "not conducive to the maintenance of standards." He continued, explaining that this reliance could "only be a temporary expedient" because UC protocol required instructors employed for more than a few years to gain promotion in salary and rank. Moreover, if the university did not follow its procedures and promote the instructors, "the capable men resign; only the less capable remain. This type of deterioration," Sproul cautioned the governor, "will become serious unless additional funds can be promptly supplied." Nonetheless, despite Sproul's dire predictions, by 1939–40, while the ranks of Berkeley professors had swollen to 234, with 132 associate professors and 100 assistant professors, there were also 83 instructors and 65 lecturers conducting classes. This was an improvement over the 1930 numbers, but the increase was still in no way proportional to the growth in the student population.[66] Like all public universities, the University of California coped with its funding difficulties by cutting back while trying to preserve the university's essential core and continue fulfilling its mission. This was never an easy task, but a new source of funding lightened the load by the middle years of the 1930s.

If the universities could not count on their respective state legislatures to provide sufficient resources for the maintenance and expansion of their institutions, they could at least turn to a newly important source of funding, the New Deal agencies of the federal government. At Ohio State, as it became clear that the university could no longer rely on the state legislature for adequate support of itself or its students, President Rightmire and others began looking to the federal government for institutional and student aid. In early 1934, Rightmire requested more than $67,000 in federal loans to create jobs for students unable to attend Ohio State without them. In his June 1934 report to the trustees and the governor, Rightmire introduced sections entitled "Federal Aid for Students through Part-Time Employment" and "Government Assistance through C.W.A. [Civil Works Administration], F.E.R.A. [Federal Emergency Relief Administration], P.W.A. [Public Works Administration], and C.W.S. [Civil Works Service]." He explained that 1,272 students had found part-time jobs financed with federal loans and that federal money had made possible much of the facilities maintenance that the state could not afford. This aid, consisting of loans and grants totaling well over $100,000, supported landscaping projects around the Olentangy River as it flowed by the campus, the remodeling of the university armory, the cleaning, washing, and painting of university buildings' interior and exterior walls, as well as the construction of additional university dormitories. This construction included the creation of dorm rooms within the existing football stadium structure, an addition Rightmire characterized as "not only an economical utilization of the stadium structure" but one that also had "the greatest social significance; it is deeply appreciated by the people of Ohio."[67]

The University of California could also look to federal government agencies, particularly the National Youth Administration (NYA) and the Works Progress Administration (WPA), for financial support during the middle and late 1930s. In 1939, Sproul summarized the importance of this assistance, writing, "Had it not been for the timely aid of the Federal Government through the N.Y.A. the University would certainly not have discharged its teaching and public service responsibilities as successfully as it has." According to Sproul, the NYA had provided more than five hundred thousand hours of employment for students at all seven branches of the University of California; and the NYA had also provided the university's branches with more than one million hours of labor that "facilitat[ed] the general operation of the institution." By spending more than $200,000 on the seven campuses to provide file clerks, library workers, and research assistants, among other workers, the NYA had allowed both the student body and the university to get through many lean spots.[68]

The NYA had been vitally important, but it was its sister New Deal program, the WPA, which enabled university leaders to focus on continuing research programs. The WPA's money for research projects allowed professors, whose "active and original minds found themselves in a ceaseless round of classroom routine," to pursue ambitious projects otherwise impossible to fund. The WPA spent $750,000 on research activities in one year alone, amounting to approximately two million working hours over a two-year period. Throughout the decade, the University of California consistently defended to the public and the alumni the value of "pure" research, and the WPA allowed many faculty members to continue with their vital work. This institutional investment in faculty research paid off handsomely in 1939 when Professor Ernest O. Lawrence won the Nobel Prize for Physics for his work with the cyclotron.[69]

Evidence from the University of Texas highlights the fact that the nation's universities looked to the federal government for aid before the creation of the New Deal agencies, but that the amount of assistance grew greatly under Franklin Delano Roosevelt's administration. For example, in late 1932 University of Texas president Benedict asked the university's investment statistician, C. D. Simmons, to investigate the lending conditions imposed by the Reconstruction Finance Corporation (RFC) to see if the "terms [are] onerous or could we never pay back and get out of jail, etc., etc., etc.?"[70] Simmons confessed that he had "been concentrating such energy . . . on University funds invested in other people's projects" that he had devoted no time to "getting them to invest money in ours." Simmons explained to Benedict that the university would probably be justified in asking for RFC money to build dormitories because the dormitories could, in theory, meet the criterion of paying for themselves over the next twenty years. Whether they actually would or not, Simmons wrote, was "somewhat beside the point when the building achieves one of the purposes of the act in giving work to unemployed." Benedict and the university continued petitioning for federal funds to help finance building projects. By December 1936 the Public Works Administration alone had loaned the university $1,867,000 and had granted the school $931,500.[71]

Once again, it is important to note the importance of personal connection and interests within large, impersonal institutions and agencies. During the most trying times of the mid–1930s, the University of Tennessee also looked to New Deal programs for help, just as the federal government looked to the university for assistance in administering the Tennessee Valley Authority (TVA). The university's personable president, Harcourt A. Morgan, during the late 1920s and early 1930s was one of the country's leading experts on the Tennessee valley region. As such, he was an obvious choice to help run the TVA. The university gave Morgan a one-year leave of absence in 1933, and in August 1934 he left his university position for a permanent job with the TVA. At the same time, the Roosevelt administration had many reasons, in addition to the general humanitarian ones, to grant federal aid to the state of Tennessee. Roosevelt's secretary of state, Cordell Hull, hailed from Tennessee; and probably more importantly, Tennessee was not as solidly Democratic as most other southern states. In other words, partly to prevent Tennessee from returning to the Republican fold, as it had in the 1928 presidential election, Roosevelt's New Deal was very generous to Tennessee.[72]

Even with such strong state and institutional connections to the federal government and federal agencies, the University of Tennessee failed to take full advantage of the potential government aid. Helped by the fact that the main WPA administrator for Tennessee was also a trustee of the university, the university received well over $300,000 in WPA funds to pay for labor costs in construction projects. The cautious attitude of university president Hoskins and limited university resources, however, severely restricted the university's ability to benefit from PWA and other government projects. Since the PWA required petitioners to provide 55 percent of the necessary funds, to which the federal government would match 45 percent, to take full advantage of the program, Tennessee would have had to come up with substantial sums on its own. In most cases university officials could not do so.[73] According to James Montgomery, in 1938 Tennessee "stood last among southern states for the amount of PWA money appropriated to colleges and universities," having received only $166,909, while Louisiana collected $4,675,272 and North Carolina received $2,357,618.[74]

Like other large public universities, the University of Tennessee used the federal money it did receive to improve the physical facilities of the main campus and to employ students in various research and construction projects. Using CWA funds, Knoxville students labored to preserve manuscript collections, collect sociological data on the residents of the Tennessee Valley, clean library bookshelves, surface tennis courts, and paint the interiors and exteriors of buildings, among other tasks. The university also used WPA money to add onto the football stadium, twice, not only adding seats, but, like Ohio State, also adding residential rooms in the form of Reserve Officers' Training Corps (ROTC) barracks, in the stadium's interior.[75]

This addition of residence hall space under the football stadium's bleachers did not have universal support. The university's dean of students, F. M. Massey, wrote to President Hoskins in January 1938 to "vigorously assert that it [was] not fair to sacrifice the welfare of students to help pay for a new stadium." Massey based his argument on the assumption that "any institution that builds a dormitory for men or women with any other objective than the maximum cultural service to students involved is breaking faith not only with the present student body but with those that are to come." Despite Massey's objections, the university continued the project and made the additions to the stadium and to the number of available rooms for students.[76]

With its proximity to the nation's capital, the University of Maryland at College Park was the state university best situated to take advantage of federal largess during the Great Depression, and the institution capitalized on its location and on its leaders' personal relationships with federal officials to help finance an amazing building program during the 1930s. Throughout the decade, federal programs added greatly to the university's landscape and to the budgets of the university and its students. As Callcott noted, in an era of lavish federal spending on colleges and universities, "great leeway remained for a politically astute university administration to cash in on the wide range of opportunities." President Byrd was, if anything, politically astute. The university not only benefited from the annual $100,000 for agricultural work granted by the Bankhead-Jones Act of 1935, but also profited from Byrd's political connections and acumen. Byrd got the Civilian Conservation Corps (CCC) to establish a regional headquarters at College Park and also landed a $50,000 grant for campus landscaping from the agency. In 1936, a Maryland administrator wrote to the Baltimore administrator of the NYA, telling him, "The aid rendered to students under the National Youth Administration has been a great benefit to the students, and has helped many to secure education who otherwise would not have received it." At one point, more than 20 percent of Maryland students worked for the NYA, helping their university just as the federal government helped them.[77]

The federal programs certainly helped the university as an institution survive the Depression equally as much as they did the students. Benefiting primarily from the PWA and the WPA, the University of Maryland ultimately received approximately $3,000,000 for campus building projects, easily one of the largest totals given to a university. This was not coincidental but rather the product of location and clever politics. For example, at one point in 1938, the generally conservative Democrat Byrd met secretly with President Roosevelt, and shortly thereafter the university received even more than the $1,000,000 Byrd had requested from the federal government. Perhaps not coincidently, a few months later Byrd spoke out against the reelection campaign of Millard E. Tydings, one of his university's most loyal supporters, a personal friend of Byrd, and a vocal opponent of the New Deal. After Roosevelt's congressional purge attempts failed, Byrd quickly reconciled with his former classmate and continued to work successfully with Tydings to get the university more money from federal coffers.[78]

The influx of federal money and a slowly recovering national economy helped the nation's public universities return to somewhat normal operating procedures by the late 1930s. Although officials at the University of California still referred to the 1938–1940 period as "one of the most difficult in the history of the University," most other university leaders by that point seemed relieved to have survived the worst of the Depression with their institutions intact. The year 1938 saw Ohio State officials noting that they had exited the "trough of a depression" and Tennessee voters electing a new governor who would push for increased university appropriations and work with a legislature that was more willing to support the state's main university. Meanwhile, the combination of Byrd's personality, large gifts, and federal funds delivered optimism to the University of Maryland campus; and by 1937 the University of Texas was able to restore most of its salaries to the pre-Depression levels. By the late 1930s, most US public university officials recognized that the worst was over and that the universities would emerge intact, if not strengthened.

This confidence was evident in many places by the late 1930s, but it had not always been there. It is important to note the very real difficulties these universities faced and the dramatic measures their leaders took in order to continue operations. Facing geometric growth in student populations and gutted budgets, large public universities looked to the federal government for help to prevent further cuts in staff positions, teachers' salaries, library subscriptions, and the numbers of classes and degree programs offered.

There was a genuine sense of crisis on US campuses during the 1930s, but despite the determination of most universities to present themselves as cost-effective educators, as essential, non-frivolous agencies, the primary area that did not suffer dramatic cuts in operations and that certainly never truly confronted cancellation was the universities' athletic programs. In the context of a very real sense of financial and social crisis, a complex combination of institutional, political, ideological, communal, and commercial values worked to preserve and protect the athletic operations of US public universities during the Depression, just as they worked to protect the universities themselves.

CHAPTER 2

★ ★ ★ ★ ★

Financed by Football

The Economics of Big-Time Athletics during the Depression

> *A very large percentage of colleges have had their athletic income reduced. In spite of this, and the most remarkable part of it to this writer, is the fact that we have been able to keep our athletic programs almost intact. Very few colleges have abolished sports. They are to be congratulated. It is an unwise policy to eliminate. If something must be done it is far better to modify.*
>
> —C. E. BILHEIMER, GETTYSBURG COLLEGE, 1933.

After a decade of remarkable expansion for intercollegiate athletic programs in the United States, the shockwave of the early Great Depression years threatened to destroy all that prosperity and planning had built. Despite mounting losses and dim hopes for an immediate financial recovery, however, during the 1930s most US universities did almost anything they could to preserve their men's intercollegiate programs. This was an effort to provide athletic opportunities and important moral and character-building lessons for male students. By the end of the 1930s these programs had regained their audiences and their solvency, primarily because their football teams had managed to retain their profitability, if not their profit margins, and because administrators had been able to adjust the scale and cost of their athletic offerings while also adopting a more commercial and consumer-focused approach to their men's athletic programs.

US men's intercollegiate athletics persevered for financial, ideological, and cultural reasons. While later chapters examine the ideological, social, and cultural supports of intercollegiate athletics, and the economics and intended lessons of women's programs, this one examines the economics of big-time athletics and the patterns of responses to the financial challenges of the 1930s. Across the nation, schools responded in similar ways to the shared crisis. This was in large part because extravagant spending on physical facilities of the 1920s limited the number of options available to the universities during the 1930s. A form of institutional inertia protected men's intercollegiate athletics; given the cost of recently constructed facilities, it was easier for universities to keep most athletic programs rather than abandon them.

During this period the classification of big-time athletics encompassed an extremely wide range of programs and universities, but in each of these institutions, football remained the cornerstone of the program and the main provider for the budget.

Although football would become much less profitable during the 1930s and much less able to support minor sports programs, in most places it *did* remain profitable. A third pattern was that, when confronted with red ink, athletic officials became even less troubled by the commercialization of athletics and more concerned with the continuation of them, relying upon football revenue, in general, and "big-game" hype and revenue, in particular, to sustain their programs. By the end of the decade, contrary to reformers' wishes, university leaders were treating college athletics much more like a business rather than less like one.

The 1920s were a golden age for college football programs, whose popularity and magnitude exploded. With the expansion in attendance numbers and scale came increased athletic revenues. During that decade, as attendance doubled and income tripled, US colleges and universities inaugurated an unprecedented athletic building boom. In 1920, only Yale University could seat more than seventy thousand in its campus football stadium; by 1930, more than seven schools could, most of them in the Midwest and the West, including both Ohio State University and the University of California. Many of these institutions reaped great financial rewards from their athletic programs.

For example, in the 1920s, the University of Alabama gained $150,000 from intercollegiate athletics in one year, most of which came from football revenues. Harvard University's football team produced $429,000 and supported the rest of the school's athletic programs, still leaving a profit of $131,000. The University of Washington's athletic programs produced $230,000 and cost the university $192,000, producing a profit of $38,000. Finally, epitomizing the excess of 1920s college athletics, the Yale University Athletic Association produced a profit of $348,500 in the 1927–28 academic year, out of a gross income of $1,119,000. Although most universities did not conduct athletics on such a profitable or grand scale, the groundswell of support for men's intercollegiate athletics, especially football, at all levels and in all regions throughout the 1920s inspired athletic officials to borrow great sums of money to finance construction in order to meet the actual and anticipated demand.[1]

The golden age, however, ended rather abruptly with the dawn of the new decade, and universities in the United States had to address the twin problems of declining revenue and increased commitments. US universities shared the burdens of paying off the debt from the previous decade's building spree, and many also felt compelled to continue building new facilities during the 1930s as college enrollment increased. Having made large physical and institutional commitments to athletics during the 1920s, American university officials (especially those with their jobs on the line) were reluctant to retrench during the hard times of the 1930s. Most schools made cutbacks, some in the numbers of "minor" programs offered, almost all in the numbers of games played and trips taken by the minor sports teams. Although these universities continued to rely upon football as the one sport that enabled the schools to fund and offer the others, during the early years of the 1930s football revenue declined precipitously, even though at many places attendance levels remained relatively stable.

Most US public universities were eager and willing participants in the athletic building boom of the 1920s; a large number of them built or committed to building new stadiums or gymnasiums during the decade with the understanding that the profits reaped during the 1920s would continue to pour into the university's coffers. They were mistaken. Their experience in the 1930s stood in stark contrast to that of the preceding decade. In 1933, a Northwestern University professor reminded the attendees of the College Physical Education Association meeting of the good old days when "it was almost impossible to spend the income that came pouring in." An Ohio State professor similarly recalled the 1920s as a time when the football team generated more money than the athletic department could spend without expanding facilities; so build they did.[2]

The University of California represented the upper end of the national spending spectrum during the 1920s as it dedicated its 76,000-seat California Memorial Stadium in 1923.[3] Given the financial success of its football teams in the 1920s, the Berkeley administrators had no initial reasons to regret their decision to expand. With one year's athletic income totaling $486,162 (more than $450,000 of it coming from football) and with athletic profits that year exceeding $170,000, Berkeley was able to pay off most of its massive debt in 1930, three years ahead of schedule. In fact, in the early 1930s, California administrators recommitted themselves to creating a more expansive recreation plant. Using money lent by the board of regents and to be repaid out of athletic revenues and student fees, the university paid $1,400,000 for three city blocks of land adjacent to campus, intending to build football and baseball practice fields, a 25,000-seat track and field stadium, a new gymnasium, intramural sports fields, tennis courts, handball courts, and others recreational facilities.[4]

Still, even in the prosperous golden age, Berkeley officials realized the need to achieve stability in the school's athletic revenues. Anticipating the lean years to come, the general manager of the Associated Students of the University of California (the ASUC was the body that oversaw athletics at Berkeley.), W. W. Monahan, argued in February 1930 that the university's athletic situation was not as rosy as it appeared. Monahan explained that playing five postseason or intersectional football games within the previous six years had produced an extra $275,000 for the ASUC, but he did not believe that the university should or could continue to rely on these irregular income infusions to balance the ledger books. In fact, Monahan noted that over the same six-year span, the ASUC had had to borrow between $75,000 and $80,000 each year simply to continue operations during the spring and summer. Monahan fervently hoped that "we will within the next few years place ourselves in a position where this will not be necessary."[5] His wishes for balanced budgets would not be granted in the early 1930s, and the University of California resumed its athletic plant expansion by the later years of the decade.

Like California and many other schools, Ohio State built an enormous, on-campus football stadium during the 1920s.[6] In the late 1910s, after a series of very successful football seasons, Ohio State officials and supporters perceived a demand for a much larger football stadium than then existed in Columbus. In 1920, the university began a massive fund-raising campaign financed by athletic profits, soliciting gift and "stadium subscriptions" from students and faculty members and from alumni and friends in Columbus and far away. By early 1921, devotees of the university had pledged more than $1,000,000 to a stadium fund, and the university accepted a $1,341,000 bid on the stadium construction. The trustees placed all responsibility for the stadium in the hands of the Athletic Board, with the stipulation that the university itself would not have any financial obligations and that the stadium would cost no more than $930,000. Unfortunately for the Athletic Board, the final cost of the stadium was almost twice what the trustees had approved.[7]

In late 1927, after spending more than $800,000 in athletic revenues on the stadium's construction, the Athletic Board turned over to the university an impressive athletic plant including forty-six new tennis courts, new walking and running tracks, baseball fields, intramural fields, and additions to the stadium worth $1,900,000. The trustees accepted this gift with great gratitude and with the expectation that the Athletic Board would be responsible for all remaining financial obligations. With the onset of the Depression, however, it became clear that many of the stadium subscribers would not fulfill their pledges. In 1936, the Athletic Board finally officially recognized that it would never see the $165,000 still owed by subscribers and finally closed the books on the stadium project.[8]

Ohio State had also committed itself in the late 1920s to building many other athletic facilities, including a men's gymnasium, a natatorium, a golf course, and a new field house. By 1931, the university had begun work on all but the field house, but as an Athletic Department report bluntly explained, "the depression caused a sudden and complete change of circumstances." The university had utilized $550,000 in state funding to construct the men's gymnasium, but it had to rely upon its own resources for the remainder of the projects. The board had in the early 1930s, "in anticipation of surplus receipts," borrowed a grand total of $310,000 to build the natatorium, but these surpluses did not materialize.[9] For several years the Athletic Board could pay only the interest on its financial obligations for the golf course and the natatorium, even though it leased the golf course land for livestock grazing in the early 1930s. Finally, in 1936, with the promise of substantial assistance from the Works Progress Administration (WPA), the university was able to continue its construction of the golf course, completing it in 1939 with a total expenditure of athletic revenue exceeding $360,000.[10]

Although the University of California and Ohio State spent much more on athletic infrastructure than most other US universities, the building programs at the University of Texas, the University of Tennessee, and the University of Maryland illustrate that they were all part of a national movement. For example, the University of Texas Athletic Council moved in 1929 to build a new gymnasium and new locker buildings for the football and track teams at the football stadium, one that could hold forty-two thousand spectators. That same year the University of Tennessee loaned more than $120,000 to its Athletic Association to refinance one debt and to finance additions to the football stadium, bringing its seating capacity to more than thirty thousand.[11]

In the late 1920s the relatively young and small University of Maryland also joined in the national athletic construction boom, adding new stands for its athletic fields and proposing many more improvements. After finishing construction of a new 1,500-seat baseball stadium, a new track, and new tennis courts, in February of 1930 the Maryland Board of Regents granted a request made jointly by the student government association and the university's Athletic Board to launch yet another wave of athletic construction projects. Instituting a $10 student activity fee to finance the projects, the regents approved spending $105,000 on a host of additional facilities. A breathless correspondent for the *Maryland Alumni News* informed his readers of the good news: "Great strides have been made in the last two years and when the proposed field house, revamped concrete stands, swimming pool, golf course, and some additional recreational spots are provided, the Old Line University will have the best all-around athletic plant in the South."[12]

In May of 1931, the regents authorized spending an additional $140,000, with $120,000 to come from athletic bonds and $20,000 from the state legislature, on a men's field house as well. The January 1932 dedication of the new field house, its prestige enhanced by the attendance of the governor and other dignitaries, produced more banner headlines on the front page of the alumni publication.[13] This commitment to athletic construction developed all across the nation during the 1920s and early 1930s, and the erection of these prominent and expensive facilities made it virtually impossible for schools to jettison their intercollegiate athletic programs, even if they had wanted to do so, with the University of Chicago the most notable exception to this rule.[14]

Even though many schools enjoyed the positive publicity that accompanied the unveiling of impressive new athletic facilities, athletic officials also had to deal with less-flattering press coverage of their activities and programs. A series of dramatic headlines in the early 1930s called attention to less favorable developments in US intercollegiate athletics, the literally declining fortunes of many of the nation's intercollegiate programs. In the January 3, 1931, edition of the *New York Times*, under the headline "Football Viewed as Facing Crisis," appeared this introduction: "College athletics in general and football in particular, still suffering somewhat from the growing pains of super-salesmanship and ballyhoo, have been abruptly brought to face with somewhat critical conditions for 1931."[15] Citing a "cross-fire of criticism leveled at intercollegiate football during the final week of the old year" and the "combined ills of over-emphasis and the effects of considerable depression in the region of the box offices," the Associated Press author reported that college and conference officials across the country had begun taking steps to limit the perceived negative effects of football.[16]

Five months later, another *New York Times* report further undermined whatever optimism remained in athletic circles across the country. Citing a recent Carnegie Foundation report, the author reported that undergraduates and the general public had become less enthusiastic about intercollegiate athletics and that the economic depression had finally caught up to intercollegiate athletic programs. Purdue University's football program in the 1930–31 academic year, for example, had generated $97,000 less than planners had predicted, leading to an operating deficit of $40,000. Overall, the *Times* article reported that 80 percent of surveyed institutions had been forced to cut back on their athletic programs in terms of sports offered, number of games played, or both.[17]

Reflecting the national economic trends, the early years of the decade brought with them dramatically reduced athletic revenues for US universities. Nonetheless, university administrators remained committed to continuing their intercollegiate athletic programs in as complete a form as fiscally possible; and by doing so, they ensured the preservation of the men's intercollegiate athletics.

Few public institutions at the beginning of the 1930s had athletic incomes surpassing those of the University of California and Ohio State, just as few flagship state universities earned less than the University of Maryland from its teams. In terms of athletic revenue in the 1920s and 1930s, the University of Texas and the University of Tennessee fell into the vast middle ground between these two poles. Despite their vast differences in scale, these and other US universities shared similar responses to the revenue crunch of the early 1930s: they fought to continue football on its previous scale and to sustain the other programs as well as they could. The shrinking pool of available money and the continued dominance of football also led in many places to considerations of cutting out all or many minor sports. Ultimately, most institutions did not completely cancel their minor sports programs, but most did limit the numbers of games, the amount of travel, and the numbers of participants for a variety of sports.

Athletic profits dramatically declined at universities across the nation in the early 1930s. For example, at the University of Maryland the football team produced an annual profit between $25,000 and $30,000 a year in the late 1920s; but by 1932 sharply reduced revenues led the university's athletic director to proclaim publicly that the decline in fortunes would *not* lead to a corresponding reduction in the numbers of sports offered at Maryland. A mere three months later, a different story emanated from College Park as the *Washington News* reported that Maryland officials were leaning toward canceling all spring intercollegiate sports. At that time, University of Maryland vice president and former football coach Harry C. Byrd confirmed the seriousness of the situation in a private letter to University of Georgia president Dr. S. V. Sanford, writing, "All our athletic money is impounded in a bank and under the relief bill now before the legislature, we shall be able to draw out only 2% per month. I see nothing in front of us except to call off all spring sports."[18] Ultimately, the University of Maryland was able to fund and field an entire slate of spring varsity and freshman sports teams in 1933, but its leaders were not alone in considering canceling programs and schedules.[19]

The situation at the University of Texas was in many ways analogous to that in College Park and most other public universities: officials had become accustomed to deploying football profits to finance the schools' other athletic activities, but they had to adjust their expectations to fit the new reality. As at Maryland, football revenue produced the vast majority of the University of Texas's athletic income entering the 1930s, but there the numbers were much larger. In the decade's early years, football continued to provide the largest piece of the pie, even as the entire pie kept shrinking. Despite producing income exceeding $120,000 in the 1927–28 academic year and more than $150,000 in both 1928–29 and 1929–30, the University of Texas intercollegiate athletic program continued to operate at a deficit, in part because operating expenditures in these years consumed at least two-thirds of the income and in part because of large debt payments on the new gymnasium and sports field. In August 1928, Longhorn intercollegiate athletics had a deficit of $29,000; in August 1929, it was $37,000. By August 1930, the deficit had climbed to $48,000, and officials estimated in early 1931 that by August of that year the deficit would expand to more than $63,000. In the context of this ominous trend, officials could not have been pleased to see another related trend, that of declining football revenues.[20]

The University of Texas's income from its most profitable and popular sport steadily and sharply declined in the early 1930s. With an alternating schedule dictating where the most lucrative games were played, during the years 1928 to 1931 gross football receipts hovered between $150,000 and $125,000; meanwhile, net football receipts remained remarkably stable, actually increasing by a little more than $1,000 a year, from $101,236 to $103,802. The next three years were not as kind to the financial managers in Austin. In the 1931–32 and 1932–33 academic years, the gross football receipts took a 30 percent plunge before stabilizing just above $100,000 but then dropping again to $68,724, a figure only 46 percent of the total a mere four years before, while the net football receipts declined proportionally as well, even when adjusted for deflation.[21] Between 1930 and 1934, football continued to turn a profit, but the margin narrowed dramatically over the four-year period. After an encouraging profit increase from $63,677 in 1930 to $71,284 in 1931, the profits fell to $47,364, to $37,283, and to $15,722 for the following three years, respectively. Throughout this period, all other University of Texas intercollegiate athletic programs continued to lose money and to rely on football revenues for support.[22]

The main branches of the University of Maryland and the University of Texas were not exceptions to the rule; their experiences were the rule in the early years of the 1930s. J. W. Coombs, a southern intercollegiate baseball coach, wrote to the A. G. Spalding and Brothers Sporting Goods Company explaining the plight of minor sports programs across the South. Of the twenty-three Southern Conference schools, Coombs reported in November 1932, twenty-one fielded baseball teams; but he warned that this ratio would not survive without some help. Coombs cautioned his equipment distributor, "We are simply up against it here in the South. Our minor sports program is being reduced, our baseball schedule is being cut to the lowest possible level and unless some concession can be given to us by the manufacturers of our equipment, it will not be long before baseball will fall in the tracks of the minor sports, the same as it has done in several of our Southern Conference Colleges."[23] Across the South and the rest of the nation, it was becoming clear that the reduced football profits could no longer support minor sports to the extent that they had during the 1920s. The question was how to respond to the new reality.

Given the declining athletic revenues of the early 1930s, the commissioner of the Big Ten Conference, John L. Griffith, also spoke about the necessity of negotiating equipment discounts for his member institutions. Big Ten institutions faced the fact that the earlier-predicted continuation of prosperity had not materialized. Looking back in 1937, Ralph Aigler, the University of Michigan's chairman of the board in control of physical education, could note with irony that the borrowing and building spree of the late 1920s had "seemed a perfectly safe procedure." As Aigler noted, however, the drop in Michigan's football income from $400,000 in 1929 to $152,000 in 1935 had made him reconsider, even though the athletic programs had somehow been able to stay "in the black" and had avoided defaulting on any loans. Although Aigler remained confident that a general economic upturn would remove insecurity from all aspects of athletic financing, he expressed hope that "the time will also come when the intra- and extramural sports program will no longer depend upon the efforts of boys playing football for its chief support."[24] That time would not arrive during the 1930s.

Ohio State had no other option but to rely upon its young men playing football if the university was to maintain its commitment to a large, men's intercollegiate athletic program, and it most certainly did intend to keep the program intact. As at almost all other institutions, football served at Ohio State as the chief revenue producer and as the

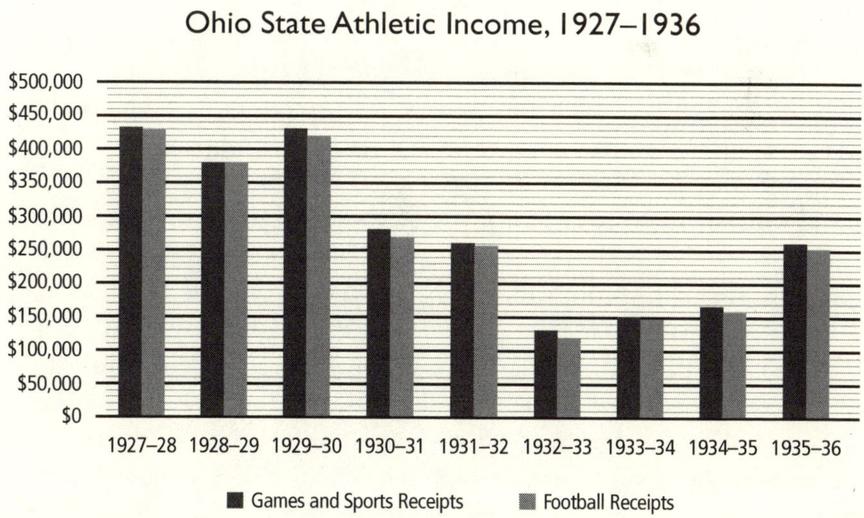

Figure 2.1

chief source of funding for all other athletic programs, in addition to dominating the campus's social calendar.[25]

The reliance on football as the main source of income becomes clear when one examines this chart (fig. 2.1) highlighting the close correlation between Ohio State's "games and sports" receipt totals and the football receipt totals. For example, in the 1927–28 academic year, when the games and sports receipt total was $434,464, football generated $425,586, almost 98 percent of the total. The next year football generated more than 99 percent of the total games and sports receipts. Throughout the 1930s, the Columbus Athletic Department would continue to rely upon football for the overwhelming majority of its athletic revenues. Even in 1932–33, when the total receipts had plummeted to $129,111, football produced $118,789 of that figure, more than 92 percent. The chart's data also show that university budgeters clearly recognized their dependence upon football receipts. The 1935–36 games and sports total was an estimate in April 1936, based on the known football receipt total of $252,536.[26]

Some of Ohio State's counterparts in the upper echelon of athletic spending experienced less dramatic, but still substantial, revenue reductions in the early 1930s. In the 1929 calendar year, the University of California's football team brought in $622,547 and cost the university just more than a quarter of a million dollars, leaving a net profit of $372,125. The rest of the Berkeley intercollegiate athletic program ran a deficit of $84,338, not considering general overhead expenses, but the football profits still allowed the ASUC to claim a $225,004 profit from athletics. A mere three years later, football profits had dropped by more than one-third, to $244,525; in 1933, the football profit margin was only slightly higher at $246,330. These numbers, though lower than the university had come to expect, help illustrate the continuing profitability of football at many schools during the Depression. While officials were able to deal with stabilizing football profits, the overall athletic financial picture at California was not quite so rosy. In the academic year ending in 1933, California athletics still made money, but instead of the school earning the $225,000 from 1929 or even the $142,055 from 1932, athletics brought in only $68,042. Make no mistake, other institutions would have loved to have had only the problems of reduced profitability that California officials faced, but the problems of relative decline were real to the administrators who faced them.[27]

Reflecting the national economic picture, the period between 1932 and 1934 represented the lowest point for the athletic programs of US public universities, large and small. By the 1933–34 school year, athletic revenue streams had slowed to a trickle instead of continuing to gush, as irrationally exuberant officials had predicted in the late 1920s. The University of Illinois provides another useful example of how universities experienced the fluctuating fortunes of the early and mid 1930s. In the chart (fig. 2.2), one can see how the University of Illinois's athletic fortunes reached their nadir in the 1932–33 academic year before beginning a slow recovery. Even if the overall numbers are not completely representative—most US schools did not bring in more than $400,000 from athletics in the late 1920s—the general pattern held at most other universities.[28]

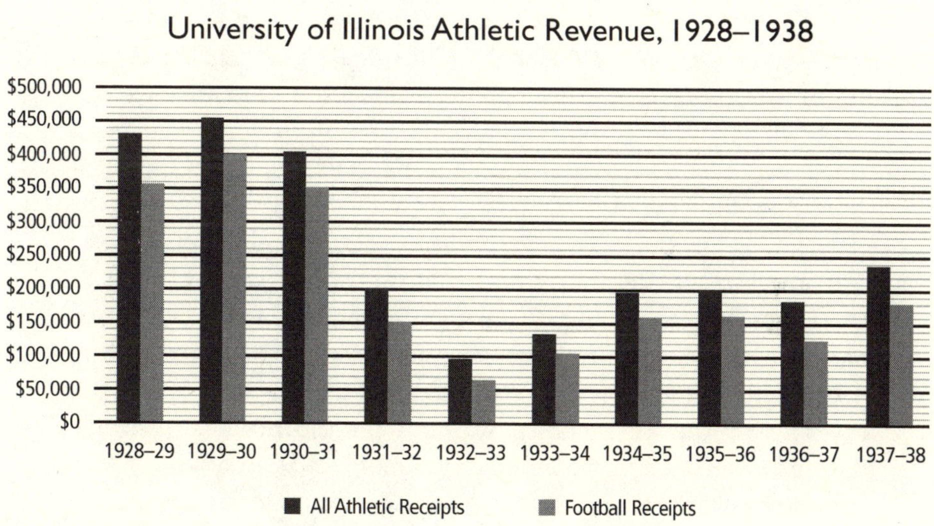

Figure 2.2

If universities relied almost solely upon football to finance their athletic programs, then it was usually "big game" revenues that kept the sinking football programs afloat. University officials had recognized early on that with the increased public interest tied to playing a traditional rival or a novel, high-profile game came much-needed cash infusions. They realized that playing more enticing match-ups would allow them to charge higher ticket prices while also drawing larger crowds. As one author pointed out in December 1931, one thing was clear, "the public with less money to spend is going to be more critical in making purchases, and this will also apply to its choice of football games." He continued, warning his colleagues that "practice games with easy opponents will not fill the stands. Schools that are anxious to hold their spectator interest therefore will have to be careful in building their schedules to include more teams that offer close and interesting rivalry." The author expressed optimism that if officials followed this advice then football could "hold its own in the new scale to which the public will adjust its spending."[29] Schools would have to market their athletic products to the consumers better than ever before.

To many officials and to much of the general public, "attractive" games meant challenging one of the established, elite universities, including those that had reputations for excellence in academics as well as athletics, especially Harvard University and Yale University, and those that did not, the University of Notre Dame most explicitly. Affiliation with the elite institutions through athletics was a well-established practice by the 1930s, with the excitement surrounding a 1929 Yale football team visit to the University of Georgia serving as a perfect example of how schools used sports to affiliate themselves with others and "betters." In 1931, the University of Texas football team traveled cross-country to play against the Harvard squad, a journey made despite reservations about the "large deficit and commitments of [the] athletic association." As it turned out, the university made $19,320 from the trip, making the game the second most lucrative in terms of revenue that year, missing first place by only $314.[30] Still, without knowing this, the regents provided $2,500 to finance a band of forty musicians to also travel to Cambridge because some Texas officials wanted to put on a "big show" and because some thought that the band would "add much to the impression made by [the] team on its first trip east."[31] As anyone familiar with the advertisements of the era knew, first impressions meant everything.

Some schools used athletics to confirm, not create, status, while also generating revenues. The University of California considered itself to be the academic peer of Harvard and Yale, and its officials sought to solidify that status by using athletic competition to demonstrate their relative equality. In the mid-1930s, University of California president Robert G. Sproul pushed for a track meet pitting a team representing all California campuses, including Berkeley, Los Angeles, Davis, and San Francisco, against a unified Harvard and Yale or a combined Oxford and Cambridge team. Either way, officials wanted to compete against "some team representative of two first-class universities."[32]

Unfortunately, even prestige-enhancing track meets would not have paid the bills, so the California officials also pursued a football game with the perceived polar opposite of the "first-class universities," Notre Dame, a university that then had a much less flattering academic reputation than it now enjoys. In 1931, as athletic receipts were beginning to bottom out in Berkeley, the dean of men presented several arguments for an athletic relationship with Notre Dame. Dean Thomas Putnam pointed out that the football team would miss only a total of five days of class during the entire 1933 football season and only three days during the 1932 season; therefore Sproul would not look like a hypocrite in endorsing the games after insisting that academic work must come first. Secondly, Putnam refuted the argument that "we would lose caste academically if we played Notre Dame" because California already competed against many other lesser academic institutions. "Ideally," Putnam noted, "we would like to play institutions of our own standards, both academically and athletically. Few, if any, institutions have this privilege and certainly we do not." Thirdly, Putnam contended that California's "local prestige [would] be greatly enhanced amongst all football followers, and in general with alumni," if it played Notre Dame. If California chose to decline the offer, Putnam warned, Stanford would surely accept, and California would enhance its "snobbish" reputation while the "athletic prestige" of Stanford grew.[33]

However exciting and lucrative single games against prominent foes could be, most universities relied more on traditional grudge matches for their regular revenue boosts. For the University of Texas during the 1930s, the University of Oklahoma and the Texas Agricultural and Mechanical University served as the principal rivals and the main draws at the gate, as the chart (fig. 2.3) indicates. Although in the 1931–32 and 1935–36 school years these two rivalries did not provide the two highest-grossing games of the Texas football seasons, they both always ranked in the top four income-producing games. Comparing the money received for these two contests to the receipts from another annual rival, Centenary College of Louisiana, highlights the fact that most football profits, and therefore most athletic revenue, at Texas came from a small number of games and that tradition alone would not pay the bills.[34]

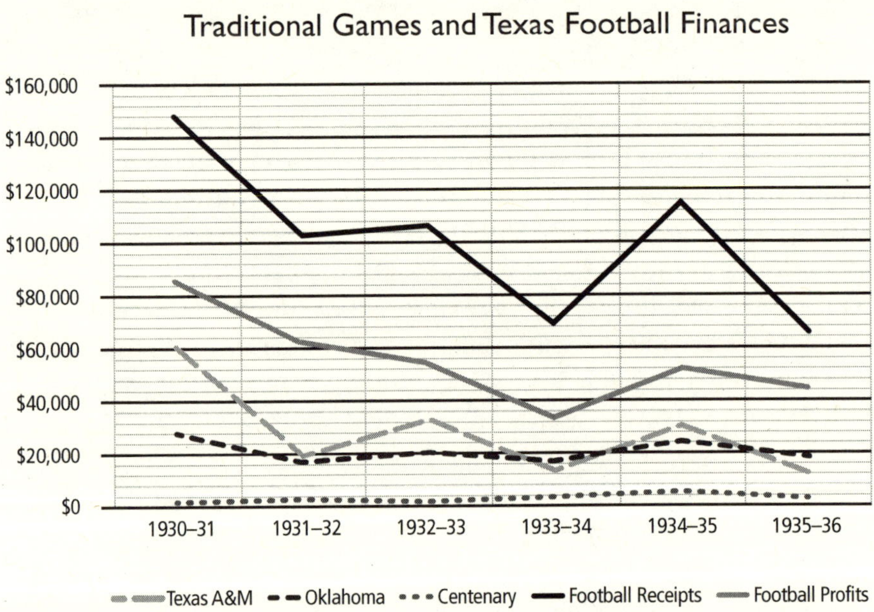

Figure 2.3

Similarly, the revenue from the Ohio State–University of Michigan football games traditionally produced the most interest and revenue for those schools and continued to do so throughout the worst years of the Depression. While the Michigan game maintained its position as the most important and lucrative single event, the early 1930s witnessed a steep decline in total game receipts for it and other games at Ohio State. During the eight years between 1927 and 1936, the Michigan game was always one of the top two money-producing contests for the

Buckeyes, but as the chart (fig. 2.4) indicates, even this annual and attractive game was not able to preserve its revenue levels during the lean years of the early to mid 1930s. Fortunately for the institution, Ohio State officials were wise enough to schedule additional games against other very attractive opponents during the 1930s, producing spikes of not only additional fan interest but also spectator dollars. For example, the 1929 and 1930 Ohio State–University of Pittsburgh football games together produced more than $92,000 in receipts. In 1930 and 1931, games against the Naval Academy (Annapolis, Maryland) nearly equaled that amount. Another home game in 1935 against Notre Dame generated almost $180,000 for the two schools to split, just when they needed it most. As the overall total declined, the percentage of the revenue coming from these two or three "big games" became much more significant.[35]

The Ohio State–Notre Dame game deserves special attention because it was an outstanding game and because it reveals the limits

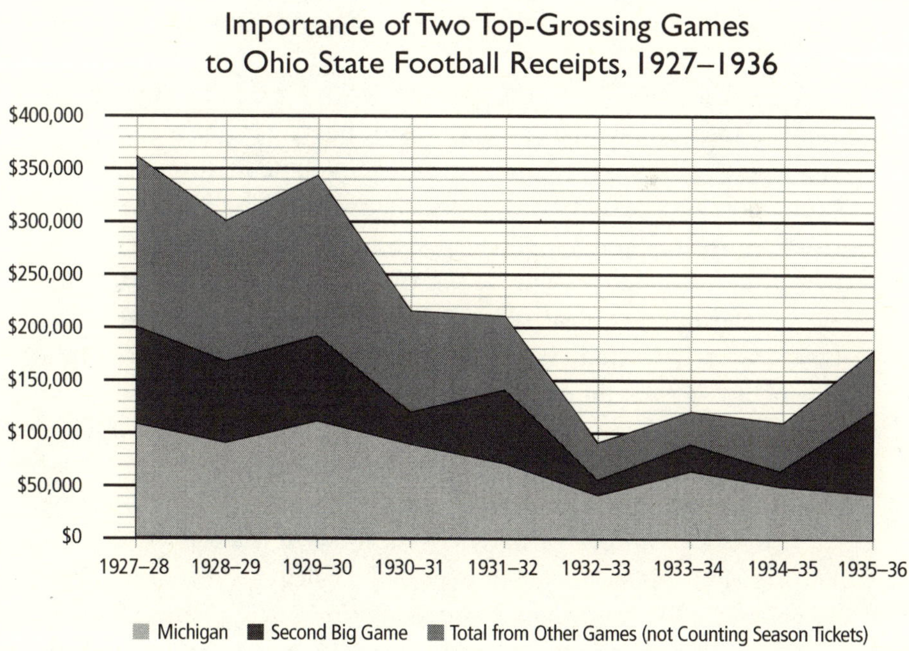

Figure 2.4

of the "big game" appeal to some administrators. The passions and events surrounding the Ohio State–Notre Dame football series in the 1935–36 school year most clearly illustrate the divisive effects that "economic, racial, and religious" disputes could have on campuses and the uneasiness among officials that these disputes caused as they threatened to destroy the campus community. Matching two powerful football squads from neighboring states, the series generated tremendous increases in game receipts when Ohio State desperately needed them; however, it also revealed a decidedly unwelcome sectarian split in the Columbus and campus communities. In 1935, the home game against the Fighting Irish attracted a sellout crowd of more than 81,000 and grossed more than $175,000. As a point of comparison, Ohio State's next highest home receipt total that year barely exceeded $60,000. This game was an unqualified success on the field as well as in the ticket office, with Notre Dame rallying from a 13–0 deficit to win on the game's final play. In 1950, sportswriters recognized this thrilling game as "the greatest college football game of the half-century." Millions across the nation heard the broadcast on CBS, and the next year Ohio State pocketed an additional $65,000 from another close loss, this one in South Bend.[36]

This clearly was a profitable relationship for Ohio State and for Notre Dame, yet the series ended in 1936, not to resume for decades. One wonders why, in the midst of financial difficulty caused by the Depression and facing a hostile legislature, the Ohio State Athletic Board chose not to pursue this seemingly natural and certainly lucrative rivalry. After all, the number of tickets sold and the high prices paid for them clearly indicated public interest. James Pollard unsatisfactorily noted this odd discontinuance with this simple statement: "Despite the excitement it produced this series was never renewed." In fact, according to their athletic director, Lynn St. John, Ohio State officials chose not to renew the series precisely because of "the excitement" surrounding it.[37]

Ohio was a hotbed of nativist sentiment in the early twentieth century. In the 1920s, many Ohioans had participated in the national revival of the Ku Klux Klan and its anti-Catholicism. In fact, a student organization using hooded robes, scare tactics, and the name "The Klandestine Klan" had even helped to raise money for the football stadium, receiving favorable front-page coverage in the student

Ohio State playing Notre Dame in front of a packed house in 1935. *Courtesy of The Ohio State University Archives.*

newspaper for its efforts. During this same period Notre Dame's student body and football players grew accustomed to the passions their school's Catholic heritage aroused. Millions of Americans feverishly supported the Fighting Irish in assertion of their own Catholic pride, while perhaps even more despised and jeered them in a prejudiced backlash, amplified, undoubtedly, by jealousy of Notre Dame's athletic success. According to Murray Sperber, a historian of Notre Dame football, by the mid-1920s Notre Dame had secured the allegiance of most of the nation's urban Catholics as a result of their gridiron successes. The power of that allegiance, even in Columbus, became readily apparent when Notre Dame visited Ohio State in 1935.[38]

The *Columbus Dispatch* reported that twenty-four special trains were necessary to carry all of the interested football fans to Columbus, including the entire Notre Dame student body. According to Sperber, these trainloads of Notre Dame boosters "encountered extremely hostile crowds and anti-Catholic taunts." At one point, the football team had an audience of fifteen thousand anti-Catholics serenading them with jeers.[39] With this reception, one can understand why Notre Dame might have chosen not to play at Ohio State again; however, Notre Dame's entourage had experienced this sort of reception, and much worse, numerous times before. Ohio State's officials, on the other hand, were not used to the divided loyalties the visit revealed and the threat to campus cohesion it created. In their eyes, college athletics were supposed to create community, not destroy it.

In 1940, frustrated by the lack of additional contests between the two institutions, one alumnus wrote to St. John and pointed out the seemingly obvious reasons to renew the series. He wrote, "It's a natural—short distances—neighboring states—outstanding Foot Ball Teams—great universities—Large following (in and out of the university families)—Popular [Institutions?]—Crowd draws—clean athletics—good spirit. etc." He even goaded St. John, telling him that Chicago's football fans compared Ohio State with the University of Chicago, a Big Ten school that had recently abolished football. Neither his logical nor his emotional arguments, however, could persuade St. John to renew the series.[40]

St. John's confidential response to his correspondent reveals a great deal about the important role intercollegiate athletics played in creating community in the 1930s as well as about the depth of prejudices against Catholics many people in central Ohio had during that period. St. John absolved all Protestants and blamed the Catholics themselves for the turmoil surrounding the contest, writing that "the attitude of all the Catholics who attend such a game and who very obviously look upon it as a contest between the Catholic church and other people" was at fault. He cited a friend who explained anti-Catholicism as simply the result of "an inferiority complex that, without justification, gets into the mind of the average Catholic." St. John bemoaned the fact that while Ohio State had as many Catholics on its squad as did Notre Dame, all of Ohio State's Catholic faculty members and students rooted for Notre Dame. This was entirely possible, if not probable, considering Ohio State's demographics in the mid-1930s. During the academic years 1935–36 and 1936–37, Catholics were the third largest religious group on campus, numbering 1,178 and 1,347, respectively. In both years, the Catholic students constituted just fewer than 10 percent of the entire student population. Finally, St. John wrote that football could be a "rallying point for the spirit of an institution and of a community," but that the inability of Catholics to put anything above their church made "intercollegiate football under those conditions . . . a liability and not an asset."[41]

In 1938, Griffith, the commissioner of the Big Ten Conference and the president of the National Collegiate Athletic Association (NCAA), wrote to St. John asking for his opinion about why the members of the Big Ten had won only four football games out of forty-three with Notre Dame over the prior forty-two years. St. John succinctly explained the problems, as he saw them, of playing against Notre Dame. St. John contended that Notre Dame's superiority sprang from its ability to use its Catholic heritage to recruit nationally. He also argued that the Notre Dame athletes enjoyed unfair advantages, writing that in South Bend they had "no interference on account of studies with their daily football work" and got to live in "what amounts to a big training club." Still, St. John insisted, Ohio State would have continued playing Notre Dame if the students and faculty had not "place[d] their loyalty to the church over their loyalty to the Ohio State University." Again, he argued that the Ohio State team had featured "ten or twelve good Catholic boys," at least four of whom started. The competition with Notre Dame produced a tremendous amount of money, two fantastic games (and two tough Ohio State losses), a great deal of national attention, as well as campus and community division. In this case, arguing that "financial return cannot possibly make up for the breaking down of the unity and solidarity in a university community," St. John and others decided that three out of four was not good enough.[42]

These big games, including the Notre Dame ones, were important to Ohio State for several reasons. First, they satisfied a customer base, interesting large numbers of potential university supporters and often eliciting favorable national attention and media coverage. Second, they induced people to spend their precious disposable income at the stadiums' ticket windows. Finally, these games allowed the universities to charge much higher ticket prices and, therefore, to make much more money from the marquee contests than from regular games.

During the 1930s, the ability to charge full prices for game tickets was a rare privilege, and universities took advantage of every opportunity they had to make spectators pay high prices to witness games (fig. 2.5).

The 1935 Ohio State–Notre Dame game provides the best example of how schools used attractive games to justify escalating their ticket prices. Ohio State sold 54,504 tickets to that game: 4,061 box seats for $4.00 each, 45,828 for $3.30, and 4,615 for $2.20. In total, Ohio State sold over 49,000 tickets at more than $3.00. To put this number into perspective, disregarding the 16,120 season tickets Ohio State sold that year, the university sold only 2,028 additional tickets for as much as $3.00, and none for more than $3.00, out of the other 90,348 tickets it sold for home games that year.[43] The higher ticket prices permitted by the attractiveness of high-profile games were much more important during the early 1930s as university athletic programs felt forced to slash their prices in order to get people to attend their other games. At Ohio State and other places, the depressed circumstances compelled the universities to lower many of their ticket prices in the hopes of retaining interest and fan support. Understandably, most were not eager to do so. In early 1932, the director of ticket sales, Henry D. Taylor, wrote to the athletic director, Lynn St. John, that he had a "sinking feeling" as he presented his proposed list of reduced football prices. Still, Taylor believed that, "with conditions as they are, it might be advisable to offer such a bargain."[44]

These "bargains" were seen in the prices for less notable games as well as in the ticket prices for the Michigan game. A quick comparison illustrates exactly how the declining ticket prices affected athletic finances. In 1930, Ohio State played nearby Mount Union College in football, attracting 10,217 fans who paid a total of $12,543 to see the game. Three years later, the University of Virginia's football team visited Columbus, and more than 49,500 fans witnessed the spectacle. The much larger crowd did not translate, however, into much larger profits. On the contrary, 42,987 of those fans (almost 87 percent) paid only ten cents for "children's" tickets to see the game, and only 351 paid more than $1.00. Despite the enormous crowd, the Virginia game brought in less than $10,000 of ticket revenue for Ohio State.[45] It is clear that looking only at attendance figures to document continued public support of athletics misses the important fact that the cost to individuals of supporting Ohio State was often almost nothing.

In what must have been a more troubling scenario, Ohio State even had to reduce the prices of coveted Michigan tickets during the early 1930s. In 1930, Ohio State offered no tickets for the Michigan game for less than $3.00, and the university sold 54,251 tickets for $3.00 and 4,560 for $4.00. Two years later, while almost 22,000 spectators paid $3.00 or more for their tickets, single-ticket sales for the Michigan game fell from 58,811 to 35,533, even though the Buckeyes also offered $2.20 and $1.50 tickets. By the 1934 home game, Ohio State sold only 2,079 tickets for $3.00. In contrast, 75 percent of the 50,000 fans paid either $2.50 or $2.00 for their tickets, and 20 percent paid less than $2.00. In other words, four years after the minimum ticket price for the Michigan game was $3.00, 95 percent of the paying customers got in for less than that. The chart (fig. 2.5) illustrates how, even with the 1934 and 1935 seasons' popular and lucrative home games against Michigan and Notre Dame, respectively, lower-priced tickets came to represent a much more significant percentage of overall ticket sales in the early to mid 1930s.[46]

Following the logic of Ohio State's St. John when he explained in

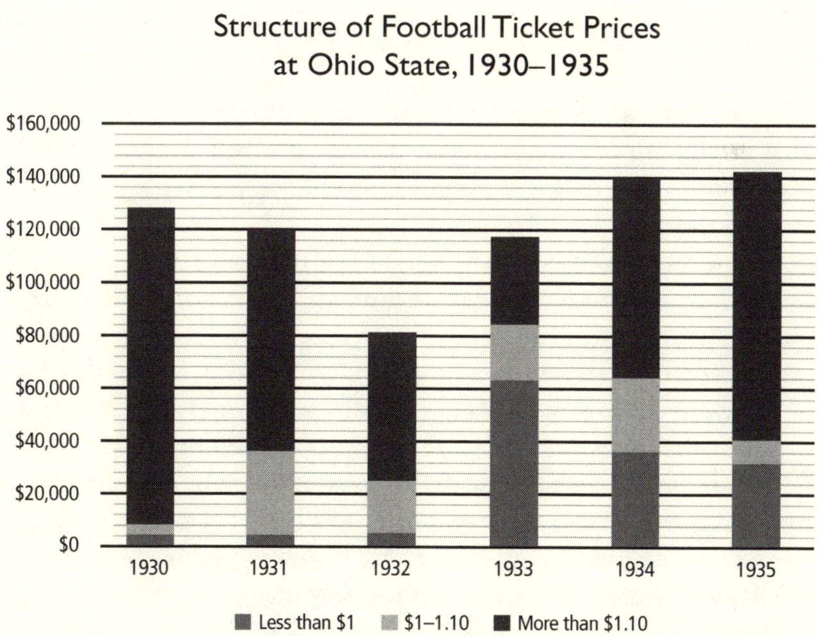

Figure 2.5

1932 that it was neither "reasonable nor good business for us to charge the same prices for the Indiana game here as we do for the Michigan game," other athletic departments around the nation adjusted their ticket prices during the 1930s, seeking the perfect price point that would allow them to continue attracting large numbers of fans, but also recognizing that the fans might be reluctant to spend as much as earlier for tickets.[47] For example, the University of Texas charged only $1.10 for all tickets to the 1933 football contests against Southwestern University and the Mines College, and it priced the "choice seats" for the Centenary game at $2.00, allowing the "majority seats" to sell for $1.50. Most other games that season followed the same price structure as the Centenary game. The next year, however, Texas officials reduced the best Centenary seats to $1.50 and sold the rest for $1.10, while the university approved lower-priced ticket options for most of the other games as well.[48]

It is clear that "big games" and "big money" could mean much different things to different universities during the 1930s. Without formal classifications such as those that exist today, when commentators discussed "big-time" college athletics, they spoke generally. Using such generalizations today, however, obscures the wide range of athletic income and spending that existed even among the major state universities.

The University of Maryland represented the lower end of the big-time spectrum, entering the decade of the 1930s with average football net profits between $25,000 and $30,000 a year. In 1930, university officials believed that they had finally found a cash cow, a football series against the Naval Academy with one game in Annapolis and two in either Baltimore or Washington, D.C. The contract arranging the contests specified that if a game in the series grossed more than $80,000, then the universities would split the net proceeds in half, but with the Naval Academy getting an additional $6,000. If the net total were less than $80,000, then the division would be a true fifty-fifty split. Based on the 1932 financial summary of the game, the nitpicking about what would happen once the revenue topped $80,000 had been an exercise in futility.[49]

After printing almost 60,000 tickets for the game, Maryland and Navy sold precisely 8,761 of them. This produced a net profit of $5,989 that the universities, as they had agreed, split in half. Despite their puny share, Maryland athletic officials must have been happy to make a profit at all, considering that the next week's financial report indicated a net loss of $299.92 for an away game against Washington and Lee University witnessed by 738 customers.[50]

While Maryland spent the rest of the decade hoping to net $2,000–2,500 a football game, which was necessary to make football "self-supporting," other institutions across the nation set their sights much higher, still relying upon glamorous big games to make their budgets work. The University of Tennessee, for example, grossed more than $73,001, netting more than $50,000 from a 1934 football game against the University of Alabama, Tennessee's traditional rival; and the university reaped more than $100,000 from its 1940 appearance in the Rose Bowl, a game the football team lost.[51]

Just as the economic pains of the early 1930s were shared across the nation's universities, so were the reactions, as university officials responded to the economic slowdown and athletic revenue shortfalls of the 1930s with a variety of standard measures. Without exception, they slashed administrative costs (but not their own positions), and at many institutions athletic officials only grudgingly accepted the salary reductions that were mandatory in all other university departments. Schools and conferences almost immediately targeted minor sports programs for reductions in the number of programs, games, or both. Recognizing the potential pitfalls that lay ahead, Griffith adopted the industrial rhetoric of the day and warned his colleagues in 1931 that the universities might have to act more like private businesses and discontinue unprofitable lines: minor sports.[52]

At Ohio State, the Athletic Department officials initially resisted all suggestions that they submit to salary reductions as all other university employees had to do, basing their argument on the independence they saw as granted by separate athletic revenue sources. Ultimately, athletic personnel grudgingly worked out an agreement with the board of trustees, one that required reductions only on the salary portions that came from non-athletic sources.[53] This reduction can be seen most clearly in the Athletic Department's "administration and general expenditures" in the years 1929 through 1935. The university had allocated more than $128,000 for this line item in the 1929–30 fiscal year, but when the university began suffering from economic difficulties, administrators cut the expenses to $112,000, then to $89,000, and finally to the mid to upper $50,000s, where the expenses remained from 1931 until 1935.[54]

At most schools athletic officials were reluctant to follow the same salary guidelines as other university employees, but this was a public relations battle they could not win. Speaking in 1933, a Northwestern University professor noted, "The problem of salary adjustment is a most difficult one. I do not think that any member of the coaching staff can expect to avoid the cuts that have fallen the lot of the entire faculty of his institution." He continued, discussing the "several instances where coaches and directors were granted exemptions and the ill feeling and criticism that it aroused on the faculty cost the unfortunate individuals far more than they gained."[55]

Athletic officials and coaches felt entitled to exemptions from university-wide salary reductions because universities had already established the precedent of treating them differently, especially in matters of compensation. This practice only highlighted the existing and growing divide between the academic and athletic arms of the universities. In fact, one of Howard Savage's primary criticisms of intercollegiate athletics in his *American College Athletics* was the elevation of professional coaches to positions of great importance and power on the university campus. He argued that the "position of a coach whose tenure depends upon victory is both unfortunate and unfair. The situation is deleterious to sport but especially to education, however it is defined."[56]

Savage found that among the surveyed institutions, the highest-paid full professor made $12,000, while the best-compensated football coach made $14,000. The median salary for full professors was $5,000, against $6,000 for the coaches. The average professor salary was $5,158, as opposed to $6,107 for the coaches. Generally, Savage and his colleagues found that smaller institutions were doing a better job than larger schools of keeping coaches and professors in the same salary structure, but the national trends remained troubling.[57]

Even before the Depression, this broadly based criticism of coaches as a privileged elite within the university certainly applied to the state universities of California, Texas, Ohio, Tennessee, and Maryland, as well as to most other US universities. While the University of Texas was signing a three-year contract in early 1931 that paid Clyde Littlefield $6,500 a year to be head football and track coach, the University of California paid its head football coach $8,500 a year plus an additional $3,500 annually for his duties as head track coach. In January 1929 California also generously compensated the coach of its nationally prominent crew squad with a $500 raise, bringing his annual salary up to $7,500. The coming of a national depression did not deter California from giving its next football coach an even more lucrative compensation package. In 1931, after setting an internal limit of $15,000 a year, the ASUC awarded Bill Ingram a three-year contract worth $13,000 annually, and the Associated Students also provided Ingram with $3,000 to cover his moving expenses.[58]

National economic trends did force some reconsideration, however. Only two years later, California's athletic officials deemed this salary excessive. In a retrenchment move, the ASUC cancelled Ingram's $13,000-a-year contract and gave him a new one worth just more than 75 percent of his existing contract. The new one paid Ingram "only" $10,000 a year for two years. Similarly, the highly paid and very successful crew coach, who had been earning $7,500 a year, also had to accept a new contract paying him $5,750 a year for two years.[59]

Although during the 1920s and 1930s US universities paid more, in terms of attention and salary, to their football programs, they did not leave the other coaches poverty stricken. As the crew coach's salary indicates, the University of California's largess was not restricted to the football program; still, the salary structure revealed a great deal about the areas of athletic emphasis. For example, after paying C. M. Price $4,500 to be the head basketball coach (he had also been the head football coach) in the 1930–31 school year, the university signed him to a one-year $3,000 contract in April 1931 and to a two-year contract at $3,500 in March of 1932. Meanwhile, over the same years Leonard B. Allison, an important assistant football coach, earned $7,500 and then $9,000 a year. In 1932, while Price received $3,500 as the head basketball coach, another football assistant received almost double his salary, earning $6,000. In contrast, the university would not pay more than $5,000 for a head track coach. Once Allison became head football coach in November 1934, however, his salary remained stable at $9,000 with a three-year contract.[60] Even at an institution with other prominent and successful sports, football was the most important sport on campus, and the salary structure reflected its position.

The head football coach's salary at California did not reach the symbolic $10,000 figure again until the 1937–38 season, and it did not again surpass it until April of 1939, the same year the head basketball coach finally earned $5,000. While the ASUC executives decided that they could again afford these salaries, they also decided that they could not return completely to the compensation excesses of the late 1920s and the early 1930s. To make this point clearly, the executives included in their minutes their belief that "the salary of an assistant football coach should not exceed $6,000." This time they drew the line: they would pay $6,000 (and they immediately did), but not more.[61]

Many Midwestern universities displayed the same priorities as the University of California did in their athletic salary structures during the 1930s, as a one-year snapshot illustrates. During one of the worst years of the Depression, 1932–33, the average Big Ten head football coach's salary was $7,709, with the lowest being $5,000 at the University of Iowa and highest coming from the University of Wisconsin at $10,000. In contrast, the average salary for Big Ten head basketball coaches was $4,672, a mere 60 percent of the football coaches' average. Judging by these figures, Ohio State provides an appropriate sample for those wanting to observe national trends of compensation and depression-induced retrenchment. In the 1931–32 academic year the head football coach at Ohio State received $7,800; all but $300 of this total came from athletic receipts. Reflecting plummeting athletic revenues, in 1932–33 the coach earned $7,150, with $6,650 coming from athletic receipts. Over the same two-year period, the head basketball coach's total compensation fell from $6,000 to $5,100, and the track and cross country coach lost 12 percent of his salary as it dropped from $5,450 to $4,800. The university eliminated the entire salaries of the tennis, golf, gymnastics, fencing, rifle, soccer, and polo coaches, even though most of these men had made less than $600 in 1931–32, as the university relegated these sports to intramural status. By 1934 though, the Athletic Board members believed that they could afford to commit to a three-year contract providing $7,500 a year to the colorful and exciting new football coach, Francis Schmidt.[62]

Unlike coaches at many other institutions, Robert Neyland never faced a salary reduction while coaching at the University of Tennessee during the Depression. His high salary was not, however, entirely a result of his personal negotiating power and past successes; it also reflected the general importance the school placed on football. When military duties called Neyland overseas during the mid–1930s, his replacement still earned $6,000 a year, three times more than the highest-paid professor's salary. Still, that high salary did not compare to the one Neyland received after he returned to the Knoxville campus. Looking to fend off any potential suitors from other schools, the board of trustees gave Neyland a $1,500 raise, increasing his total salary for his work as athletic director and football coach to $13,500. In 1940, the university president earned only 63 percent of Neyland's salary; in fact, that year the president ran his entire office for less than what Neyland made, a sum greater than 10 percent of the entire Liberal Arts College budget.[63]

If most large public US universities did not respond to the financial problems of the early 1930s by cutting major sports programs or coaches' salaries too dramatically, they did not restrain from whittling away at their "minor" sports programs to protect these other expenses. At almost every institution, all sports but football were indeed unprofitable or, at most, barely covered their own expenses. This is not to imply that minor sports did not contribute tangibly to the athletic environment at many universities; often, institutions were able to claim national championship titles, and the resulting prestige, because these minor sports programs existed. For example, the fact that the University of California's crew team represented the United States in the 1928 and 1932 Olympics brought much positive coverage to the university; and the highly successful University of Maryland lacrosse team brought favorable press for that university as well.[64]

Colleges and universities in the United States preserved the breadth of their men's intercollegiate athletic programs to a remarkable degree during the trying years of the 1930s. Instead of jettisoning many less-popular teams and programs, athletic officials doggedly kept them operating by taking institutional and conference-wide steps to reduce costs and to minimize losses. In 1933, one professor was pleased to report to his colleagues that, although US schools "have been forced to curtail severely" their minor sports programs, "few institutions have been forced to drop outright from their program any sport that had previously met favor by the students."[65] This national observation gains credence when one examines the fates of minor sports at a variety of US public universities.

As mentioned earlier, Southern Conference institutions shared enough financial difficulties in the fall of 1932 that many, including the University of Maryland, considered dropping, or at least trimming, their spring sports offerings. Although complete cancellation proved to be unnecessary, Maryland officials took several steps to reduce the financial drain created by the unprofitable spring sports. As one news report indicated, since even popular spring sports did "not draw sufficient numbers to College Park," school officials considered "play[ing] their big games on foreign fields." The report noted especially the baseball team's ability to attract crowds in North Carolina and Virginia and the lacrosse team's attractiveness to teams in the North and in Baltimore. At the same time the University of Texas officials strongly resisted the Southwest Conference proposal to abolish baseball completely because of the Depression.[66]

Other institutions sought to maintain minor sports programs while reducing expenses by limiting the numbers of games, players, and trips. For example, Ohio State stopped sending its baseball teams on southern trips because of the expense during the Depression; and, along with other Big Ten institutions, the Buckeyes also took several other steps to minimize costs. In 1933, Big Ten member institutions voted to limit the number of baseball players that could travel to away games to thirteen, allowing fifteen if the squad would play multiple games. The schools also set limits on the wages schools could pay the one umpire for baseball games. They similarly restricted the numbers of competitions for wrestling and other sports, and Ohio State established a "hitch hike" plan utilizing private cars and personal favors to get its athletes to their competitions and to house them once there.[67]

When it came time for athletic budgeting committees to identify their funding priorities, minor sports generally did not triumph, but, importantly, most did not disappear. Instead, just as in the early 1930s athletic officials across the nation labored to maintain as extensive an intercollegiate sporting program as possible for their male students, by the mid to late 1930s many institutions were eager and able to add to their men's athletic offerings, especially programs that would utilize the new athletic facilities the universities had built or committed to building during happier times.

Ohio State, for example, added swimming as a varsity sport when the new swimming pool opened in 1931, but it could not support all of its established sports in the early 1930s. In 1930, the board of trustees cited lack of funds in its refusal to recognize boxing as a varsity sport, but by 1936 the university was able to increase its contributions to many minor sports. For example, at its November 23, 1936, meeting, the Athletic Board added budgetary line items totaling almost $2,000 to fund pistol and rifle shooting, polo, and fencing teams.[68]

The Universities of Texas, California, and Maryland took similar actions to support minor sports in spirit, if not always in budgetary line items. In 1933 the University of Texas Athletic Council authorized the designation of fencing as a varsity sport with the understanding that the council would not contribute financially to the program, and in 1936 boxing and wrestling got "unofficial probational" status, meaning that they were not intercollegiate varsity activities but that participants got certain benefits and recognition, including full use of the gymnasium and other recreational facilities. The council, however, rejected numerous applications requesting varsity status for polo.[69]

In California, after limiting all activities in 1931 in an effort to avoid large deficits, the ASUC approved polo as a varsity sport in 1934, provided that the team's expenses did not exceed its income. That same year, the director of physical education, Frank Kleeberger, argued for an expansive sports program, stating that the university should do everything it could to expose students to as many sporting opportunities as possible, including cricket, tennis, and soccer. In 1934, California officials also recognized that they had to pay more attention to their track program; with a crowd greater than twelve thousand at the last University of Southern California–University of California meet, the public interest certainly existed.[70]

Similarly, throughout the 1930s Maryland students competed in intercollegiate sports that were not officially recognized or funded by the athletic board but were assisted by the Physical Education Department. Although the Maryland athletic director recognized many problems with this arrangement, he thought the benefits to the students outweighed the problems such decentralization caused. By 1940, Maryland had elevated three of these club sports—soccer, wrestling, and golf—to varsity status.[71]

Another response to the financial pressures of the Depression was to cater to the prevailing consumer culture by encouraging more exciting styles of play and by trying to buy success by hiring brand-name coaches, men who had achieved success on their own or who had been affiliated with successful programs, often at the University of Notre Dame. When replacing its football coach between the 1933 and 1934 seasons, Ohio State hired Francis Schmidt, a coach acclaimed for the style and flair that his Texas Christian University teams had displayed, in direct contrast to the unimaginative, if successful, style of his Ohio State predecessor, Sam Willaman. According to university historian James Pollard, Schmidt "was an exponent of open football and ushered in an era of 'razzle-dazzle' play in the Stadium and on opponents' fields which attracted wide attention and greatly increased the interest in football." Pollard also noted, "Schmidt himself was equally colorful."[72] When trying to attract crowds, a little razzle-dazzle was a good thing.

In its two football coach hires of the 1930s, the University of Texas deployed the two main methods of attracting a great deal of enthusiasm for a program: hiring one coach with connections to Notre Dame and hiring another with a recognizable name and successful reputation. In 1931, when the University of Texas hired Jack Chevigny as its football coach, the Longhorns got the man who had tied the score with a touchdown in the famous Army–Notre Dame "Gipper" game and a man who had also coached at his alma mater under Knute Rockne. It would have been difficult to find an individual with more personal brushes with celebrity and success than Chevigny in 1931, and the University of Texas community seemed pleased with its hire.[73]

Although Chevigny's teams had several successful seasons, including a win over his alma mater in 1934, the personal-institutional relationship soured, and the Texas Athletic Council began to look for another star to buy. The council had to pay full price to lure its target, Dana X. Bible, away from his joint appointment as athletic director and head football coach at the University of Nebraska, where he was an established commodity. Before his tenure at Nebraska, Bible had coached Texas A & M and had won five Southwest Conference championships in a decade, a stretch that included two teams that did not surrender a point. After continuing his success at Nebraska, Bible was a star in the coaching world; in fact, Benjamin Rader has listed Bible along with Glenn "Pop" Warner and Knute Rockne as the most famous college football coaches of the 1920–50 era.[74] That kind of prestige and public recognition did not come cheaply.

The University of Texas Athletic Council offered Bible in 1937 a ten-year contract to serve as athletic director at $7,500 a year and a five-year contract to serve as football coach at $7,500 a year, and it arranged for "interested people outside the University" to give Bible a $5,000 signing bonus. The council members justified the high price for Bible by arguing that he would be able to increase the football team's profits and that he would soon earn the respect of the university's faculty members, who would, undoubtedly, initially resent his pay scale. As an additional argument for Bible, the council contended that Bible would "command and retain indefinitely the respect and cooperation of all groups interested in athletic affairs more effectively than any other possible appointee, which advantage alone justifies a large stipend."[75] Although the committee members recognized that Bible was expensive, they knew that they could not put a price tag on his anticipated ability to build stronger community ties.

The commercial orientation increasingly extended to all aspects of college athletics. Even if college officials at the University of California and elsewhere could stomach playing institutions not of their "own standards, both academically and athletically," many continued to voice real concerns about creeping commercialism, the decline of amateurism, and the interference of athletics with the intellectual pursuits of the university. Their actions, however, did not always match their rhetoric. Throughout the Depression, many officials lessened their resistance to commercial ties to their athletic teams, embracing almost any activity that could generate additional income for their universities. For example, they began signing contracts by the late 1930s that allowed commercially sponsored radio broadcasts. Although the financial benefits for the universities were small, often less than $5,000 a year, the broadcasts had the potential to bring in money and also to stir up interest among potential paying customers. In fact, the main argument against the broadcasts was not the commercial component but the fear that the availability of free broadcasts would dissuade fans from purchasing tickets to the games.[76]

The University of Texas was one of the most blatant in its straying from the paths of pure amateurism; in fact, according to the minutes of the university's Athletic Council, the subject of amateurism *never* came up in that body's deliberations during the 1930s. Throughout the decade, University of Texas athletic teams, primarily baseball and men's basketball, competed regularly against professional teams and other clubs not affiliated with educational institutions. For example, in 1929, the Athletic Council approved games against Babe Ruth's New York Yankees and the New York Giants, and the university continued to compete against professional baseball teams throughout the rest of the decade. Meanwhile, during the 1930s, the basketball team was challenging Olson's Terrible Swedes and the New York Celtics, the "world's professional championship team."[77]

Most university athletic officials believed by the end of the 1930s that the tough times were over and that athletic revenues would return to stability, if not necessarily to the levels of the late 1920s. Ohio State officials, for example, in 1936 projected that they would continue to gross more than $229,000 from their "games and sports" activities for the next nine years. This optimism was expressed after the athletic board members had witnessed the games and sports decline from $434,646 to $166,588 (with a low of $129,111) over the preceding eight years.[78] Certainly by the late 1930s athletic leaders at universities all across the country believed that they had made it through the toughest part of the crisis, and they found that they had done so with their athletic programs relatively unscathed. In most instances, they were right. These officials were able to preserve the institution of men's college athletics at large public universities primarily because football remained profitable throughout the decade, even if not to the same degree as before.

Equally importantly, the leaders of US universities developed several successful strategies for dealing with the crises of confidence and income that the Depression caused. Through a combination of spending and program reductions, increased commercialism, and creative scheduling, university athletic officials protected most of their major and minor sport programs from the financial distresses of the Depression. One reason that they did so was they had no choice: the universities had to pay the bills for the athletic construction of the 1920s and early 1930s. The officials were also motivated by their desire to protect their own salaries and stations. But they also did so because they believed that intercollegiate athletics could teach essential lessons about competition and perseverance to athletes and audiences that no other component of the university could teach and that were vitally important given the political, economic, and social challenges confronting the nation in the 1930s.

CHAPTER 3

★ ★ ★ ★ ★

Competitive Democratic Athletics for Men

"Ideals" seems to me to be a rather lofty word to use in connection with intercollegiate athletics. What about ideals of duck hunting or of chess playing or of backyard gardening? Pleasant and healthful outdoor activity is involved in all these.

—H. Y. BENEDICT, PRESIDENT
OF THE UNIVERSITY OF TEXAS, 1932.

Through our athletic programs, we can help to inculcate in our boys the American spirit. We can refuse to be influenced by the soft idealists. We can let the world know where we stand and what we are doing.

—JOHN L. GRIFFITH, COMMISSIONER
OF THE BIG TEN CONFERENCE, 1939.

Universities and their athletic programs came under ideological assault on two fronts in the United States during the Great Depression. One set of attacks came from those groups of faculty and students who were upset by what they viewed as the tendency of schools to support the status quo that disadvantaged important groups. Another type of attack came from groups and individuals who criticized the growing commercialism of college athletics and who questioned the education values of these programs. The trials of the Depression and its accompanying social conflict led athletic leaders to reaffirm and reemphasize a positive ideology of competitive men's sport that stressed the social and personal lessons athletics could teach young men. The university officials also linked the spread of competitive values to the desired maintenance of a traditional, laissez-faire capitalist social order. The effect was to politicize athletics, associating America's school sporting culture with leadership and corporate forms, as well as national vigor and strength. In the eyes of many prominent athletic organizers and administrators, competitive sports were especially important as a bulwark against radicalism and disunity, in general, and against socialism and communism, in particular. Their association of sports with traditional democratic values served to defend intercollegiate athletics against the reform impulses epitomized by the 1929 Carnegie Foundation for the Advancement of Teaching report and the social and economic pressures brought on by the Depression.

As discussed in chapter 2, during the 1930s, university presidents had to articulate their views of the role of state universities, often defending the universities' activities department by department. Of all the university programs, intercollegiate athletics received the most scrutiny and provoked the most involved debates. Depression-era American college and university officials had multiple reasons to reconsider their institutions' commitments to big-time intercollegiate athletics. The 1929 release of the Carnegie Foundation for the Advancement of Teaching's scathing *American College Athletics*, coupled with the onset of real financial difficulties in the early 1930s, gave university administrators substantive reasons to reevaluate the role and function of intercollegiate athletics.

Critics contended that these programs were the least "educational" parts of the university, but even to these skeptics, athletics remained an essential part of the modem US university. Even as people inside and outside the academy pointed out the corruption of intercollegiate athletics, very few seriously proposed completely abandoning the existing system. If they were not going to jettison all the sports programs, though, officials still had to justify keeping them. What emerged from the reconsideration of intercollegiate athletics in the late 1920s and the 1930s was an interlocking structure of justifications, rationalizations, and accommodations, all of which worked together to buttress the institution of intercollegiate athletics against the most forceful criticism it had received since the early 1900s, when the outrage over football violence reached Theodore Roosevelt's White House and led to the creation of the National Collegiate Athletic Association (NCAA).[1]

Public university presidents and officials saw the protection and perpetuation of democracy as the fundamental duty of the universities. As public institutions, according to the presidents, universities could best serve the general populations of the states by educating their youth, by preparing them for productive lives, and by coordinating other research and service programs that could benefit the states' citizens. According to historian Frederick Rudolph, US universities began to reemphasize their commitments to public service and to democracy in the 1920s. This desire to meet the needs of the general public in a prosperous decade resulted in the creation of numerous new schools of business and public administration. During the 1930s, as they needed the support of the taxpayers and legislators, public universities had no choice but to promote aggressively their abilities to aid the states' residents. These schools continued to prepare business students for leadership, just as they touted the tangible benefits of their research programs and argued that athletics could help prepare young men mentally for the competitive social and business arenas that they would soon enter.[2]

If university officials had faced only budgetary problems during the 1930s, they might not have perceived a widespread threat to their universities' and country's values or marshaled all resources, including athletic programs, to preserve these core values. Instead, the 1930s proved a tumultuous decade for American students, faculty, and administrators; and this national sense of campus crisis and the seemingly constant state of turmoil caused many officials to see almost any questioning of the status quo as a direct challenge to their universities', the country's, and their own authority and legitimacy. Athletic officials labored to preserve, for their male students, competitive ideas and programs designed to teach them the diligence, determination, and competitive zeal necessary to succeed in a modem business environment, while at the same time preserving a vital sense of campus community.[3] They frequently made their case in public pronouncements and in private letters, but they would find that their task was not an easy one during the 1930s. In order to understand the urgency and intensity of these leaders' defenses of men's competitive athletics, it is necessary to understand the level and types of turmoil and threats they were witnessing on their campuses in the 1930s.

Part of the leaders' difficulty lay in the number and intensity of attacks on some traditional ideas and customs that arose from the suffering of the Depression. The 1930s witnessed the invigoration of a politics suspicious of the traditional interests of established institutions. Attacks on compulsory military training, for example, swept across the nation's campuses as student groups challenged the conventions of tying the manpower needs of the military services with higher education. The controversies of the early 1930s prompted one historian of Ohio State to label the school year 1930–31 as "one of turmoil and trouble for the University from without and within." During that academic year, the student Liberal Club protested against the compulsory military drills required by the university. This led to a faculty vote in favor of optional military drilling, the threat of intercession by the state legislature, and a reversal of the faculty vote. These Ohio State challenges to military drilling on campus were emblematic of a national phenomenon that fed societal perceptions of a radicalizing student culture opposed to "American" values and institutions.[4]

At the University of California at Berkeley, for example, the student Anti-War Committee promoted participation in a national peace strike in April 1935, the same year that university president Robert G. Sproul reported to his colleagues that "our experience here over the years has more and more convinced us that military training as maintained under the R.O.T.C. is a valuable asset to the University." Berkeley police officers arrested the Anti-War Committee's leaders for violating a local law regulating leaflet distribution, and the vocal students received no assistance or support from the university's Associated Students organization. Shortly thereafter, more than two thousand students gathered to protest against war and militarism, but according to one report, only about 10 to 15 percent of the attendees went to participate in the rally. The others just went to watch. This drama occurred at an embarrassing time for the university because the outspoken students were drawing attention to themselves precisely when the state legislature was discussing the university's budget.[5]

The California student protests continued throughout the decade, as did the problematic public association of the university with radicalism. In his presidential report covering the years 1932 to 1934, Sproul entitled one section "Student Body Represents Sound Americanism," in which he explained that the university had told all students that "if you don't believe in America and American institutions, you have no place in the University of the State." Sproul acknowledged, however, that in a student population of almost twenty thousand, the UC system indeed harbored "youths tinged with disloyalty." His belief that the university and the state must respect these students' rights to free speech did not please all Californians, nor did the continuing activities of these allegedly "disloyal youths."[6] In 1936, California students voted by more than a two to one ratio to end compulsory ROTC training, but the board of regents did not submit to the students' wishes, maintaining the program as it existed. By 1937 the Associated Students of the University of California (ASUC) had a Peace Committee, and it sought unsuccessfully to rebut the regents' arguments for requiring ROTC training.[7]

The challenges to military training and institutional support of the armed forces also surfaced on the East Coast as officials at the University of Maryland suffered even greater headaches over the issue of mandatory ROTC. training. In 1935, freshman Ennis H. Coale, a devout Methodist and a practicing pacifist, along with a friend, asked for an exemption from the mandatory military training at Maryland. President Raymond A. Pearson, with the consent of the board of regents, promptly expelled the students for their insubordination, prompting the two to sue the university for re-admission with an ROTC exemption. This case brought national attention to College Park as it became a test case, making its way through the judicial system to the US Supreme Court, with the Methodist Church and the American Association of University Professors (AAUP), among others, supporting the petition and the *New York Times* and the ROTC backing the university's decision and decrying the case as a part of a "carefully planned Communist campaign."[8]

The US Supreme Court did not agree to hear the University of Maryland case, essentially affirming the appeals court's decision that in a free country the students were free to earn their degrees elsewhere. Further south, in Knoxville, the University of Tennessee League for Industrial Democracy, an organization connected to the National Socialist Party, also protested the mandatory ROTC training. Unsurprisingly, this organization's arguments did not convince the president of the University of Tennessee, James Hoskins. Hoskins wrote in 1935, "The mental and physical alertness, the poise, confidence, and self respect obtained through military training make it worthwhile."[9] Student activists proved unable to attract a large following in Knoxville; as part of a national strike against war, only twenty-nine Tennessee students gathered. Three of these were newspaper reporters, and many more were seemingly drawn more by the novelty of the event than its ideological content.[10]

As comments alleging a Communist conspiracy in College Park, Berkeley, and Knoxville illustrate, during the 1930s many Americans remained vigilant for any signs of radicalism, especially at public universities. University administrators accordingly acted to squelch student activism seen as leftist. At Ohio State in 1931, the *Free Voice*, a student newspaper that challenged the university's policies in many areas, briefly emerged and helped inspire the protest against compulsory military training. Although student protests and publications occasionally presented a leftist face to the public, official activities and ceremonies conveyed a different message, one much less critical of the nation and its difficulties. Many of these activities served as fodder in promoting a jingoistic American patriotism, and athletics were often central to this endeavor. For instance, the president of the American Nationalist Confederation, "a Coalition of Anti-Communist Organizations," wrote to Sproul and described how sixty-eight thousand spectators at an Ohio State game responded to the playing of the national anthem: "At that time were we convinced, that in spite of all the forces of unrest throughout the world, here was one people that would still devote their lives, their fortunes and their sacred honor to the maintenance of those high principles of Liberty, Justice, and Humanity upon which this nation was founded."[11]

The concern for the preservation of a certain brand of "American values" was evident in the administration buildings in Columbus, Ohio, and at most other US universities. At the University of Maryland, presidents Raymond A. Pearson and his successor, Harry C. Byrd, also kept a close watch on the activities of liberal students on their campus and across the nation. Pearson maintained a clipping file of activities he viewed suspiciously. One, for example, was a *Baltimore Sun* story entitled "Kansas Students Dance with Negro Girls and Lose Social Privileges" and another was "The Searchlight: Data on Subversive Movements Against the American Government, Political and Labor Radicals, Communists and the 'Pinks.'" The *Sun* story about the Kansas dance emphasized the importance of the YMCA as a facilitator of racial mixing, dating back to the mid-1920s. Pearson was especially alarmed with the "alleged radical drift of Y.M.C.A." Throughout the 1930s, Pearson and Byrd monitored campus speakers and groups' activities closely, just as they continued to correspond with the anti-radical Better America Federation and other similar groups as they sought to contain and understand "anti-American forces such as the A.C.L.U."[12]

At the University of California, student radical activity brought on public relations controversies throughout the decade. There, voices from the left were heard loudly and clearly, both across the campus and around the state. In 1931, the Social Problems Club, loosely connected to the National Student League (NSL), argued that the "extracurricular activities of university students should not be restricted to football, fraternities, sororities, and teas," but should also include substantive political action.[13] Other student organizations at Berkeley included the Young People's Socialist League and the Young Communist League. Although Sproul thought that the protests, strikes, and rhetoric of these student groups brought trouble for the university, and although he sanctioned measures designed to limit their visibility and influence on campus, he did not try to silence them completely.[14]

In 1934, however, in the context of campus turmoil, statewide labor unrest, and an election with a former Socialist, Upton Sinclair, campaigning to "end poverty in California," Sproul delivered a series of speeches intended to highlight his personal anti-radicalism. Sproul, however, would not go along with suspensions of UCLA student officers who had violated their university's rules regarding political discussions. This stance prompted the Los Angeles *Evening Post* to credit Sproul for recognizing that not everybody "with an independent idea is a Communist." Sproul's discretion, along with the continued student agitation, persuaded many Californians that their state university was indeed a seedbed for subversive activity.[15]

In addition to sharing political upheaval, many US universities faced racial unrest during the 1930s, with the challenges to the existing norms strengthening many administrators' beliefs that they faced a general political and social crisis. The activities of the Associated Students of the University of California in combating racial discrimination certainly would have been enough to convince officials at the universities in Tennessee, Texas, and Maryland that anti-American forces were at work in Berkeley. In 1939, after a local athletic club had denied entry to two students of Japanese ancestry who wanted to attend a dance, the ASUC wrote the club with this request: "Because we feel that racial discrimination is a prime factor in undermining democracy, we ask that you adopt in the future a policy of non-discrimination in admitting people to your dining and dancing facilities."[16] When the club refused to adhere to the requested policy, the ASUC voted not to hold its senior banquet at the club.[17] This type of principled stance against racial discrimination was conspicuously absent at the other schools, especially at the southern schools of Maryland, Tennessee, and Texas, but also in the Midwest at Ohio State.

At the University of Texas in 1932, the National Student League helped to publish an alternative student newspaper called *The Spark*. This paper confronted the nation's and that state's social problems head-on, discomforting the university administration, which preferred to avoid politically unsettling social unrest. The front page featured a cartoon of college graduates standing in unemployment lines, an alarming essay calling for workers and students to unite, a report on starvation in Austin, and an essay arguing that "college students and workers will be shot down to protect capitalist investments."[18] The regents were especially upset when the National Student League challenged racial segregation by prominently supporting "full social and political equality for Negroes and other minorities." One regent immediately proposed banning the National Student League from the campus entirely.[19] Another correspondent, writing as a "former stu-

THE SPARK

PUBLISHED THROUGH VOLUNTARY CONTRIBUTIONS
OF STUDENTS OF THE UNIVERSITY OF TEXAS

VOLUME I. AUSTIN, TEXAS, JUNE, 1932. NUMBER I.

UNIVERSITY WORKERS DEFRAUDED

Students and Workers! Form A United Front!

As the first issue of our paper goes to press, it seems highly probable that laborers employed on University building projects will continue to work for starvation wages. The matter has been referred to a tribunal of three judges, one of whom granted the original restraining order against the payment of standard compensations. Illusions of judicial impartiality to the contrary, the sole function of the courts, under a competitive economic order, is to protect the interests of the capitalist class. This contention is proven by the train of injunctions issued against struggling workers, and by the long list of judicial murders of those who dare to protest against legalized robbery and exploitation.

The workers and students must learn to place no faith in capitalistic judges or capitalistic politicians. These gentry promise to bring about a Heaven on Earth, in order to get working-class votes. If they do grant a few minor concessions, it is for the purpose of doping the workers into more submissive acceptance of the system. The enforcement of these same concessions in the form of innocuous statutes by the judges, the politicians, and the police reminds one of a snake chewing its own tail.

Students and workers must form a broad united front for action if the workers on the building projects receive justice. The workers themselves must organize rank and file committees to carry on an unceasing struggle for better wages and improved condition.

WAR!

College Students and Workers Will be Shot Down to Protect Capitalist Investments!

A second great war will begin in a few weeks or days, according to reliable information, concurred in by American, European, and Asiatic military quarters. It will not be an "Act of God." It has been definitely planned by men—business men, militarists, and politicians throughout the world.

The only way that capitalism can save itself is through war. Each capitalist country has a large surplus of products which it cannot dispose of, either at home or abroad. Moreover, the inefficiency and planless economy of capitalism cannot compete with the example of the efficiency and planned economy of the Soviet Union.

(Continued on page 4)

STARVATION IN AUSTIN

Result of Student Survey Reveal Appalling Conditions

It is amazing how little the people of the University of Texas know about the lamentable living conditions of the citizens poorer than they, who live in the same town. And this lack of realization is a terrible reflection upon our individualistic environment. A group of students, desiring to gain some idea of the gravity of the situation, last month undertook a house to house inquiry in a number of the poorer districts; in north west Austin, in a region including twenty-fifth street, in East Austin, and in the vicinity of south First Street. The findings were appalling.

From among the great number of poor families living in these districts, two hundred were chosen at random. In making an analysis of the results, we must take into account two factors which render great exactitude impossible. The first of these was the bitterness of suffering which often made the people unwilling to reveal the depth of their destitution. The second factor was the extreme irregularity of the incomes of most of the families, which made estimates rather than precise figures necessary. Nevertheless there is no question that the figures given below are in a broad sense true to the situation. The approximate average expenditure for food in these two hundred poor families chosen at random is **one dollar and fifteen cents per week per person for whites and seventy to eighty cents per week, per person, for colored and Mexicans.** Just try to imagine what this means. The figure given for whites.

(Continued on page 4)

AFTER GRADUATION—WHAT?

(Illustrating the benefits of a higher Education)

Political cartoon from a University of Texas student publication, *The Spark*. *Courtesy of the Dolph Briscoe Center for American History, the University of Texas at Austin.*

dent of the University and a Southern man," wanted President H. Y. Benedict to know that he was "unequivocally opposed to the equality of the Negro race, and [he] regret[ted] to see the University foster directly or indirectly through any publications coming from its students that character of propaganda."[20]

The fact that the agitators were from New York only exacerbated the outrage. Benedict felt compelled to explain to the governor, among others, that *The Spark* was not an authorized publication, that it certainly did not represent UT policies, and that calibrating the proper response was difficult. Benedict was willing to use force to suppress any violent attempt to put these proposals into action, but he also recognized that deciding "what limit to set on free discussion of changes to be accomplished by peaceful and constitutional means is a hard problem."[21] Benedict feared that he might destroy democracy while attempting to save it.

While Texas roiled over the printed words of a few radical students, the University of Maryland faced a much more serious challenge to its segregationist practices during the 1930s. The University of Maryland was one of the first institutions to face the young Thurgood Marshall in an integration court case. Since 1885, when an African American student had graduated from the Maryland law school, the institution had maintained an informal, but firm, segregated status. The color line was de facto, not de jure, but it was real nonetheless. The state helped support tiny Princess Anne Academy for its African American residents, but this institution did not offer college-level classes until the late 1920s, and the Depression robbed it of any positive momentum it had gathered. After 1932, the state provided a grand total of $600 for African American Marylanders to use when attending out-of-state schools open to them. Confronted with two applications from African Americans in 1933, University of Maryland vice president Byrd recognized the precariousness of the university's position as a whites-only institution without a formal law against integration. He wanted the legislature to pass such a law before concluding its session, because, as he explained to a Chapel Hill law professor, he was afraid that "unless we do [have such a law] we shall have some liberal minded judge granting a Mandamus forcing us to accept some Negro student, upon receipt of which I feel sure that some of us will go to jail."[22] Byrd did not get his favored law, but he did get his feared court ruling.

In 1934, after working his way through Amherst College, Donald Murray challenged the University of Maryland's exclusion of African Americans by applying to its law school. With the help of Marshall's advocacy, Murray won his case, matriculated, and eventually graduated from Maryland's law school. In June 1935, the university registrar seemed to recognize the problem with the university's practices, writing, "It will take a long, long time 'to educate' the Whites to the fact that the Negroes have a constitutional right to equal educational opportunities in schools for Whites and this despite the fact that Negroes are taxed for the support of the institutions for Whites."[23] Although the registrar saw "glaring at [him] that fateful fourteenth amendment," acting president Byrd was not willing to submit to arguments based on fairness, propriety, and the US Constitution as easily. He wrote, in July 1935, "Perhaps I shall have to go to jail, but I think we have got to keep the Negroes out. [Governor Harry W.] Nice tells me he does not mind going to jail provided I go with him, so there is some moral support anyway."[24]

When Byrd and others tried to circumvent the ruling by increasing the out-of-state scholarship fund to $30,000 and by buying the Princess Anne Academy for $100,000, Marshall was not impressed. He informed Byrd, "The Negro citizens of the State of Maryland do not believe that this [increase] was actuated by any motive of generosity on your part or of any sincere wish to aid Negro students; but rather as an attempt to set up certain high-sounding provisions to attempt to exclude Negroes from the University of Maryland." Marshall called on Byrd to "take the necessary steps to provide constitutionally for the higher education of Negroes according to the University of Maryland decision by either establishing a separate but equal State University for Negroes; or to admit Negroes to the University of Maryland."[25] University administrators caught flak from advocates on both sides of the argument for either giving too much or not enough. Race remained a contentious issue at the University of Maryland as officials there continued laboring to protect the status quo.[26]

Racial challenges also existed in the presumably more tolerant American Midwest. Although it was officially an integrated university, Ohio State faced challenges to its existing racial order during the 1930s. In 1931, for example, Ohio State administrators and trustees controversially dismissed a popular professor, Dr. W. D. Miller, for his "sociological views." Miller had allowed white Ohio State female students to congregate, eat, and dance with African American students while visiting nearby Wilberforce College. Miller's firing, according to historian of the university James Pollard, "quickly split the campus, with the faculty 'liberals' pitted against the 'conservatives' and with the administration strongly criticized for its actions." Not only did 132 faculty members officially protest Miller's removal, but the American Association of University Professors investigated the matter and sided with Miller's supporters. Along with the library budget and salary structure, academic freedom found itself threatened at Ohio State, even if football did not.[27]

Although Ohio State's percentage of African American students was very small by modern standards (out of a student body of just under 10,000, only 250 African Americans, including Jesse Owens, attended Ohio State in 1934), their presence was unsettling to many white people on the campus. In 1937, one year after Owens's Olympic triumphs, the campus YWCA and the Socialist Club endorsed the formation of a campus National Association for the Advancement of Colored People (NAACP) chapter. This advocacy inspired the campus Anti-Negro Guild to distribute across campus leaflets, complete with such subtle titles as "THE KU KLUX KLAN HAD THE RIGHT IDEA!!!" Administrators quickly identified the propagandists and spoke among themselves about the necessity of quick and decisive action. Urging prompt punishment, the dean of men, J. A. Park, reminded university president George Rightmire that "the University has been criticized, however unfairly, for its attitudes towards negroes and the circumstances of this case are widely known"; and another school official wanted to punish the two culprits as a measure to stop the "waves of propaganda and counterpropaganda which beat about our heads constantly on the campus in economic, racial, and religious matters." The trustees took a different strategy in silencing the propaganda wars raging across the Columbus campus; with only two voicing dissent, they directed the abolition of a twelve-person so-called Marxist Club.[28]

Dissent over segregation practices and race relations bubbled across the Midwest to challenge athletic policy. In 1937 athletic directors and administrators across the Big Ten Conference felt the heat of campus passions as they found themselves confronted with a petition for greater racial equality, at least in athletics. The Northwestern University Inter-racial Committee (including representatives from Northwestern's Peace Action Committee, YMCA, YWCA, B'nai B'rith

Hillel Organization, Socialist Club, and International Relations Club), in conjunction with representatives from student organizations at Ohio State, the University of Iowa, Purdue University, the University of Minnesota, the University of Michigan, and the University of Chicago, asked the conference's athletic directors to "rescind a so-called 'unwritten law' prohibiting the participation of Negroes in Big Ten basketball, swimming, and wrestling competition" at their March 8, 1937, meeting. The petitioning students argued that sports should teach desirable American values. They based their request in the language of competition and on the understanding that the racial discrimination was "inconsistent with aims of the higher education and with the spirit of the Constitution of the United States as well as with the desire of the student body to be represented in its athletics by its most qualified members, regardless of race or creed." The agenda for the March 8 meeting of the Big Ten athletic directors did not include this issue among its ten items for discussions, and Ohio State continued to field all-white squads in these sports over the next ten years.[29]

It was in this cauldron of campus controversies that universities, their leaders, supporters, and other constituencies were rethinking and refining ideas about the role of a state university in a state's life and work during the 1930s. Critical reports about university athletics added another factor to this reconsideration. In the 1920s, the chief justice of the Supreme Court, former president William Howard Taft, publicly criticized the conduct of intercollegiate athletics; then, in 1929, the Carnegie Foundation released its highly critical and very public report *American College Athletics*.[30] Moreover, in the later 1930s, western institutions had to address issues raised by the Atherton Report on Pacific Coast Conference athletic conditions. Although *American College Athletics* was by no means the only public statement criticizing the excesses of intercollegiate competition, it was the most extensive, most discussed, and most damning. It was also the one report all US institutions with big-time intercollegiate athletics simply had to address.[31]

Based on three years of extensive research, *American College Athletics* opened with a damning preface by Henry Pritchett, the foundation's president, and supported its claims with twelve chapters and 349 pages of evidence and analysis. Historian John R. Thelin described the report as an "encyclopedic survey of conditions concerning governance and finance of college sports, providing data that were sufficiently compelling to break the silence about the commercialization of college sports."[32] Thelin also pointed out that although the report caused a great deal of public discussion about the desirability and necessity of athletic reforms, not much reform actually resulted from the discussion. Still, the scope of the report, its critical tone, and its reams of compelling evidence forced administrators and athletics officials at US universities to reevaluate, if only briefly, their commitments to the status quo in intercollegiate athletics.[33]

In the preface, Pritchett wrote, "The thoughtful reader who has become aware of the transformation of college sports into professional athletic contests directed by paid coaches will wish to have answers to two questions. Who is responsible for the athletic transformation? And what is now to be done about it?"[34] Pritchett concluded that no single party deserved censure for the professionalization of collegiate sport, writing that the general trend of society, the desires of influential alumni, the reluctance of university officials to take principled stands, along with actions based on good intentions, had all factored into the equation. As for the second question, the report took a firmer stand:

> The paid coach, the gate receipts, the special training tables, the costly sweaters and extensive journeys in special Pullman cars, the recruiting from the high school, the demoralizing publicity showered on the players, the devotion of an undue proportion of time to training, the devices for putting a desirable athlete, but a weak scholar, across the hurdles of the examinations—these ought to stop and the intercollege and intramural sports be brought back to a stage in which they can be enjoyed by large numbers of students and where they do not involve an expenditure of time and money wholly at variance with any idea of honest study.[35]

The Carnegie report supported its critical generalizations with specific examples from across the nation. For example, the report praised Ohio State for keeping its coaches occupied with many sports but criticized Texas, among other schools, for hiring a full-time coach at a substantial salary and expecting him to coach only one or two sports. It appeared to the authors that "the substitution of the academic costume for the football suit represents rather a yielding on the part of university authorities to demands made by influential and skillful coaches, whose services they fear to lose, than a desire to recognize physical education" as a legitimate academic enterprise.[36] The authors also criticized some schools' willingness to spend lavishly on coaching staffs, identifying a group of high rollers, including Ohio State University, Yale University, Harvard University, and the University of Wisconsin, that spent between $35,400 and $84,600 annually on their athletic coaches. The report concluded that this extravagance "clearly reflect[ed] a distorted scale of academic and athletic values."[37]

Suffering under the strains of highly publicized criticism and financial distress, it would have made sense for university officials across the nation to jettison whatever operations of the university they deemed unessential or controversial. In a purely rational world, athletics might easily have fallen into that category. If Ohio State officials believed their students could persevere in the 1930s without any new library books, surely the same students could have received an education without a school-sponsored basketball or track team. There were, however, many powerful practical and ideological reasons for maintaining big-time athletic programs in the face of fiscal and ethical opposition.

First, institutional inertia helped protect the established programs. Once a sport had staked out a place within university budgets and calendars, and once jobs were created and filled, it became more difficult to remove them, especially since many universities still owed considerable sums for the boom in athletics construction of the 1920s. Second, even though almost every observer saw problems with intercollegiate athletics as they existed in 1929, most university officials refused to admit that the allegations of the Carnegie report, and those in other exposés, applied to their own institutions, instead pointing their fingers and accusations at other universities, identifying them as the real culprits and thus denying responsibility for trying to "fix" the problems the report's authors identified.

A third and much more important reason for the preservation of intercollegiate athletic programs during the 1930s is directly related to the second one: just as most officials did not concede that their universities' athletic programs were "professional" or "corrupt," they also continued to argue that intercollegiate athletics contributed directly to the educational mission of the university. In other words, the athletic programs were not really extracurricular at all, but they were essential tools for preparing men and women for later life.

Fourth, amid the crises of the Depression, some athletic officials offered political and philosophical defenses of intercollegiate athletics, arguing that the instruction in teamwork, discipline, competition, following rules, and handling setbacks without complaint were vital for the continuation of a laissez-faire capitalist social order. Finally, as chapter 6 explores more fully, university administrators had recognized very early on that it was easier to get alumni, prospective students, legislators, and other citizens interested in intercollegiate athletics than in geometric proofs, botany experiments, and literary criticism. By offering athletes and athletics as a product for public consumption, the universities could generate public allegiance and support. Although not all of these rationalizations surfaced at the same time at the same place, national leaders continually voiced them all, and the justifications worked together to defend intercollegiate athletics, and also the speakers' own jobs, from the forceful economic and ideological criticisms of the early 1930s.

There was no uniform response to the Carnegie report, but almost every institution had to react to its descriptions and accusations and to address the larger issues the report raised, especially regarding the described overemphasis and commercialization of athletics. University of Texas president Harry Benedict had anticipated these charges in 1928 when he had made a well-publicized attack on the over-emphasis of athletics. Although the Carnegie report echoed several of his criticisms, not every college official accepted them. Playing a semantic game, University of Maryland president Pearson wrote in early 1931, "The question of over-emphasis on football is largely a matter of what is meant by overemphasis." After explaining that over-emphasis, if it indeed existed, was an administrative problem and should be addressed on a case-by-case basis, Pearson happily reported that "there is no over-emphasis on football in the University of Maryland."[38] University of California officials had a slightly different and more representative interpretation of the problem. Although they were concerned about the attention given to intercollegiate athletics, especially football, and thought that colleges could do more to offset this interest, they believed that any perceived over-emphasis was the product of sportswriters and a "noisy minority of the student body and alumni."[39]

After the publication of the Carnegie report, California leaders, particularly university president Sproul, were also more willing than many of their colleagues to acknowledge privately the problem of commercialism in the supposedly amateur games, calling the existing levels of commercialism a "disgrace to American Universities."[40] In a separate letter that same year, Sproul warned that, without reform, "the end [of intercollegiate athletics] is not far off." He argued that the professionalism and commercialism were turning people away from the college game and attracting only people with no real affiliation with the university. Sproul continued, arguing that "even those who are University men and women are coming to look on the contest as merely a great show."[41]

Given these general agreements with much of the report's conclusions, it is unsurprising that University of California officials expressed great admiration for the report and its goals. Writing to a local high school student in early 1930, California's then president, W. W. Campbell, gave the report a very positive review, calling it "incomparably the best publication" about college athletics. Although Campbell thought that the report overstated the problems at times (while, at the same time, probably underestimating the problems at certain institutions), he still thought the report would "be of great value in correcting some of the exceedingly unfortunate policies followed in many educational institutions."[42] This recognition of real problems in the operation of intercollegiate athletics led California's leaders to become firm advocates of having a strong conference commissioner to regulate and control commercialism.

The conference system was one important preexisting bulwark against the criticism expressed in the Carnegie report, with the nation's conferences serving, in Thelin's words, as "the crucial collective unit for instilling standards in college sports."[43] This does not mean that the University of Tennessee's and the University of Maryland's affiliation with the Southern Conference, the University of California's membership in the Pacific Coast Conference (PCC), the University of Texas's membership in the Southwestern Conference, and Ohio State's membership in the Big Ten Conference insulated them from athletic improprieties, just that they had conference standards that worked, or were supposed to work, to create the proverbial level playing field. During the 1920s and 1930s, the NCAA, despite the "national" part of its name, was not as powerful or important to the daily operation of the individual programs as the regional athletic conferences were.

During this period the Big Ten Conference provided national leadership for other conferences in a variety of ways. It was the first to hire a professional commissioner, John L. Griffith, and a professional staff; it also established what became national guidelines in the areas of athletic control, eligibility, and scholarships. The member institutions took the formation and enforcement of their rules very seriously, and they were eager to report violations, at least those allegedly committed by their competition. Having a strong commissioner's office with the power to enforce findings and even to expel institutions served the Big Ten well during the 1930s as institutions sought to implement various reform measures and to prevent corruption.[44]

Institutions in other regions replicated the Big Ten's response to complaints of commercialism, corruption, and professionalization. The Big Ten's model inspired reform-minded officials across the nation to agitate for similar structures and powers in their conferences. For example, in 1930, California president Sproul wrote to his dean of men that he was "not at all satisfied with present [intercollegiate athletic] conditions, particularly in California, and unless strongly persuaded to the contrary [was] strongly disposed to lead a crusade for reform." This reform effort would begin with the "appointment of a commissioner with the widest possible powers, from whom may be expected an honest and vigorous attempt to clean up the athletic situation on the Pacific Coast, which [to Sproul] is deplorable and getting worse."[45] During the 1930s, the PCC hired a full-time commissioner, and in 1938 Sproul finally received what he had earlier desired, a monumental investigation of PCC athletics and associated improprieties.[46] Southern Conference officials debated the propriety and feasibility of hiring a commissioner during the early 1930s, but the schools could neither agree on the desirability of a strong commissioner nor afford to appoint one at the time.[47]

With his institution about to undergo intensive conference scrutiny in the late 1920s, the University of Tennessee's faculty advisor for athletics, Nathan W. Dougherty, had a different interpretation of the Carnegie report. In a seventeen-page summary and rebuttal of *American College Athletics*, Dougherty argued that Howard Savage and the other authors revealed their biases against "practical" American universities beginning with the opening lines of the report, which emphasized and lauded the European antecedents of American universities. In a chapter-by-chapter analysis of the report presented to the Tennessee president, Dougherty cast doubt on the report's conclusions and characterized its interpretations as being overblown and inappropriate. For example, responding to the report's position that large budgets for paid, professional coaches epitomized the "distorted scale of academic and athletic values," Dougherty dismissed this conclusion with a metaphor: "This is a natural conclusion for an American business man but not a sound one for a College Professor. It might just as well be said that since the smoke of the locomotive can be seen farther than the locomotive that it is the most important part of the railway train." He argued that coaching is a "specialized activity, and specialized service is always expensive."[48] While Dougherty was undoubtedly accurate with his assertion that specialized service was expensive, he never addressed why the university considered that service vital enough to justify the high cost; he just assumed that it should.

Other prominent southern university leaders did articulate forceful arguments for the value of intercollegiate athletics during the 1930s. In January 1938, R. A. Fetzer, the University of North Carolina athletic director, and Howard W. Odum, the director of the Institute for Research in Social Science and one of the most prominent sociologists in the nation, wrote to athletic directors across the South asking for detailed information. Odum and Fetzer explained that the Institute for Research in Social Science had spent the previous ten to fifteen years conducting regional studies on southern progress and institutions, contending in several reports that southern institutions should be doing better with the facilities and abilities at their disposal. The institute often used intercollegiate football as an "index to show how, when the southern institutions wanted to do something well, they did it." Football, then, in the eyes of some very accomplished scholars and educational leaders, had intrinsic value as a focal point for regional pride and as a case study of regional accomplishment.[49]

The reaction of the officials at the University of Texas to the release of the Carnegie report more closely resembled California's reaction than Tennessee's. The November 1929 issue of *The Alcade*, the publication of the Texas Ex-Students Association, summarized the scope and findings of the report in one article, following it with another written by the director of athletics and giving "the Texas side of it." Dr. H. J. Ettlinger noted, "While the report only covers the dark side of the picture, [Texans] must, nevertheless, admit that the facts as presented are true." Ettlinger continued, pointing out that "in the Southwest conditions in the past few years have been very bad," despite the numerous regulations designed to prevent the very violations and corruption *American College Athletics* documented. The Texas athletic director advocated following one of two paths to rectify the situation: one, change the rules to match existing practices, or two, enforce the rules and punish those that need punishing. Either through permitted professionalism or through more rigidly enforcing amateurism, "the benefits of intercollegiate athletics" in creating loyalty to schools "must be preserved."[50]

Like the University of California, the University of Texas and its officials devoted a great deal of time and print space to discussing efforts to reform intercollegiate athletics. During the late 1920s and early 1930s, *The Alcade* carried numerous articles on the Carnegie report and the university's response to it and on other investigations of the university's practice of hiring athletes to serve as physical education teaching assistants. Most of these essays were substantive evaluations of arguments, featuring thoughtful analysis of the evidence offered, but not all were. Instead, some tried to illustrate, through humor and pseudo-science, the absurdity of advocating a single, rational program for intercollegiate athletics. In December 1929, Texas president H. Y. Benedict vowed to "out-Einstein Einstein and out-Newton Newton" with his proposal of a gridiron-based graphing system that would provide the solution to the "Great Super-Einstein Intercollegiate Athletic Problem." Benedict used his graph to show that there existed an entire spectrum of rational opinions about the proper conduct and place of intercollegiate athletics, but that when charting these opinions, one would still be likely to be "irrational and absurd everywhere in all his opinions throughout the entire curve."[51] Impartial, disinterested reason and algebraic formulas could not alone, in Benedict's eyes, account for all of the variables involved in administering and controlling intercollegiate athletics.

University officials across the nation shared Ettlinger's and others' belief that intercollegiate athletics, while problematic, were too valuable for universities to abandon, and they offered many reasons why. The authors of *American College Athletics* agreed that properly conducted athletics were valuable and took comfort in the observation that colleges and universities had made progress over the previous three decades and implored their readers to "let that improvement continue—let [athletics'] physical, moral, and spiritual potentialities in the education of youth be clearly understood and sincerely acted upon, [so that] their value in our national life will be immeasurably enhanced."[52]

By removing commercialism from athletics, colleges and universities would go a long way toward realizing their potential to shape properly the young men of America, but Savage and the other Carnegie authors demanded more. In their view, "the American college must renew within itself the force that will challenge the best intellectual capabilities of the undergraduate," recognizing that athletics did not prevent intellectual growth and that they could be a powerful socializing force, promoting "courage, independent thinking, cooperation, initiative, habits of bodily activity, and above all, honesty in dealings between man and man."[53] By making athletics pure, officials would make them purposeful.

For many, that purpose was clear. Most defenders of intercollegiate athletics agreed that not all important lessons could be learned in a classroom, that universities should labor to create the types of competitive men that could lead the United States properly, men who valued teamwork, sacrifice for an ideal, and striving for victory. These university leaders echoed the sentiments of the Carnegie report's authors and earlier idealists who presented athletic programs as a teaching tool, with the games and practices serving as additional laboratories for vital learning. According to a prominent line of argument, intercollegiate athletics served the universities' and nation's common good by teaching virtue to athletes, by inspiring other students to participate in sports, and by showcasing positive attributes to all spectators. These justifications, and the dozens like them, drew upon a preexisting and prominent vision of competitive sport as a crucible of American values. As Mark Dyreson has argued, "progressive" Americans living between 1880 and 1920 tried to use athletic programs and team sports to produce "civic virtue and national vitality."[54] This desire to create a "sporting republic" was an attempt by the new middle class to minimize the problems of industrialization and modernization by teaching Protestant, professional, and republican values through sports. By focusing on the benefits of sound minds and bodies, regulated activity, and the ideals of "fair play" during competition, these idealistic reformers sought to foster social cohesion through sport.[55]

The belief that athletics could inculcate desirable traits in collegians, however, remained strong throughout the 1920s and beyond in US colleges and universities as the public and private statements of athletic officials illustrate. In 1922, the University of Michigan's Fielding Yost argued that university athletics offered much more than mere "technical exhibitions." Yost contended that college athletics had three "underlying aims . . . to develop and maintain the physical health of all the students; to promote recreation through self-expression, and a wholesome spirit of competition and rivalry; to form habits and inculcate ideals of right living." Similarly, Big Ten commissioner Griffith defended intercollegiate athletics in 1929 by reasserting the thesis that "the main value of athletics lies in the fact that they serve to develop qualities that cannot be measured by an intelligence or physical efficiency test." Griffith explained that even spectators could learn valuable life lessons from observing intercollegiate athletics, just as he asserted that games taught participants to play by the rules, a vital skill in a democracy. Griffith did not offer in 1929, however, as he would in the 1930s, an unqualified defense of American democracy; instead, he wrote that some criticized college athletics merely because of its scale, arguing that "in a democracy such as ours we are apt to place a premium on mediocrity and to be suspicious of men, organizations and activities which are highly successful." These comments display a persevering progressive attitude toward sport throughout the 1920s, but they do not include the explicit associations between intercollegiate athletics and the preservation of American business and political norms in the face of "radical" alternatives that dominated the correspondence of the 1930s.[56]

The argument that intercollegiate athletics could use competition to help prepare male students for the real world was not just a sophistic rationalization concocted by self-interested administrators to justify keeping programs popular with students and alumni. Instead, not only was it the natural product of a long history of "character-building" claims for athletics, it was also the logical extension of the progressive educational theories of John Dewey. Scholars have noted that Dewey's ideas found footholds in US universities during the 1930s. This new educational outlook stressed the importance of practical, as opposed to theoretical, education, preparing students for life's challenges through experience. This pedagogical theory lent itself well to ideological defenses of universities' athletic programs. After all, many reasoned, where better could students experience the thrills of success and the agony of failure than on the athletic fields and courts, and where else could universities better teach students that life has rules, winners, and losers?[57]

According to this theory, intercollegiate athletics served as a vital teaching tool on university campuses, as an integral part of the undergraduate educational apparatus rather than a frivolous diversion. In fact, according to the official and public pronouncements of the Southern Conference, "athletics are valuable only in so far as they serve fundamental educational purposes, namely, to develop leaders of the highest type."[58] Similarly, University of Texas football and track coach Clyde Littlefield wrote for the Texas alumni publication in the early 1930s, "Athletics are, and should ever remain a contributory factor to this main object of college training," which is "to become better educated and become better fitted for life." To this end, Littlefield argued, intercollegiate athletes inspired other students to play sports, thereby exposing additional students to life's lessons as taught through athletics. Moreover, "athletics benefit even those who do not participate at all. By the example before them, all tend to hold in higher esteem the qualities of determination, service, loyalty, which are fostered by athletic competition."[59]

Despite these common defenses of men's intercollegiate athletics,

University of California physical educator Frank Kleeberger spoke for many when he cautioned in an internal memo in 1930 that "the fundamental organization of athletics here and elsewhere renders its control impossible as a wholesome educational influence." The next week his own university president insisted to an outsider that the "football team . . . be a normal outgrowth of the institution and not an exotic flower grafted onto it."[60] Even a critic such as Kleeberger admitted that he enjoyed the excitement athletics could bring to campus, but he also argued that football fever had too many negative side effects, including teaching dishonesty through the violation of established rules, putting an institution's focus on the profit potential instead of proper morals, and celebrating athletes above all other students, all in the name of higher education. Kleeberger thought that California had the opportunity in the early 1930s to "rebuild athletics . . . on a sound educational basis," but if the time was not yet at hand, he implored the president to establish real controls so as to "subdue the undesirable symptoms of the disease and accentuate the limited educational values inherent in the present system."[61]

Athletics could indeed teach students, but Kleeberger and others warned that students were learning the wrong lessons about celebrity, dishonesty, cheating, and the importance of money. As the Carnegie report and rigorous self-studies in the 1930s illustrated all too well, the type of idealistic synthesis of the educational and athletic worked much better in theory than in practice. Nonetheless, despite Kleeberger's and like-minded critics' warnings, most defenders of intercollegiate athletics presented the programs as purveyors of positive lessons, or at least harmless diversions, that deserved a place on university campuses.

University officials became more anxious to promote certain habits and virtues as campus and national disruptions convinced them that core American beliefs and practices were under attack. While many intellectuals, reformers, labor leaders, and politicians discussed and sought changes in the structure of US society and government as a means of meeting the crises of the Great Depression, athletic officials across the country defended the established order and their position within it. They did so by expanding upon idealized images of competitive, democratic, and successful American athletes as the future leaders of capitalism and the saviors of Western civilization.[62] These athletic leaders built upon earlier beliefs linking competitive athletics and American values and began using explicitly political rhetoric and arguments to make their point that intercollegiate athletics were important tools, not only for continuing the amateur tradition in American life, but also for preserving competitive, democratic capitalism itself from its many serious challenges during the Depression.

The connection between athletic competition and the preferred American way of life was not limited to the minds of aging Progressive reformers and self-interested athletic officials. Instead, throughout the 1920s and the 1930s, the rhetoric of competition helped provide the infrastructure for both political parties' platforms. Despite their disagreements about the proper role of government in regulating the economy and the social sphere, both the Democrats and the Republicans saw competition as a central component of the American system.[63] Although some of his opponents saw President Franklin D. Roosevelt as a wild-eyed leveler, a "traitor to his class" who wanted to destroy the American capitalist system, he was not. In fact, many historians have since argued the exact opposite point, that Roosevelt served as one of industrial capitalism's most valuable protectors. As several scholars have pointed out, many of Roosevelt's programs worked to buttress, not undermine, the US economic system.[64]

During the 1930s, many Americans looked to their national government for assistance, and most also expected the government to continue preparing the country's youth for economic revival and for democratic participation. The New Deal did exactly that through the Works Progress Administration (WPA), which adopted the progressive model of using athletics and physical training to teach "proper" American values. During the 1930s, athletic officials at US universities did likewise, using laissez-faire rhetoric to marry athletic competition to the nation's capitalist future.

The changes brought by the New Deal helped to turn one prominent athletic official against the Roosevelt administration, specifically, and the Democratic Party, generally. At the University of Tennessee, the head football coach was also a major in the US Army Corps of Engineers. Major (later General) Robert Neyland's administration of a dam and electric power came under scrutiny by Roosevelt's Tennessee Valley Authority in the summer of 1933, and while no charges were ever filed against Neyland, he held a grudge against the New Deal power brokers for decades. After retiring as a brigadier general from military service after World War II, Neyland wrote that he had been "brought up a dyed-in-the-wool 100 percent Democrat," but he lived long enough to hear his dad proclaim, "If these damn New Dealers are Democrats, I ain't." Neyland (and his dad, presumably) was against "the New Deal, Fair Deal, or any other sort of Deal" that offered "the national graduated income tax that is Requirement [No.] 1 of the Communist Manifesto" and "the Social Security laws which constitute the most barefaced and gigantic fraud upon our present population and upon millions of those yet unborn."[65]

The experiences of the Ohio State University and the Big Ten Conference during the 1930s provide an excellent example of this politicization of sports. Before the Depression struck, Ohio State had built one of the largest and most successful athletic programs in the nation. When the crises of economic collapse mounted, however, the resulting pressures threatened the very continuation of intercollegiate athletics. Ohio State officials, led by the director of athletics, Lynn St. John, and acting collaboratively with their counterparts in the Big Ten conference, sought to protect sports programs by coupling those programs to the safeguarding of particular values. In a revival and modification of the arguments of a previous generation of progressive reformers, St. John and his colleagues argued that colleges and universities could and should use intercollegiate athletic programs as tools to produce the business leaders, field generals, and virtuous citizens necessary to secure a safe, democratic, and capitalist future for the nation. Their political rhetoric was both self-serving and highly charged by the ferment of the Great Depression, and the political associations they made would not disappear as most Americans returned to prosperity, and to the Cold War, in the 1940s, 1950s, and beyond.[66]

Clearly, by the late 1930s, even the most isolated athletic official could not have failed to notice the social upheaval and the challenges to the institutions of the day, challenges to community that were rooted in long-term social problems, and challenges to the economic and political status quo sparked by the Depression. In the midst of this economic and social disruption, most US universities maintained and even strengthened their commitments to providing athletic opportunities for their student populations. The question, then, is why did they emphasize seemingly extracurricular activities when the core of the university, the academic programs and infrastructures, found themselves under financial siege?

One important answer is that the academic and athletic administrators did not regard athletics as extracurricular at all; instead, they believed athletic experiences to be vital to the universities' duty to prepare the competitive leaders of a capitalist nation. With the continuation of men's intercollegiate athletic programs, leaders sought to preserve the political and social systems, not only of the university, but also of the nation during a time of great unrest. Many working in US universities maintained and came to reemphasize their faith in the ability of sports programs to shape the beliefs and habits of individuals to fit into a corporate, laissez-faire capitalist mold, to create a sense of community, and to teach American democratic values through competition. In the 1930s, however, the rhetoric became more politicized, as the officials drew sharp distinctions between an idealized, competitive American way of life and the socialist and communist alternatives they saw threatening their campuses and their nation.[67]

In 1931 a discussion about the proper place of athletics in institutions of higher learning consumed the time of athletic directors and college presidents across the Midwest. On October 29, 1931, David E. Ross, a member of the Purdue University Board of Regents, delivered a controversial and widely discussed lecture criticizing the professionalism of college sports and the importance that financial considerations had when setting policies and schedules. Ross claimed, "While the public apparently demands these [intramural and intercollegiate] contests it may be seriously doubted" that the state legislatures would pay for them if asked. He declared that football stadiums "by long odds ... [are] the most ineffective expenditure of money made for practical purposes" and continued to say that the lack of real public interest in minor sports made them very difficult to finance. Nonetheless, as his fellow critic Kleeberger had done before, even Ross acknowledged the positive influence intercollegiate athletics could have on a university environment, calling them the best vehicle "for giving character and unity to that vital thing we know as the spirit of an institution."[68] Ross also lauded the ability of intercollegiate athletics to foster citizenship and to "inculcate in [athletes] ideas of fairness, sportsmanship, and integrity." Despite some problems, athletics still appeared to Ross to be essential tools for shaping competitive all-American boys.[69]

None of the above seems very controversial or specifically related to the Depression; in fact, Ross's acknowledgments of the virtues of intercollegiate athletics fit neatly into the well-established cannon of athletic defenses, just as his criticisms echoed those voiced earlier. Ross, however, concluded his speech with a call to remove scheduling from the hands of those interested in gate receipts; and, most threatening to some, he asked that "those vested with authority . . . at least discuss conference pooling of athletic contest funds" so that universities could continue the education of athletes on and off the field without charges of professionalism.[70] These final thoughts did not find receptive ears in the Ohio State University administration's hallways or in the Big Ten Conference headquarters. Later that same year, J. L. Morrill, Ohio State's junior dean of education, hastily drafted a response to a questionnaire that the Big Ten had based on Ross's speech and distributed.[71] Morrill contended that Ohio State's athletic programs were "of great value educationally to the members of the teams, the student body and the public, of the moral concept of loyalty to an ideal (represented by the University) and of self sacrifice for the sake of an ideal."[72]

Morrill also defended the athletic administration and oversight system in place at Ohio State, rejecting any suggestions of impropriety. He argued that athletics, while treated as any other educational program of the university, received much more supervision and scrutiny than any other program, thus rendering athletics safe from all excess. In other words, it was the same, yet different. He agreed with Ross that football's role as the main revenue-generating sport was "unfortunate," but he declared it easily "defensible." Sidestepping a question about the salaries granted to "highly paid and highly professional" Athletic Department personnel, Morrill replied that the correct standard of evaluation should be the recipient's character, not his salary. Despite acknowledging the powerful hold athletics had on the general public and on alumni, Morrill denied that the publicity sports programs provided necessarily helped the university. He also mildly dismissed Ross's proposal of rotating schedules to remove the temptation for scheduling "money" games.[73]

Morrill's valuations and defenses of Big Ten intercollegiate athletics fit nicely into a well-established pattern. He saw athletics as a vehicle for moral uplift that certainly belonged in US universities. Of course, people rarely, if ever, acknowledge their complete range of motivations to themselves, much less to others. As suggested before, the athletic administrators of the 1920s and 1930s must have wanted to protect college athletics, in part, in order to protect their own jobs. Moreover, some of the vehemence in Ohio State's arguments against "collectivism" might have come from the fact that Ohio State, leading the conference in athletic revenue for much of the decade, would have had to share more of its wealth than others. Still, pragmatism aside, during the Depression, as they were surrounded by tremendous economic, racial, religious, and political challenges to the status quo, many of the nation's athletic administrators imbued their work with explicit political implications.

While Morrill couched his disapproval of Ross's rotation idea in very moderate, apolitical terms, Ohio State athletic director St. John employed starkly political language to convey his disgust. St. John called Ross's proposal to pool conference athletic funds a "really wild idea" and "utterly foolish." According to St. John, that idea, when combined with the rotating-schedules plan, "border[ed] somewhat on rank communism of a dangerous type."[74]

St. John and Morrill were not the only high-ranking athletic officials to defend the status quo during the early 1930s, nor were they the only ones to frame their arguments in politically loaded terms. Griffith, the Big Ten commissioner, NCAA president during much of the 1930s, and one of St. John's very good friends, unsurprisingly shared many of St. John's views as well as his method of expressing them. In a public response to Ross's statements, Griffith offered several business analogies comparing universities' athletic programs to manufacturers' production lines. He stated that, just as in a business setting, the unprofitable lines (read: minor sports) might face abolition or at least reduction if the Depression grew much worse. Griffith also denied Ross's assertions that athletic administrators designed football schedules based on their profit potential, arguing that they emphasized, instead, "traditional games," which coincidentally just happened to attract the most attention and produce the greatest revenues. Maintaining these traditional rivalries was essential to maintaining public interest; therefore, rotating schedules would prove counterproductive. Griffith saved his strongest rhetoric for Ross's proposal that conference members consider pooling the conferences athletic revenues to ensure all students equal opportunities and to prevent revenue-based schedules. Griffith dismissed this revenue-sharing plan as a "socialistic theory which our manufacturers and business men would not be willing to put into effect in terms of their own business."[75] What would not be good for General Motors would not, in Griffith's eyes, be good for the Big Ten Conference.

Athletic directors and administrators in the United States further politicized their rhetoric by explicitly connecting conference policies and athletics to larger world events, making the public and private debates over the proper values of intercollegiate athletics carry even more importance. The correspondence among St. John, Griffith, and other conference athletic officials throughout the 1930s and the early 1940s reveals a shared vision of politics as well as athletics, highlighting the connections between the two fields as they traded swipes at Roosevelt and his policies. Griffith, for example, constantly included political discussions in his official correspondence with the conference athletic directors. In one 1932 letter, Griffith told St. John about how Iowa's voters had recently voted out a senator who had spent the previous ten years attacking the existing "capitalistic and economic system and by implication at least advocating the redistribution of wealth." He followed that example with an "Exhibit B," the story of an athletic conference removing a commissioner who had been critical of intercollegiate athletics. Griffith hopefully concluded his message with the belief that he and St. John might "witness an era of sanity in which the demagogues and the inveighers against the constructive systems of athletics and wealth will be less prominent than they have been." During the 1930s, as consistent opponents of Franklin Roosevelt and the collectivism that he and the New Deal represented to them, Griffith and St. John would find their search for "sanity" to be a continuous struggle.[76]

No statement better illustrates the continuing connections that conference and university officials made between politics and athletics than the following from a confidential memo entitled "Reconstruction," sent by Griffith to Ohio State's St. John:

> I start by assuming that although the United States is in a temporary slump that she will come out of the slump. If there is a world war between the Orient and the Occident; if the nation's

> economic structure is destroyed and a new social, economic and political philosophy takes the place of our present national philosophy then it will not be necessary for anyone to give heed to that which we have come to think of as college athletics. Our entire philosophy of athletics is inextricably interwoven into our American philosophy of life.
>
> We are a capitalistic nation and so we believe in champions and championships. We believe, however, that the champions should win by fair means. As President Hoover has pointed out communism would hold the speed of the swiftest to that of the slowest. Is it not clear then that if we continue to hold to the American conception of competition that we are going to continue along familiar and similar lines in athletics?[77]

Griffith continued his analysis by arguing that "wars, business depressions, and athletic problems" resulted directly from "human greed, disregard for the rights of others, arrogance, selfishness and suspicion." So, who were the culprits Griffith singled out in 1932? They were the Japanese for invading Manchuria, the bankers for lending unwisely just to draw interest, and football coaches for conducting unauthorized practices in violation of Big Ten Conference rules. Griffith doubted the necessity of adopting "Ghandiism to lessen the chances of war," just as he challenged the need to "follow the Stahlin [*sic*] principles by way of guaranteeing every man three meals a day." Instead, he proclaimed, colleges must continue teaching the importance of competition, if not only for the American system, then to prevent young men from abandoning their pure amateur status to find competition and corruption in professional events. "The colleges must go on," Griffith exhorted, "or others will take their place."[78]

Or worse yet, the United States itself would forget how to compete, relying instead on leaders who were promising Americans, in Griffith's words, that "they will give us security, that we won't have to pay for our sins, that they will share the wealth created by others with us, etc. etc." This was not anti-radical rhetoric intended to rouse a crowd and demonize an opponent. Instead, these were private and confidential expressions of the deeply held beliefs of the future NCAA president, as was Griffith's letter to Colonel G. L. Townsend, a retiring Ohio State athletic official and commandant of the Military Science Department. Griffith wrote, in 1938, "Aside from what you have meant to athletics at Ohio State and in the Conference, I have rejoiced that you were in charge of military affairs at Ohio State. The Pacifists and the crackpots from the lunatic fringe have been very active in recent years and we need men such as you to help preserve an even balance of the ship of state."[79]

While commissioner of the Big Ten and president of the NCAA, Griffith also voiced these ideas publicly, producing numerous patriotic and politically charged speeches and articles during the 1930s. St. John's collection of his friend's writings included, among many others, an *Athletic Journal* essay entitled "Athletics Exemplify the American Way," in which Griffith argued that "our form of democracy is a glorified athletic game." Having praised the importance Germany and Japan placed on coordinated physical education programs in 1922, the commissioner of the United States' most powerful athletic conference stressed in this essay the political importance of competitive college athletics to the country. He argued, "Since most people will agree that the American way is better for Americans than the Communist way, the Nazi way or the Fascist way, we will not discuss that point. Instead we would like to call attention to some similarities between the American way of life and the athletic way." Quoting Abraham Lincoln on the virtues of competition, Griffith argued that "1) Competition, 2) Rules governing competition, 3) Leveling up process, 4) Courage and the will to carry on" characterized both the American and athletic way of life. He concluded by exhorting his readers to "preserve the American way and let us exemplify it on the playing fields of our country."[80]

In open letters to all Big Ten coaches, Griffith used much the same rhetoric. Emphasizing the importance of competition, he warned the coaches to take "one look at Europe today [to see] clearly what happens to a people grown soft. . . . If there are more softies in America than there are fighters, we will go the whole way to state socialism." That was unthinkable to Griffith, but fortunately he again had a solution. "Through our athletic programs," Griffith wrote, "we can help to inculcate in our boys the American spirit. We can refuse to be influenced by the soft idealists. We can let the world know where we stand and what we are doing." According to Griffith's reports, the business world already knew what his conference was doing. Griffith reported to the Big Ten's athletic directors in 1938 that they had the support of the nation's business community, telling the athletic directors that Americans were regaining confidence after the failure of Roosevelt's court-packing plan and the Reorganization Bill and that several eastern associates had expressed their "highest regard" for the Big Ten "because they felt we were conservative and sane and were keeping athletics on a sound foundation."[81] To Griffith, the debate was not just a discussion over the pay of baseball umpires or the number of players allowed to travel with their squads; the battle over athletic policy was a fight over the future of American democracy and economy as he and his colleagues understood them.

Griffith was not speaking only for himself when making these explicit connections between competitive athletics and a specific set of American values, beliefs, and institutions. Instead, as seen in the proceedings and publications of the national physical education associations, these views were common throughout the profession. In 1933, a Gettysburg College professor argued, "In these days of stress, strain, and uncertainty the college student should be sent out into the world with a strong competitive spirit"; "today, competition is keen and our students should have the benefit of that disciplinary training which they can only receive by engaging in some type of athletic activity."[82] This disciplinary training was enhanced by the ability of physical education programs and athletic activities to "preserve values and enrich life" while restoring morale.[83]

Many authors and speakers made explicit their contention that athletics offered the best vehicle the universities had for real "democratic training." In 1931, the University of Michigan's athletic director, Fielding Yost, quoted a Harvard educator as arguing that athletics provided the best emotional training for democratic participation. Another physical educator argued in 1931, "Social relationships are learned on the playfields. The contribution from our program to a useful citizenship surpasses that of any other." He continued, "Our democracy is dependent upon a high type of team work"; by teaching proper values, college programs removed "impediments to a smooth running community, state, and national life."[84]

Unsurprisingly, an article entitled "The Relation of Physical Education to the Purposes of Democracy" advanced the same general thesis: proper athletic training can create citizens better able and more inclined to protect the American democratic system. The author argued that "no other phase of the whole school curriculum offers as many, as potent, or as real opportunities for inculcating the principles of tolerance and the democratic attitude and habits of conduct as does physical education."[85]

This article's author, like many other male physical educators, echoed an argument common among contemporary female physical educators: democratic training worked best when all got the opportunity to participate. Although the men were not willing to sacrifice their varsity programs as the women's leaders had been, most still recognized that their rhetoric implied the need to expand their programs as widely as possible, especially as the threat of war approached. While almost all physical educators argued that their profession had a unique ability to prepare the nation's youth for the mental and physical challenges of a potential war, few phrased their thoughts as colorfully as William Hughes from Teachers College, Columbia University. Hughes wrote in 1940, "Men die of hardening of the arteries, nations die of softening of the spine." His solution was simple; reemphasize in the nation's colleges the physical rigor and the democratic training of athletics. As he put it, "those who believe in athletics feel that the concrete that has gone into stadia will be more effective than that in the Maginot Line."[86]

Throughout the decade, athletic officials continued expressing their concern with the potential subversive influence of those on the political left on US campuses, just as the university presidents did. In November 1934 Griffith asked St. John to tell him if there were "any liberal clubs such as the League for Industrial Democracy at Ohio State." He also desired a confidential report about the numbers involved and the "pedigree" of the leaders. St. John quickly replied with the ominous news that there were three such groups active on the Columbus campus. The groups shared a core of twenty to thirty "very loud and articulate" members. St. John also warned Griffith that "in this nucleus . . . there is a great majority of Cleveland Jews" and that two of the groups were "quite frankly communistic." In a student body of over ten thousand students, the presence of fewer than thirty students challenging the economic and political systems of the United States still threatened these local and national athletic leaders.[87]

Nor did the fear of socialism in the athletic policy of the US government dissipate as conditions began to improve.[88] Many of Griffith's Big Ten contemporaries shared these ideological and political reasons for valuing men's intercollegiate athletics. For example, Glenn Frank, the president of the University of Wisconsin, in late 1936 equated the desires for universal and high standards in intercollegiate athletics to the progressive struggles "enlightened doctors, lawyers, and business men" fought for their own standards. Frank later listed these standards in the form of a creed that labeled losing one's temper as "treason to the team," and he portrayed football as "as effective an instrument of moral and intellectual discipline as any enterprise the American university fosters." That is either a ringing endorsement of athletics or a condemnation of all other university activities, and it seems clear that Frank intended the former. Frank pointed out the need for competition and sportsmanship in the ranks of American business, finance and politics; and he argued that university athletics could be, as the Greek games once were, "a force for democracy, for self-control, for honesty, for patience, and for temperate living."[89]

If one believed everything Frank claimed, one could no longer question the place of athletics on a campus, but one might wonder about the importance of academic education to an institution boasting a properly run athletic program. Still, underneath Frank's hyperbole rests an assumption that many of his colleagues shared: intercollegiate athletics were necessary, not only to ensure the proper development of mature students, but also to safeguard the future of American democracy and society. While discussing a conference move to restrict Ohio State's football practice length, the University of Minnesota athletic director, Frank McCormick, demonstrated the comfort level that Midwestern athletic directors felt about expressing their laissez-faire political sentiments. McCormick wrote, "I don't think it is possible for them to put over such a regulation. If they start making everything fair and on an equal basis, the first thing you will know we will be as socialistic as our present form of government at Washington."[90] It appears that the "domino theory" appeared in American minds long before Eisenhower endorsed it. Once a committee started restricting the length of football practices, Columbus and Madison might as well have been suburbs of Moscow or, for that matter, Hyde Park.

The threat of world war did not dissipate this fear; in fact, it intensified the apprehension. In May 1941, Griffith still worried about the threat of an internal radical revolt more than anything else. He argued that the United States should not challenge Adolph Hitler on his own turf, three thousand miles from home, or in the neutral territory of South America. Concerned by rumors that any Nazi attack on the United States "would be an inside job," Griffith worried about what would happen even if the United States defeated the Nazis in a war. He was afraid that "these people who want collectivism, supervision, and regimentation may gain their wish if we spend one hundred billion dollars or more on a European war, repudiate our debts following the war and perhaps experience some sort of a revolution." "What profit," he inquired, "would it be to us to have licked Hitler" if "the collectivists who wanted regimentation should take over our country?" A collectivist regime would be unacceptable to Griffith because, by his definition, any organization that opposed competition—or college football—was un-American.[91]

The men making all of these arguments were some of the most prominent athletic officials in collegiate sport. They were conference commissioners, presidents of professional organizations, prominent athletic directors, respected professors of education, and the shapers of policies on their own campuses. Through their wide range of responses to the twin pressures of reform agitation and economic difficulties, these men protected the institution of intercollegiate athletics during the Depression. Their responses, buttressed by institutional inertia and continuing football profits, included public discussions of the Carnegie report, the move to create and empower conference commissioners to deal with the identified problems in intercollegiate athletics, and the modification of an existing ideology supporting athletics to address the perceived social and political radicalism of the Depression. Their actions guaranteed that men's intercollegiate athletics would emerge from the potential pitfalls of the 1930s essentially unchanged and unscathed. If the economic and reform pressures indeed offered, as the University of California's Kleeberger hoped, a "strategic moment to rebuild athletics," then that moment passed without fundamental changes in the American way of athletics.

CHAPTER 4

★ ★ ★ ★ ★

Communal Values and Women's Sport

Come join a sport and find real pleasure;
Joy Without Measure the whole year through
Where skies are lighter, and smiles are brighter
Play the Game, not for fame, but for friendship true,
At California, hail Alma Mater, through all
The year we'll ere be gay.
With voices raising, thy honor praising.
We'll be true, loyal to W.A.A.

—GRACE JOHNSTONE, CLASS OF 1927
(to be sung at a 1929 W.A.A. meeting
to the tune of "Neapolitan Nights")

Games like basketball and baseball are combative sports. They develop ugly muscles—muscles ugly in girls—as well as scowling faces and the competitive spirit. As an inevitable consequence your girls may find it more difficult to attract the most worthy fathers for their children.

—QUOTED IN INA GITTINGS,
"WHY CRAMP COMPETITION?" (1931)

In stark contrast to what happened with men's college athletics, the decline of ticket revenue did not directly threaten the existing financing and operation of women's athletics on US campuses. The era's financial pressure along with a consistent concern about how to educate and prepare properly feminine and democratic young ladies did, however, affect the ways female physical educators thought about their duties, programs, and jobs. The resulting programs and ideas shaped the athletic opportunities for generations of college women.

During the early twentieth century, female physical educators worked under the constant fear that they might lose their jobs to men who would not share their ability to prepare, or interest in preparing, young women's bodies and temperaments for a proper life. This anxiety only increased in the 1930s as the possibility of emergency budgetary cutbacks threatened all that female physical educators had built. These women constructed a combination of philosophical arguments and athletic programs that worked to protect their positions, their authority, and the women under their care. They contended that only women could provide the expertise, supervision, and guidance that the young college women needed. They reaffirmed and strengthened an existing ideology that stressed the fundamental differences between men's and women's bodies and social needs, and they structured their programs completely differently than men's, so that no one would dispute the desirability of female experts molding the nation's young ladies.

They did all of this in the name of "democratic" sport. The version of democracy taught to college women through athletics, however, was not the competition-based, individualistic, victory-oriented democracy that the men learned; instead, the women's vision of democracy and society was much more egalitarian and collective, based on the principles of absolute equality of opportunity and the denial of individual acclaim and attention.

The different structures of the men's and women's athletic programs both revealed and perpetuated the different sets of values university officials intended each gender to receive from their athletic programs. The men's highly publicized and celebrated varsity programs, particularly football, acted as the core of men's athletics; in contrast, the women's intramural programs served as the backbone of women's college athletics throughout the 1930s, protecting college women from the excesses seen both in men's intercollegiate athletics and in women's industrial league athletics. In short, while men's and women's athletic programs both celebrated "democracy," they taught polar opposite visions of democratic participation and the value of competition.

Depression circumstances did not create these gender-based interpretations of how college athletics programs could teach desired values, but they did help solidify and institutionalize the beliefs. These different visions of the proper nature of men's and women's sports, coupled with the universities' unwillingness to finance women's athletics on anywhere near the same scale as men's sports, therefore, made it highly unlikely that serious attempts to expand women's athletics would emerge. Yet, such a movement did develop across the nation by the late 1930s.

It did so, in part, because some educators recognized that their female college students were not satisfied with only the types of athletic opportunities endorsed by the professional orthodoxy. Simply put, some physical educators had a difficult time reconciling their anti-competition rhetoric with the realities they faced on their individual campuses and in their own lives. Promoted by a younger generation of physical educators who were less restricted by the orthodox professional views of women's roles and the nature of women's athletics and also encouraged by the significant advances many women had made in public life, the urge to expand collegiate women's athletic opportunities was as much a product of the 1930s as was the resolute resistance to the new ideas. Though moderate in many ways, the move to create a women's NCAA and to launch a national intercollegiate golf tournament for women overtly challenged the beliefs of most American female and male professional physical educators. While the leaders of this movement accepted the notion that women's organizations should oversee women's sports, they posited that, contrary to the beliefs of most physical education professionals, a proper form of femininity and controlled competition could coexist.

Although firmly entrenched, the challenged orthodoxy had been in place less than a decade when the Depression began. Beginning in the 1920s and extending through the 1930s, the mantra "A Girl for Every Game, and a Game for Every Girl" guided the athletic policies and shaped the athletic programs for most women attending US colleges and universities. As part of a dominant national and international movement, female physical educators worked to protect their female charges from the "evils of sports for women" and to prevent women's college athletic programs from becoming as corrupt, competitive, and commercialized as they believed the men's programs to be. The white, university-level physical educators also defined themselves in contrast to the emerging working-class and existing African American models of sport. During difficult financial times, the educators labored to preserve their own positions within the academy; and, by establishing approved structures of athletic organization and operation, they sought to teach their athletes a certain set of gender-specific, often racially determined, middle-class values and habits.

Almost from the beginning, women attending US colleges desired access to athletic opportunities. As Susan Cahn has pointed out, during the late 1800s and early 1900s, "student social life at some schools thrived around active women's sports programs."[1] This was especially true at several northern women's colleges in the late nineteenth century, where "trained physical educators and resident physicians were urging [female college students] to lay aside their corsets (and their inhibitions) and exercise as they never had before." Between 1870 and 1900, students at Vassar College in New York and at Smith College and Mount Holyoke College, both in Massachusetts, often picked up bats and baseball mitts when they laid their corsets aside, consciously choosing to play "America's game," one associated directly with masculinity and manliness.[2]

Although most Americans had come to associate baseball with masculinity by the late 1800s, basketball did not have that immediate connection. By 1895, even though James A. Naismith had invented basketball only a few years earlier, women in all sections of the United States were playing basketball, with women's colleges in the South and East hosting some of the most enthusiastic contests, and western colleges also supporting intercollegiate competition vigorously. At Smith College and Radcliffe College (also in Massachusetts), the annual tournaments pitting the basketball teams of each class against each other became campus institutions, attracting the interest of the entire campus community. These games were not just popular or frivolous exercises. Instead, officials at schools where women played basketball saw the sport primarily as a teaching tool—an exercise that could build more fit bodies, more cooperative players, and quicker-thinking young ladies. With the rough and tough men's game as a counterpoint, educators developed rules for less strenuous, distinctively women's versions of basketball in order to combat the possibly perceived negative results of basketball.[3]

The first "inter-institutional" women's basketball game occurred in 1892 when the University of California squad played Miss Head's School, and the nation's intercollegiate schedule began to fill up shortly thereafter. Mount Holyoke College (Massachusetts) and Sophie Newcomb College (Louisiana), for example, both began playing in 1893. In many places, including Ohio State, by the early 1900s women's intercollegiate basketball games attracted large crowds. In Columbus, women's games drew crowds of five hundred to a thousand fans, numbers even more impressive when one considers that the Buckeyes never had more than five hundred female students during this period.[4]

The 1920s saw the emergence of the athletic "new woman" and of a new challenge to male physical superiority as women's sports continued to expand, both in and out of collegiate settings. Although historians usually highlight the accomplishments of, and the attention given to, male athletes such as Babe Ruth and Red Grange when referring to the 1920s as the "age of sports heroes," several women also emerged as iconic sports figures during this era.[5] During the 1920s women demonstrated their athletic prowess as such athletes as Sybil Bauer broke the world's men's backstroke records and Gertrude Ederle swam the English Channel more than two hours faster than any of her five male predecessors. Moreover, tennis stars such as France's Suzanne Lenglen and America's Helen Wills brought increased public attention to women's athletics during the 1920s as their eras of dominance overlapped.[6]

Significantly, however, the attention these and other female athletes attracted and the discussions they sparked were not focused solely on the women's athletic feats. Although relatively few female athletes had to deal with the demands of athletic expectations, fame, and constant media attention that male stars confronted, *all* female athletes had to navigate their way though a confusing maze of larger societal expectations. The expanding athletic opportunities between

1900 and 1930 had different meanings for white American women of different social and economic classes, and some of the most striking departures from the expectations of "proper" behavior were seen in the athletic activities of the US working class and among female athletes competing outside the control of school or college supervisors, often in strenuous basketball and in track and field events. Men controlled this developing working-class, extra-scholastic model of sport, and it presented formidable challenges to Victorian ideals of propriety and the notion of separate spheres. Directly contradicting middle-class expectations, the working-class model emphasized competition among permanent teams in front of mixed-sex crowds, using women's teams to advertise sponsoring companies and utilizing athletes' sexuality to make the advertisements effective.[7]

While concerned female physical educators designed school sports programs to give working-class women the mental and physical tools necessary to improve their stations in life, the same middle-class professional leaders intended for physical education activities in schools and, especially, colleges to create more refined, poised, and respectable "ladies." By the 1920s, however, it was clear to interested observers that professional physical educators and their ideals could not and would not control all women's sports, particularly those of the working class.[8]

This lack of control was the product of an explosion in the number of women's competitive-sporting opportunities outside colleges and schools. Throughout the early twentieth century, industrial recreation programs in the United States and Canada offered leagues, clubs, and tournaments for employees of all skill levels. In 1923, for example, more than 500 of Chicago's Western Electric Company female employees participated in the company's bowling program, while more than 120 rode horses and almost 100 competed in rifle-shooting competitions. These company- and industrial-based leagues catered to a new demographic section, a population of young, single, urban, working women who wanted to keep playing basketball and other games even after leaving the schools where they learned them.[9]

While part of a broader industrial strategy known as welfare capitalism, which was designed in part to replace workers' ethnic loyalties with loyalty to their employers, these industrial leagues also provided fantastic corporate advertisements. They did this by selling the sex appeal of the female athletes while at the same time fostering wider recognition of the companies' names. The time-honored practice of using male athletes to advertise institutions and organizations shifted, and it became more commonplace to use working-class women in the 1920s. In Texas, exceptionally talented and successful women's teams attracted regular, paying crowds of one to two thousand, and the teams often competed before audiences numbering over five thousand in tournament finals. By 1930, almost fifty women's basketball teams received regular coverage in Dallas's newspapers, coverage that included pictures, box scores, accounts of games, player interviews, and discussions of upcoming games. These games were so popular that, in 1931, leaders of the Southwest Conference recommended that the conference loosen its officiating so that the men's college game would more closely resemble the more popular women's industrial league games.[10]

Women increasingly found even more opportunities to compete outside the industrial leagues, colleges, and schools. Responding to women's demands, the all-male Amateur Athletic Union (AAU) added events for female athletes, beginning in 1916 with a national swimming competition, adding in 1924 a track competition and, in 1926, a basketball tournament. While never matching the public appeal of the men's tournaments, such women's competitions attracted enthusiastic crowds of hundreds and sometimes thousands. This expansion of competitive opportunities fostered even greater press coverage of women athletes and contributed to the introduction of American women athletes on the international stage. Although women had exhibited their golf, tennis, and archery skills at the 1900 and 1904 Olympics, not until 1920 did the United States send female skaters and swimmers to represent their country in the Olympic Games.[11] Again, this escalation did not represent progress to many US physical educators, male or female; in fact, by the 1920s, physical education organizations in the United States actively campaigned against women participating in international competitions and especially in the Olympics. They based their opposition on fears that women would start to play sports for the wrong reasons, that the athletes would be exploited in almost countless ways, and that a societal focus on training and celebrating elite athletes would reduce the opportunities for all women to participate in athletics.[12]

These educators were equally upset that US women athletes attracted notoriety and acclaim for their physical appearance as much as, if not more than, their physical skill. In both the industrial leagues and the male-controlled AAU contests, the display of athletic, feminine bodies drew extensive public notice. The abundant media descriptions of female athletes as "alluring" and "nymphs" makes clear that, in Susan Cahn's words, the "athletes were clearly perceived and portrayed as attractive, erotic women."[13]

This appeal was conscious and intentional, if not always by the women, then certainly by the male event promoters. Just as French tennis star Suzanne Lenglen "modernized" tennis in the 1920s by wearing shorter skirts and makeup during matches, the industrial leagues often used more revealing uniforms, made of shimmering, brightly colored fabrics, to accentuate the sexual appeal of the female athletes. The basketball team of one of Texas's most successful and significant industrial teams of the 1920s and 1930s replaced its traditional, "appropriate" uniforms with "panties of bright orange satin" and similar jerseys. Not only did these new uniforms allow for greater freedom of movement for the athletes, they also generated enough controversy and interest to boost the team's average crowd size from the low hundreds to around five thousand.[14] In 1931 the director of women's physical education at the University of Cincinnati, Helen Smith, scandalized her colleagues with her account of a local tournament hosted by a "well-known sporting goods house" that required one women's team to play basketball in "a sort of peach colored bathing suit."[15]

The striking advances made by women athletes in the 1920s raised serious questions for a male-dominated society. If assertive women could best men physically, then men might have to stop considering themselves as the guardians of the "weaker sex." In short, if the "new" woman became the typical woman, then all members of society would have to reevaluate the entire spectrum of male-female interactions. As Cahn has suggested, the growth of women's sports symbolized the blurring of traditional gender-based power relations.[16] Despite living in the first decade of women voters and greater sexual freedom, most Americans, and especially most university educators, regarded this upheaval as undesirable.

Media presentations and the cultivated, public personas of many prominent women athletes presented clear challenges to the existing middle-class model of gender stereotypes in the 1920s and 1930s. Forsaking the ideal of "moderation" that had governed the activities of most female athletes in the 1900s and 1910s, many athletes in the 1920s sought unmoderated excellence in athletic endeavors and unabashed freedom in personal matters, refusing to succumb to traditional, middle-class norms of respectability.

Tennis star Lenglen embodied wider societal trends of the 1920s by displaying more of her athletic body than any of her predecessors had and by overtly showcasing her sexuality.[17] In contrast, her American counterpart, University of California alumna Helen Wills, earned the nickname "the American Girl" by rejecting Lenglen's flapper mode of dress and behavior and presenting a more controlled and moderate public image. What the middle- and upper-class fans of tennis considered "American" was far more conservative than what Lenglen or her kindred spirits in the US industrial leagues and AAU embodied.[18]

The best-known and most-accomplished, and also one of the most-controversial, American female athletes of the twentieth century was Mildred "Babe" Didrikson of Beaumont, Texas, whose story illustrates well the conflicting messages attached to women's athletics in the 1920s and 1930s. In this era, in contrast to the working-class women of the industrial leagues, "respectable" women were expected to become healthier from exercise without advertising their feminine sexuality by exercising in front of male crowds or in revealing outfits. At the same time they were supposed to guard against becoming too masculine by developing large muscles or competitive instincts. Didrikson had a difficult time reconciling her extraordinary talent and desires with society's expectations.[19]

Incredibly gifted in every sport she attempted, the working-class Didrikson was the sole representative of the Employers Casualty Company at the 1932 AAU women's track and field championships, where she broke four world records and won six gold medals all in one afternoon. In the 1932 Olympics, Didrikson built upon that success by winning two gold medals, forfeiting a third only because she had used an unauthorized technique in the high jump. But her unrivaled athletic ability did not win Didrikson universal public acclaim; instead, her skills, accomplishments, muscular physique, competitive drive, and "mannish" manner only highlighted tensions created by other athletic women who were also challenging gender expectations. Seeking to feminize this intimidating athlete, male reporters continuously juxtaposed her numerous athletic medals with the cooking prize or sewing prize—the reporters were never quite clear about which domestic art she had mastered—she had won as a youngster. Moreover, it was not until "Babe" married an undeniably masculine man, a large former wrestler named George Zaharias, and took up the genteel game of golf as her primary sport that many sportswriters and observers viewed her as sufficiently respectable and feminine. By providing evidence through her publicized, married life that she was a heterosexual woman who could cook and clean, while also playing and dominating more "feminine" games, Didrikson-Zaharias achieved a greater level of public acceptance in the late 1940s than she had enjoyed in the 1920s and 1930s.[20]

The development of the institutionalized, anticompetitive, antielite mentality that dominated the academy and the women's physical education profession after the early 1920s was grounded, in large part, in opposition to this working-class, ethnic, "other" that Didrikson personified. The expanding model of extra-collegiate women's athletic activity and the omnipresent specter of commercialized, competitive, elite men's intercollegiate athletics constituted the two dangerous poles that the female physical educators tried to navigate between when designing and supervising their programs.

In the early 1920s, female leaders of women's college sports led a conservative reaction to this wide array of social and athletic changes. This legion of "respectable" women believed that they should control the development and administration of women's sports.[21] Historian Ronald Smith has effectively categorized the complex system of justifications these women constructed in support of their claims for authority by separating the argument into five categories. First, the women wanted to "prevent the exploitation of women in their sports activities," as they felt the AAU and industrial leagues were doing. Second, they wanted to "develop womanly qualities and protect women's reproductive functions," to preserve proper femininity and to avoid overexertion that might damage athletes' abilities to reproduce or attract men with whom they could conceive children. Third, the women planned to "develop educational and character-building opportunities not fostered in men's athletics," in other words, to infuse the athletes with desirable beliefs and character traits. Fourth, concerned physical educators argued that they wanted to be "democratic" and give equal athletic opportunities to all women, not just the most skilled, as opposed to the practices they observed in men's college athletics. Finally, to this well-documented list of concerns, Smith added a fifth motivating desire, one he characterized as based on "exploitation" and "hypocrisy." He asserted that the desire of professional female physical educators to separate the women's athletic activities completely from men's also stemmed from the selfish, if understandable, desire to preserve their professional autonomy and careers.[22]

They did so by working through several interconnected organizations to protect their own status as the proper administrators of women's college athletics. One can temper Smith's provocative characterization of the physical educators as Machiavellian exploiters and still recognize that women, after struggling to achieve professional and professorial status, laboring in a university system that offered women few leadership positions and a society that offered them even fewer, could rationally adopt plans designed to preserve their authority and autonomy. As Barbara Harris explained in 1978, "if the 1920s saw a slowing down of the entrance of women into the professions, the 1930s spelled disaster. Under the impact of the Depression, hostility to female employment reached new levels of intensity." This hostility was especially evident when married women continued to work, and its targets included university professors. During the 1930s, the numbers and percentages of female college teachers declined by almost one-fifth, dropping from 32.5 percent of all university teachers to 26.5 percent, a downward trend that would continue until the 1950s.[23] The female physical educators had every reason to be apprehensive, and they responded by creating organizations and ideologies to preserve their positions and protect the young women under their supervision.

In 1917 the Committee of Women's Athletics (CWA) was formed as a part of the existing American Physical Educators Association (APEA) in one of the first steps to create the protective and controlled athletic system for women that the physical education professional establishment increasingly came to promote and defend. CWA members almost immediately focused their attention on the perceived dangers posed to female athletes by the male-controlled AAU and by the male, elitist, exploitative model of athletics they saw in the Olympics and men's intercollegiate athletics. They argued against female participation in the Olympics and AAU competitions and worked instead to create a well-rounded athletic program that would adequately prepare all participants for the vaguely defined "varied emergencies of life."[24]

An organization featuring many of the same people and promoting an almost identical agenda as the CWA emerged in 1923 as the Women's Division of the National Amateur Athletic Federation (NAAF). As historian Joan Hult explained, the CWA and the Women's Division "formed a united front that opposed the AAU, collegiate, and any other efforts to provide elite and varsity athletic competition for women."[25] Historian Benjamin Rader emphasized the Women's Division's lasting importance, writing that its 1923 platform "served as a guiding principle for women's athletics until the late 1960s."[26] This enduring importance was the result, as Ellen Gerber explained, of the Women's Division platform being "endorsed in toto by all groups most concerned with women's collegiate sport."[27] Operating under the principle of "a game for every girl and every girl in a game," such organizations as the Women's Division advocated extensive intramural programs and no intercollegiate ones.[28] Based on the belief that varsity teams and intercollegiate contests shifted attention and resources away from the vast majority of undergraduate women in order to support "a few super-athletes to represent the group and entertain the mass," most members of this influential organization opposed all efforts to encourage or continue women's intercollegiate competition.[29]

Other organizations, often populated by the same people, joined the fight for this same anticompetitive agenda during the 1920s and 1930s. Working within the APEA, the National Section of Women's Athletics (NSWA) replaced the CWA in 1932 and began publishing a variety of playing and coaching guides, health-related pamphlets, and standards guides, which spelled out precisely what benefits should result from women's sports and the potential dangers coaches and athletes should avoid. By 1936, the NSWA had established a network of state associations to oversee the development and operation of all women's athletics within those states, and by 1937 more than 750 women worked on at least one of the NWSA committees. The NWSA worked closely with the Women's Division of the NAAF for most of the 1930s, but by the end of the decade both groups recognized that their assumed roles as the rule-makers and gatekeepers overlapped. In June 1940, the Women's Division merged into the American Association for Health, Physical Education, and Recreation. Even though the organization itself ceased to exist after 1940, the Women's Division's legacy in the movement for the "controlled development of collegiate sport for women" was secure.[30]

The opposition to women's intercollegiate athletic competition had much wider roots than mere fear of "super-athletes" dangerously attracting public attention. Indeed, female physical educators saw multiple reasons to resist intercollegiate competition. First, as their motto of "a game for every girl and every girl in a game" suggests, the women controlling women's college athletics had a specific, egalitarian, and "democratic" vision of women's sport: their understanding of a feminine democracy centered on cooperation and consensus, not the more masculine model of conflict and competition. They wanted their mostly white, middle-class charges to have precisely equal athletic opportunities, with no one advantaged over others, intentionally avoiding elevating the elite athletes above the rest. This egalitarian approach also applied to the amounts of instructors' attention and the schools' physical resources that, the argument held, should be available equally to all female students.[31]

The educators believed that treating all women as if they were exactly the same would prevent the undesired inflation of skilled students' egos and would also ensure that the tight budgets allocated to women's sports—budgets that would shrink even more during the Depression years—serviced all of the students, not just the elite athletes. This concern about adequate resources was legitimate. For example, in 1930 Anna Hiss, the University of Texas director of women's athletics, agitated for more equal funding for women's intramural athletics. The Texas Athletic Council, populated entirely by men, provided only $1,800 to Hiss, even though she argued repeatedly that the women were entitled to at least $2,500 in addition to a share of a student activity fee. Two years later, a mere three weeks after allocating $300 to fund four male tennis players' trip to Pennsylvania, the Athletic Council decided that, "in view of the present large deficit [and] the uncertain future of our financial condition for the coming year," it could not support a $300 raise necessary to make a women's physical educator a full-time employee.[32] Later that same year, the council declared that "because of its present financial condition, [the Athletic Council] would be limited to $4,500.00 for Intramurals for Men and $1,625.00 to Intramurals for Women; that the Athletic Council feels that the requests of the two above departments are meritorious."[33] At Texas, and elsewhere, the women's physical educators' fears for their budgetary survival were meritorious as well.

The universities' athletic leaders also wanted to use sporting activities to teach these young women "proper" values and habits in addition to creating the desired democratic or egalitarian balance in athletic offerings. Such goals had existed from the very beginning of women's college athletics, and the values physical educators wanted to teach women differed greatly from the competitive ones they wanted to teach men. Female physical educators labored to prevent their supervised athletic contests from becoming disruptive, publicized, competitive spectacles. Still, in a society that, by the 1930s, had come to accept, and in a few instances celebrate, increased competition by women outside colleges, many officials felt compelled to explain their stance.

Countering criticisms that the Women's Division abhorred all competition, a historian of the group noted in 1941 that all games involved some sort of competition and that the Women's Division existed to promote games and sports for women; therefore, by definition, the Women's Division endorsed some forms of competition. It disapproved, however, of an "intense, highly specialized type of competition" because this activity "tends to tear down real values and set up false ones."[34] This explanation raises the questions: what were these "real values" and how were they promoted through college athletic programs during the 1920s and 1930s?

According to a Women's Division spokesperson and many of her like-minded educators, competition was permissible only if it was controlled and if participants focused on the fun of the game, not the score on the board. As long as the proper attitude prevailed, games were

University of Texas intramural tennis champions, 1938. *Courtesy of the Dolph Briscoe Center for American History, the University of Texas at Austin.*

a great character-building tool, with competition serving as a "means to wholesome, healthful enjoyment, rather than an end to itself."[35] In other words, competition was fine as long as it did not become corrupt, exploitative, or competitive like men's or extra-collegiate women's athletic programs. In an important article published in 1930 entitled "'Evils of Sports for Women," Helen Smith indicted the men's athletic situation: "Competition is stressed over play and enjoyment. Great national organizations have developed whose members are, for the most part, men who are dependent upon sport for a livelihood. . . . To be sure these men have developed and produced world champions, individuals, and teams, but for the most part they have forgotten American youth as a whole and the fact that there should be opportunity for all, rather than a few."[36] The women's programs, Smith argued, were better because they "emphasiz[ed] the spirit of play and fellowship in their athletic activities for women," while the men and "those in charge of industrial athletics" for women did not.[37]

Another essential part of female physical educators' efforts to foster the correct attitude toward sport and self was their desire to "protect" young women athletes. This desire to protect had many meanings and manifestations. Some educators argued against women's intercollegiate competition because such contests would require loosely supervised, overnight travel, removing the young women from the protective custody of *in loco parentis* policies of their respective institutions. To address this difficulty, innovative educators devised a more controlled and cheaper way to allow college women to test their abilities against counterparts from other institutions without traveling by holding "telegraphic meets." For these events, officials at participating colleges and universities recorded their own athletes' efforts and then reported the results to a central location. While this tactic allowed a very controlled type of competition, it also eliminated the perceived problems of adoring crowds, personal rivalries, and overnight travel. Since they required no travel or overnight stays, the telegraphic meets were much cheaper than face-to-face competitions and thus offered practical (as well as philosophical) advantages to physical educators overseeing small budgets.[38]

Physical educators also wanted to guard against the twin terrors of the inappropriate use of or development of the women athletes' bodies. Certainly well aware of the sexual innuendos that were an integral part of press coverage of women's athletics, the use of sex appeal by the industrial leagues as part of the marketing of the games and of the sponsoring companies, and the development of the combination beauty contests–basketball tournaments run by the AAU in the 1930s, female physical educators did not want to corrupt their young women by presenting them as sexual objects. They certainly did not want their young, middle-class women playing for softball teams named "Slapsie Maxie's Curvacious Cuties" or "Balian Ice Cream Beauties."[39]

One way the educators tried to prevent this sexualizing of female athletes was by creating separate facilities for women; another way was by advocating more traditional and modest athletic uniforms for their college women. In most instances, the women received separate but unequal athletic facilities. Although some schools, including the state universities of Maryland, Texas, and California, included women's gymnasiums in the overall athletic building boom of the 1920s and early 1930s, in most places, the women got the old gym when universities built new ones for the men.[40] Howard Savage's *American College Athletics* summarized the situation this way, "In comparison with the facilities lavished upon men students, the gymnasium provisions for women usually leave much to be desired. When a new gymnasium is erected for the men, the older, disused structure is generally turned over to the women. . . . Sometimes . . . a temporary wooden frame structure, partly given over to other uses, is built for the women." Among the nation's institutions, he singled out the University of California, Coe College (in Iowa), the University of Iowa, Ohio State, and the Oregon Agricultural College for their "excellent gymnasiums for their women students."[41]

Many state and national associations spoke out about the desire for proper women's athletic attire. Smith highlighted the required use of bathing suits as basketball uniforms in 1930s, and at the 1938 Texas Athletic Federation of College Women convention, the members resolved that individual Women's Athletic Association (WAA) chapters should dedicate themselves to upholding national guidelines, including requiring "proper clothing for sports."[42]

The guardians of women's college sports did not want to see their young ladies' sexuality exploited in athletic arenas or by athletic promoters or observers. They also wanted to ensure that the sporting activities they sponsored did not rob students of their vital femininity. As Cahn has argued, "the primary problem in twentieth century American women's sport has been breaking down the socially constructed barriers separating ideals of athletes and real women; the physical educators of the 1930s helped to buttress these same barriers."[43] By trying to create more feminine types of games, complete with different rules and expectations, female athletic leaders endorsed the idea that the desire for strenuous competition was a masculine quality, inappropriate for proper females.

One male physical educator summed up the problems inherent in combining high-level sports and femininity with these telling words: "Speaking bluntly, one of the most precious qualities of girls' characters is endangered. . . . Games like basketball and baseball are combative sports. They develop ugly muscles—muscles ugly in girls—as well as scowling faces and the competitive spirit. As an inevitable consequence your girls may find it more difficult to attract the most worthy fathers for their children."[44]

Perhaps revealing fears of race suicide, many men shared the women's fear that competitive sports not only could create more masculine-minded women but also could make the athletes less physically attractive, and therefore less likely to produce the "right" kind of children. Writing in 1929, Frederick Rand Rogers asked his audience in the *American Physical Education Review* to "imagine the international marathon race for women, or a boxing championship. In these activities the competitive elements rise to the greatest prominence." He continued, explaining how the rise of the competitive elements in females was undesirable: "Such events only tend to destroy all that is womanly in girls, whether the qualities considered be physical beauty, grace, social charm and adaptability, or capacity and desire for motherhood. But other *competitive* activities are only less harmful." Dr. Rogers never explained how distance running would "destroy . . . [the] desire for motherhood," but he did suggest that "fancy diving, where victory is determined by *graceful execution alone*," would provide acceptable competitive opportunities for women.[45]

The University of Tennessee devised another solution, combining a running race with a needle-threading contest as an official intramural event of the 1930s. The Tennessee student newspaper described the competition in this way: "four pledges ran the length of Jefferson Hall, one at a time, carrying with them a needle in one hand and thread in the other. A fifth pledge threaded the needle, returning it to the other, who ran back. Then another started until all four had run."[46] Physical fitness and domestic dexterity: what more could a properly trained physical educator want from a program?

The physical educators of the 1920s and 1930s consciously created physical education and intramural sports programs that protected college women from these identified dangers and reaffirmed the proper, desired values. The emerging ideologies of the 1920s effectively ended openly conducted women's intercollegiate competition, replacing almost every intercollegiate athletic program with a host of intramural and interclass contests. The variety of these programs illustrated the difficulty of putting a set of codified ideals into effect, no matter how often they are articulated or how many profess agreement. Through the health components of the athletic programs, the physical education curricula, and the extensive intramural programs established for women, physical educators at US colleges and universities sought to indoctrinate their female students with the newly triumphant, democratic sport orthodoxy.

In order to implement their new set of ideas, the leading physical educators first had to eradicate women's intercollegiate competition from the universities. They were largely successful in doing so, although their success was neither immediate nor absolutely complete. Ellen Gerber analyzed the results of several well-known surveys conducted by a prominent spokesperson of the anti-intercollegiate movement, Mabel Lee, in 1923, 1930, and 1936 about the status of women's intercollegiate competition. Gerber concluded that Lee's statistics indicated that relatively few universities had featured varsity women's athletics before 1923 and that over the ensuing years the numbers of institutions sponsoring varsity women's programs declined, as did the numbers of sports offered by those schools that maintained a varsity presence. This decline played out in a variety of ways at the institutional level, but at most places it did indeed occur.[47]

For example, at the University of Tennessee, the decision to abandon women's intercollegiate athletics resulted from the combination of several factors. Ideologically, the growing prominence of the university's women's varsity basketball team during the 1920s caused concern for many: the women were attracting headlines as individual stars, traveling to games as far away as Kentucky and Virginia, competing against teams coached by men, and drawing attention away from the nonathletic women. As Adam Hornbuckle put it, "by the mid-twenties, varsity basketball at Tennessee reflected the skilled and competitive aspects which the [Women's Division] condemned in women's sports." In fact, a student editorial defending women's varsity basketball only highlighted the aspects that many educators found problematic: "Basketball is the only activity on the 'Hill' in which coeds compete with coeds of other colleges and universities," and through which they could earn "recognition, honor, [and] glory."[48]

Practical concerns united with ideological concerns in the mid-1920s to deny University of Tennessee women their desired attention and acclaim. The practical problem was that the move to disband women's varsity programs had great success among Tennessee's rivals, leaving the team without adequate numbers of teams to play. Hoping to continue their programs, the university's leading athletic officials, both men and women, sent a questionnaire about the continuation of women's varsity basketball to their colleagues at regional universities. The replies were overwhelmingly negative, so Tennessee's leaders decided in the spring of 1926 to end the women's varsity basketball program.[49]

This saga had parallels in countless schools across the nation, as almost all followed the same general pattern. On November 19, 1923, the University of California played Stanford University in a women's field hockey match; according to Le'Ellen Kubow, the participants did not "realize it then, but this was the last intercollegiate hockey game they would play for almost twenty-five years."[50] To explain the program's abolition, Kubow cited the growing importance of the Women's Division standards, the same standards that led to the demise of almost all openly conducted women's intercollegiate athletics during the following years.

Physical educators addressed their concern about the proper development and control of young's women's bodies by insisting that only women administer women's athletic programs and by including health and sanitary regulations in the athletic programs themselves. The 1923 Women's Division platform articulated this position very well, including the resolution that "competent women be put in immediate charge of women and girls in their athletic activities even where the administrative supervision may be under the direction of men"; and another resolution called for women to work "toward the establishment of a future policy that shall place the administration as well as teaching and coaching of girls and women in the hands of carefully trained and qualified women."[51]

Other national and local publications voiced these desires throughout the 1920s and 1930s; in fact, the Women's Division opposed the inclusion of women in the 1932 Olympic Games, in part, because participation "places men in immediate charge of athletic activities for girls and women." Even a cursory examination of the Women's Division's state leadership structure reveals how seriously the members took this desire for feminine leadership. All of the forty-eight state "chairmen" for the 1931–32 academic year were women, and all but six were directly affiliated with specific colleges, universities, or high schools.[52]

This national desire for female leadership can also be seen at the local level. At the University of Texas, both male and female administrators spoke out in the early 1930s against combining the men's and women's physical education and athletic departments. Anna Hiss argued that the physical and philosophical differences between men and women made such a combination dangerous. Since women "differ anatomically and physiologically from men," and since women's athletics emphasized the "development of all students" while men's intercollegiate athletics were for "the development of the few and for the interest of the spectators," the two were simply incompatible. Hiss also worried that, under the control of men, the women's physical education courses and intramural sports would become a "practice school" for aspiring teachers, an "experimental field" for budding researchers, and ultimately a concern subordinate to all men's activities. After all, the increasing dominance of the YMCA over the YWCA during the 1920s had demonstrated that when men's organizations took an active interest in women's athletics, the women's smaller and less well-funded organizations had great difficulty in preserving their ideals and their domains.[53]

A male physical educator at the University of Texas, L. T. Bellmont, agreed with Hiss's conclusions, admitting that many of her concerns had merit. After all, in his eyes as well, "the aims and ideals of intercollegiate athletics are foreign to all other interests involved and must be considered as a separate problem." Essentially, both Hiss and Belmont argued that women should continue to direct women's athletics because, in Belmont's words, "a spirit of harmony [could] best be obtained by completely separating all interests."[54]

Doctors had long made the same distinction that Hiss made, that women were anatomically and physiologically different than men and that those differences should affect how they participated in sports. Anatomically, the argument went, women had several disadvantages when compared to men. Women had, according to one scholar's summary, "smaller and shorter bones, smaller and shorter arms and legs, . . . more body fat, larger thighs, . . . a lower center of gravity, . . . smaller hearts, narrower chests, and more visceral organs than boys." Moreover, women were considered physiologically different because they had less muscle strength, less endurance, and fewer opportunities to push themselves to their physical limits.[55] These anatomical and physiological differences alone, however, did not necessitate trained women's control over women athletes. For the women of the physical education associations, another biological difference did.

Most female physical educators believed that women should oversee college female athletes because only women possessed the special knowledge essential to preventing dangerous overexertion during the menstrual cycle, thus avoiding damage to women's reproductive organs. Only women could, according to Marjorie Bateman in 1935, understand the special "problems and troubles" of the female athletes.[56] After decades of concern about and restrictions on women's activities during their period, in the early 1930s a few sought to lessen the strictest prohibitions on activities. In 1932, Ethel Perrin, the associate director of the American Child Health Association's Division of Health Education, contended that although there was "a general trend toward advocating normalcy of behavior during the menstrual period," women should still avoid certain activities during their period. While some doctors declared that walking, golf, dancing, and "exercises which [did] not involve undue fatigue or jumping" were acceptable, "strenuous gymnastics, tennis, basketball, and horseback riding" were not because they might damage the uterus. In contrast, the American Student Health Association declared in 1932 that educators and athletes should not consider the menstrual cycle a "period of disability from the ordinary physical and mental activities of college life."[57]

Despite the emergence of a professional debate, concerns about women's reproductive organs led most athletic officials to believe that women should continue to avoid "abnormal" athletic events, "including those of a highly competitive variety where outside pressure gives to the winning of the game an exaggerated importance." Perrin explained, "The temptation in such a situation to go beyond one's strength is a disadvantage at all times, and particularly during the menstrual period."[58] She did not have to explain that, unlike men, properly trained women physical educators would not let such a competitive situation arise in the first place.

The women running the intramural sports programs at the University of Texas in the mid-1930s incorporated these specific health concerns into their official statement of goals. Like most of their colleagues, these educators required medical examinations before and after athletic competitions, and they wanted to create "a system of supervision that shall assure a reasonable and sane attitude toward participation in activities at times of temporary physical unfitness." Not coincidentally, the same document also stressed the desirability of having activities "managed by professionally trained women."[59]

In accordance with these beliefs and concerns, university physical educators structured their physical education and intramural sports programs so that they would reward college women for meeting certain health and cleanliness standards. For example, WAA officials at the University of Maryland established a point system that allowed female athletes to earn athletic awards in multiple ways, including bathing and having good posture. Maryland women could earn a "blazer with a circle M" by accumulating 1,200 points, an "M" by earning 800 points, and "numerals" for 400 points, and they could earn these points in a variety of ways. Students could earn a total of 100 points, one quarter of the minimum necessary to receive an athletic honor, by meeting certain standards in the "Leadership, Scholarship, and Health" category. Maryland women received 25 athletic points for grade-point averages between 3.5 and 4.0, and they earned 15 points for averages between 3.0 and 3.5. Moreover, they could earn a total of 25 athletic points by following certain health rules. For example, if a female Maryland student had "an A grade in posture maintained thru the year," she received 15 points, the same number she earned if she raised her B or her C posture grade to an A during the year. Students could also earn 10 athletic points simply by having an A for "general health" during the year.[60]

The University of California's WAA had even more explicit health rules in place for its female athletes. Originally adopted in 1925, these health rules allowed individual women to earn 10 athletic points for their respective classes in a university-wide competition. According to the September 23, 1929, "Women's Athletic Association Bulletin" the "Minimum Health Standard" had four requirements: "get eight hours of sleep five nights a week"; "eat a balanced diet of three meals at regular intervals"; "eat no candy or similar sweets between meals"; and "take a cold or tepid shower, plunge or sponge, daily."[61] At a minimum, the University of California athletes should have been well rested, well fed, and clean.

The California WAA did not stop at identifying the absolute minimum; instead, the same bulletin identified the six components of the "Recommended Health Standard." If the University of California's female athletes had followed their advisors' recommendations, then they would have gotten at least sixty hours of sleep a week, eaten raw fruit and vegetables every day, had a minimum of one pint of milk daily, relaxed "completely for at least 15 minutes a day," exercised outdoors for an hour a day, and given themselves "sufficient time" for all of their meals.[62] Virtually all health professionals would still agree today that most women and men would be better off physically and emotionally if they followed these guidelines, but in the 1930s only university women received points toward athletic honors by following basic health rules. Varsity men certainly did not.

Unfortunately for ideological educators, even at schools that emphasized such health rules, most college women did not want to follow them. Louise S. Cobb, in a 1929 review of the California WAA, admitted that replies to a "health standard questionnaire" were not encouraging. She reported that "the minimum health requirements were being 'moderately' kept by the majority" of California women, and that the percentage observing the rules declined as the students progressed from freshmen to seniors. Although the results from her questionnaire dissatisfied Cobb, they did not surprise her. In fact, she noted, "Few colleges have reported any attention to health rules and standards." Still Cobb and other physical educators did not believe that they should abandon their mission to teach specific body care and control standards just because most students did not follow health regulations.

Maryville College in East Tennessee had an even more explicit set of health rules as part of its women's athletic honors program. According to the "Point System of Athletic Awards," Maryville women could earn one-sixth of the points required to "letter" by following proscribed health regulations. As at the University of California, these rules addressed almost all aspects of the women's daily lives. For example, to get maximum credit the women were supposed to sleep "from time lights cut out until 6 a.m., during any 23 days out of 30 consecutive days," with the windows "open top to bottom." As at California, the rules required the athletes to take daily baths in water not "too hot or too cold," even during their menstrual periods. The Maryville women could not snack unless the morsels had administrative approval, and they were to wash down "unmasticated food" with water. They could never drink "coco cola." Finally, the women had to change their underwear daily and to evacuate their bowels daily, "at regular time, if possible preferably after breakfast."[63]

Just as the directors of women's athletic programs tried to use athletic programs to teach proper dietary and cleanliness lessons, they also tried to use their athletic programs to teach their students desired attitudes toward life and athletics. Since the same women generally operated both sets of programs, these curricular and extracurricular activities worked together to teach and reaffirm in the women the same set of values and attitudes about sports and competition. The interlocking physical education and intramural programs that dominated the college woman's athletic landscape of the 1930s best illustrate how this attitude instruction worked.[64]

The physical educators in charge of US universities' women's intramural athletic programs structured their programs so that they would teach and reinforce the goals of the Women's Division and other official organizations. Administered by trained women who were eager to protect the college women from physical and mental harm and from all sorts of exploitation, the intramural offerings available to most collegiate women were not conducive to attracting much individual attention and certainly not much individual publicity. The educators sought to fulfill the democratic dream of a "game for every girl" through a wide and increasing variety of sports and activities. Although by definition these sports and games involved competition, the nation's intramural programs sought to diminish the significance given to competition and to the spoils of victory, athletic awards with real value. If everything went according to design, the college women would be content to "play for play's sake." The evidence shows, however, that everything did not always go according to plans.[65]

The decline of intercollegiate athletics and the rise of the new athletic orthodoxy during the 1920s and 1930s led to increased emphasis on women's intramural programs at colleges and universities across the nation. After closing the books on its intercollegiate women's programs in June 1926, the University of Tennessee allowed its director of physical training for women, Anne Huddle, to replace the intercollegiate program with a point system based on winning honors. Female athletes earning 1,000 points by participating in athletic activities would earn a letter sweater and a "T"; those who accumulated between 500 and 1,000 points received only a "UT" monogram. In keeping with the practice of coupling athletic programs with personal development agendas, Tennessee women with A academic averages received an additional 50 percent of their earned athletic points, and those with B averages got a 25 percent bonus.[66]

Despite Huddle's best efforts to make the point system comply with the Women's Division's desire for greater participation, between 1926 and 1929 the system became just as much a haven for elite athletes as the varsity program had been before it. In the first year of the new point system, only ten women earned letter sweaters, a number fewer than had in 1921 when women's varsity basketball had been prominent in Knoxville. As a consequence, in 1929 Huddle installed another type of intramural program in the place of the point system, emphasizing inter-sorority, inter-dormitory, and individual competitions as a way to attract fuller participation. As the program developed, however, barriers to an all-inclusive system remained. In the early 1930s, the sororities at Tennessee were the primary clients of the intramural system, dominating especially the team competitions, and it was not until the 1935–36 academic year, when independent students (those not in sororities) had their own athletic club, that all women gained full access to the intramural offerings at Tennessee. In 1937–38 this athletic club won the intramural championship. By the late 1930s, the modified structure of the University of Tennessee intramural program had succeeded in attracting more total participation among Knoxville's undergraduate female population, but this participation was still centered on the winning of championships. In order to fulfill the primary "democratic" goal of the physical education associations, Tennessee administrators had to sacrifice allegiance to some of the profession's lesser goals, including diminishing the importance of championships. At Tennessee at least, students wanted to play for more than "play's sake."[67]

The University of California also changed its structure of women's athletics in the late 1920s and 1930s; and, following the same pattern as Tennessee, these changes produced failure before eventually achieving qualified success. During the 1920s, the California WAA experienced a marked decline in membership, both in terms of total numbers and in percentages of active female students. Out of a female student population of 4,111 in the 1921–22 school year, the WAA's fall participation total was 1,601 and the spring total was 1,488, respectively 39.2 percent and 36.2 percent of Berkeley's student population. These numbers held relatively steady through 1926–27, normally falling between 26.8 percent and 39.0 percent. By 1929–30, however, the fall participation rate was only 10.6 percent and the spring rate was less than half of that, 4.2 percent of a female student population exceeding 4,200. California officials installed an intramural program in 1929 to reverse this downward spiral of interest and participation in WAA activities while not competing directly with the more formal and organized WAA sporting events.[68]

The first years of the intramural program did not go as smoothly as the WAA membership and leadership had desired, and the program's ability to further the goals of greater participation in women's athletics attracted serious scrutiny. Announced in the "Women's Athletic Association Bulletin" in February 1930 as "a new project, but one worthy of all the support we can give it," the intramural program almost immediately registered more than two hundred women and more than twenty organizations for swimming and archery meets. This initial enthusiasm did not last. In fact, as WAA faculty advisor Louise Cobb explained in her fall 1930 review of the WAA, many "Californians" doubted the wisdom of even continuing the intramural program after its first year, so disappointing had its results been. Cobb reported, "The Intramural program which has been fostered by W.A.A. for the particular purpose of increasing interest in sports among a greater number of campus women has failed for two semesters to accomplish this purpose." Cobb concluded her brief report with this stark assessment of the intramural program and its sponsoring agency: "The whole subject of W.A.A.—its place among student activities and how to increase its value to women students—must be seriously considered. Students," Cobb declared, "should not be spending time and effort on a needless enterprise."[69] Neither Cobb's assessment nor student participation rates were a ringing endorsement of the intramural program or its democratic ideals.

The next term's report by the intramural manager stated that the previous pattern of initial enthusiasm followed by an absence of sustained interest had repeated itself on the Berkeley campus. In fact, the report indicated that an "enthusiastic burst" launched the semester's intramural activities, with twenty-two of thirty-six residential or sorority houses represented; but, by the third and final archery meet, only eight athletes showed up, representing a mere five houses. The last swimming meet, held during a general campus field day, attracted seventeen swimmers from six houses and "a large audience." While these numbers might have been mildly encouraging, the attitudes of the participants certainly were not. Considering that the intramural program had as its stated goal to increase interest in athletics and to promote the joy of playing for play's sake, the intramural manager was not optimistic when she reported, "It was felt by several staff members present, that the girls who participated were not particularly enthusiastic, and did not seem to be enjoying their participation in the events."[70]

The failure of the intramural program to inspire more enthusiastic participation (or even much participation at all) led to continuous discussions about the program's fate and about how the administrators could reshape the program to meet their goals. Addressing the existing situation and Cobb's concerns from the previous term, the intramural board of the WAA again debated whether it should let the intramural sports programs die a natural death. Board members initially agreed to give the program another test, but the committee eventually decided not to try again under the existing set-up.

Not willing to concede complete defeat, the WAA restructured its programs and tried again. With the faculty advisor's consent, the WAA established an executive intramural board, with four women representing four different houses. Each executive board member had clear responsibilities for one of the following categories: secretarial duties, eligibility, recreational swimming, or publicity. However well conceived, the new organization could not overcome the lack of general student interest or the executive board's lack of administrative ability. In September 1931, only 233 students signed up for their health examination, with 80 signing up for tennis, 63 for swimming, 49 for Ping-Pong, 43 for horse riding, and 30 for golf. By the end of the semester, only 4 women of the 30 had qualified and had retained their interest in a golf tournament, compelling the intramural board to cancel the tournament.[71]

The intramural manager, Frederica Bernhard, noted the problems in the operation of intramurals and made several telling suggestions about how to remedy the situation. She reported that despite the "great deal of time and effort" the women had expended on intramurals, "on account of the inefficiency of the chairman, the delays in publicity, [and] the lack of definite information and cooperation, the response and enthusiasm were very poor." To rectify the problem, Bernhard made a suggestion that addressed the reality of the circumstances at the University of California but went against the established philosophy of the professional physical education societies regarding athletic awards. She recommended, "Unless a system of points can be worked out which would permit honors to be won by the House, there will not be sufficient incentive to make a success of recreational sports." In other words, Bernhard formally acknowledged that the women of California were not satisfied with merely playing for play's sake, that they needed prizes and honors to make their athletic activities seem worthwhile and interesting. The next term, the WAA developed precisely such a plan and, once again, resolved to improve its publicity efforts.[72]

The results of the increased publicity and the new incentives for the houses encouraged the members of the WAA. The numbers of participants increased in all measured categories from 1932 to 1933. In 1933, sixteen organizations participated, compared to ten in 1932; and 66 women signed up for at least one archery event while only 21 had the year before. In the other intramural sport, swimming, 120 signed up in 1933 for at least one event, compared to 84 the year before. The rising interest led some in the fall of 1933 to consider expanding the intramural program in order to "include all the girls on campus in some activity as soon as possible," but the intramural board decided against expansion for the moment, preferring to concentrate on doing only a few things very well.[73]

Over the next few years the program at the University of California expanded to include a rising number of individual and team sports. These additions included badminton, fencing, golf, riding, tennis, and volleyball, and they attracted a much wider pool of interested athletes. In both the fall and spring terms of the 1936–37 academic year, more than 340 women participated in intramurals, representing more than thirty organizations. Frederica Bernhard reported, "Intramurals have grown considerabl[y], and [are] still growing. Many changes and improvements are constantly being made." By the spring of 1939, the intramural program had become a vital supplement to California's physical education and more formalized WAA sporting activities, and the numbers of participants testified to its newfound success. That term more than 170 women played in a baseball round-robin tournament, and more than 70 women participated in badminton tournaments and swimming meets, with another 28 women testing their fencing skills against each other. All together, more than 280 different women participated in spring term intramurals, with at least 80 of them playing four or more sports. After initially languishing, the intramural program at California grew during the 1930s to fulfill its founders' goal of involving more students in athletics; however, to do this, the administrators had to compromise on other beliefs, sacrificing their opposition to athletic awards for the prize of greater participation and interest.[74]

For the University of Maryland the decade of the 1930s was also a time of expansion and experimentation in women's sports. In the 1929–30 academic year, Maryland hired its first women's athletic director and continued its already existing busy schedule of women's sports, conducted primarily on an interclass basis. The Maryland women had opportunities to participate in field hockey, tennis, "two-division basketball," rifle, baseball, volleyball, bowling, and soccer, in addition to required dancing classes for the freshmen and sophomores. That year the university shifted away from its previous policy of awarding athletic letters to standouts in individual sports, preferring instead a new honors system that rewarded participation in a multiple of sports. This conformed with the national athletic philosophy of discouraging recognition of exceptional ability and encouraging, instead, maximum participation. The Maryland yearbook reported on the new system's success: "it caused a larger number of participants to come out for each sport, and served as an incentive for many who were previously uninterested."[75]

The 1931–32 construction of a new gymnasium and the creation of a women's physical education major helped generate even more interest in athletics and intramural sports among the 325 University of Maryland women. Under the leadership of the dean of women, Adele Stamp, and the women's director of athletics, Edith Ball, the athletic program had expanded the previous year, adding track, golf, horseback riding, hiking, and archery to the athletic menu. The addition of these minor and individual sports forced another revision of the Maryland athletic point system. In the 1931–32 academic year, the students' interest caused further modifications of the intramural system; so many women wanted to play basketball that they had to form three separate teams for each class instead of the single team that had previously played.[76]

The combination of teaching physical and social skills through athletic training continued its popularity at the University of Maryland throughout the decade, but as the sports' popularity grew, so did the competitive impulses of the participants. In 1933, the student yearbook reported that the teams had played basketball under new rules but that the sport had "attracted as large a number of enthusiasts as in former years."[77] The next year, the yearbook documented a "greater interest in physical activities" than ever before, as evidenced by "the fact that the number of girls who turned out for after-school sports [was] larger than that of any preceding year."[78] That year, Maryland instructors reemphasized their dance classes because they were "very beneficial in promoting grace, poise, and good posture among the women students."[79]

While the female students of the University of Maryland were learning poise, they were also learning that the restrictions suggested by the professional physical education associations were violable. For example, the WAA contributed to homecoming festivities by promoting a series of athletic contests among the different class teams. Although women alumni were the intended audience, the connection of women's athletes with large crowds and men's football must have been disquieting to some. Moreover, instead of selecting the hockey teams based solely on class rank, the Maryland women chose them based purely on skill, trying to create evenly matched teams and more competitive contests.[80]

By the following year, the association between women's and men's athletics had grown much closer. The WAA began in the 1934–35 school year to model its basketball activities on the men's intramural programs, discarding the practice of having teams practice and play only a couple of games to determine a champion among the classes. In that system's place, the women installed "a decided innovation in women's sports," creating "a very active schedule" to decide an ultimate winner. The yearbook reported on the success of the experiment and the reasons for that success: "this form of intramurals was so popular among the co-eds that an attempt will be made to introduce it into other women's sports." It seemed that the men's style intramurals made "a fuller and better rounded out schedule of competition for the girls, in addition to allowing the individual player and groups of players a better opportunity for engaging in more actual contests than before."[81]

The University of Maryland women's desire for more competition was evident in their activities over the rest of the decade. The next year the basketball tournament expanded, including three divisions (dormitory, sorority, and nonresidential students) and a tournament among the division champions. According to reports, "there was sufficient friendly rivalry to make the games interesting for spectators as well as participants and the tournament was voted a great success." After experiencing the basketball tournament, the Maryland women made plans to emulate the men's system even further by applying the new format to other sports, including hockey and baseball, and modifying the WAA points system to recognize participation in these events. In the 1936–37 academic year, ten teams participated in the basketball tournament, with the "Day-Dodgers B" beating the "Tri Delts" in the men's style tournament and the juniors winning the regular class competition.[82] These types of tournaments gained more prominence and popularity throughout the rest of the decade, and the editors of the 1939–40 yearbook sought to explain why: "The added stress placed on intramural games was compensation [for] the dearth of intercollegiate competition."[83]

This complaint about the "dearth of intercollegiate competition" for women was one that white women at almost every US college or university could have voiced in the 1920s and 1930s. As a result of a stifling consensus among leading physical educators and their professional organizations, almost all US universities limited their women's athletic options to physical education courses and intramural programs. These two components of women's college athletes generally shared the same administrators and the same goals: to prepare ladies for active lives and to protect the women from the influences and dangers of men's and working-class women's athletics. The college women's training addressed almost all aspects of the "proper" lifestyle, ranging from posture to diet, dress, and attitude. More than anything else, educators intended the women's college athletic programs of the late 1920s and 1930s to communicate the "democratic" virtues of consensus, modesty, and teamwork and the importance of playing sports for play's sake, not for individual awards or recognition.

As the experiences of educators across the country illustrated, however, this communication of values was easier said than done, more easily planned than executed. The educators found it difficult enough to moderate the competitive impulses and desires of women within their own institutions; they would find it even more difficult to reconcile their professed belief in the evil of vigorous competition with the students' desires to test their abilities against athletes from other schools. Even in carefully orchestrated events designed to mitigate all competitive drives, this proved difficult at best and impossible at worst.

CHAPTER 5

★ ★ ★ ★ ★

"The Instinctive Urge to Compete"

Challenges to the Anticompetitive Model in Women's Sports

In the discussions to date, our group has defended the present type of Sports Day with positively religious fervor. They can't bear the thought of any compromise that involves whole teams from one college competing against whole teams from another.

—LOUISE COBB, UNIVERSITY OF CALIFORNIA, 1929

It is impossible to legislate out of an individual the instinctive urge to compete—"competition is the very soul of athletics." It is possible to guide effectively organizations for the promotion of sports toward the sound administration of women's competition.

—GLADYS PALMER, DIRECTOR
OF WOMEN'S PHYSICAL EDUCATION,
OHIO STATE UNIVERSITY, 1938

By the 1930s most white college and university physical educators in the United States, male and female, endorsed the anticompetitive model of women's sport. They designed their women's college athletic programs to inculcate in their predominately white, middle-class student population a particular style of body care and presentation as well as a certain "feminine" attitude toward athletics and competition. According to this orthodoxy, proper women neither needed nor desired high-level competition. Instead, women-controlled athletic programs with health rules and low-stress games and sports would preserve and protect the students' "vital organs," their general health, and their feminine attractiveness from the dangers found in men's college athletics and in the working-class, extra-collegiate women's competitions, events that could cause irreparable damage in stressful, individualized, and highly competitive contests. This was the overwhelming consensus, and a chorus of voices sang its praise throughout the late 1920s and the 1930s.

From the moment of its creation, however, some female physical educators refused to adopt the entire platform of the Women's Division of the National Amateur Athletic Federation and its sister organizations without question; the anticompetitive model was never completely monolithic. In colleges and universities all across the nation, physical educators labored to reconcile their profession's beliefs with many female students' desire to test their abilities in vigorous competitions, both in and out of their home institutions. According to the traditional narrative of women's sports, during the 1920s and 1930s "play days" served as the main vehicle for providing women's intra-institutional athletics, and these play days adhered closely to the stated goals of limiting competition. During the 1930s, sports days emerged as a more competitive version of the play days, but they were still closely controlled events, sanctioned and monitored by the leading physical educators of the day. The physical education establishment also recognized the legitimacy of telegraphic meets, in which university teams competed "safely" against each other by eliminating traveling and the distractions and temptations of crowds. These telegraphic meets provided gifted female college athletes limited, but real, opportunities to compare their abilities against athletes at other universities. Ominously, they also led in several instances to the type of attention and acclaim that most educators wanted their students to avoid.

While the national associations of physical educators worked to control and moderate the competitive outlets open to college women, alternatives always existed. The most subversive, controversial, and largely hidden one was the continuation of high-level intercollegiate competition. The evidence shows that the anticompetitive establishment never completely eradicated women's intercollegiate athletics and that its leaders knew it. While this limited persistence of intercollegiate athletics was, most believed, an unfortunate mistake, the isolated and unpublicized local tournaments posed no serious threat to the health and welfare of the vast majority of college women or to the jobs of their physical educators.

This dynamic changed in the late 1930s and early 1940s when a contingent from Ohio State University proposed a women's NCAA (National Collegiate Athletic Association) and a national intercollegiate golf tournament for women. While the women's NCAA never materialized, the golf tournament did. Arising out of local and national conditions, this golf tournament represented many things that the physical education establishment loathed. Importantly, it also represented many values and ideas that the national organizations endorsed, but this notable consensus went largely ignored in the contentious spring and summer preceding the tournament. A close examination of the circumstances that led up to the revival of openly conducted intercollegiate competition for women, as well as the controversy the tournament aroused, illuminates much about the prevailing consensus on how to use sports to promote certain proper feminine values, the emerging debate about what were proper middle-class, feminine activities, and the growing disagreement about the best ways to teach desired, "democratic" values to college women.

It is important to point out that the Ohio State–led challenge to the consensus was novel only among white physical educators. As a group, female physical educators at historically black colleges of the 1920s and 1930s offered the most complete rejection of the profession's anticompetitive model. Although some black female leaders argued that women should not waste their time, energy, or resources on sports, those schools that allowed women to play found that they did so enthusiastically.[1] In 1939, a survey reported that 75 percent of black colleges supported women's intercollegiate sport while only 17 percent of predominantly white schools did. Rita Liberti explained in her study of women's athletics at Bennett College (a black liberal arts college for women in North Carolina) between 1928 and 1942 that there was no uniform reaction among African American colleges to the physical educators' push to abandon women's intercollegiate athletics. In fact, as many predominately white institutions were discarding their women's programs in the late 1920s, many African American institutions were building more substantial women's programs.[2]

Officials and athletes at Bennett College and elsewhere saw no inherent conflict between ideals of femininity and competition; in fact, Bennett College president Dr. David Jones enthusiastically supported women's intercollegiate basketball as a way to breed confidence, leadership skills, and social skills in the athletes. One former Bennett basketball player explained it this way to Liberti: "Being a lady does not mean being prissy, it's just an inward culture . . . always being polite and not saying things to hurt people's feelings. You could be as tough as I don't know what on that basketball court, but you still have those same principles."[3]

Ruth Arnett, an African American leader in the YWCA and in the field of public recreation, shared these beliefs, arguing against her profession's dominant ideology and making a positive link between athletic competition and the development of proper women. According to Susan Cahn, Arnett "employ[ed] a concept of womanhood that embraced strength, self-reliance, and competitive spirit." Arnett argued that African Americans should "encourage our girls to be 'tomboys.' Let them enter any game of sport and recreation that the boy enters. Let's teach them to be real girls!"[4]

Clearly Arnett's definition of assertive, confident, and self-reliant "real" girls did not match the white physical educators' views of real womanhood, although, as historian Stephanie Shaw has pointed out, the desire to create well-mannered, well-dressed, moral ladies who could serve as ambassadors to society at large was even stronger among black female collegians than among their white counterparts. Black female students could not anticipate leading lives of leisure after graduation; therefore, they prepared most of their lives to be "self-confident, high-achieving, socially responsible adults." The more accepting attitude that most black colleges had toward women's athletics reflects this desire to prepare achievement-oriented, self-reliant adults.[5]

Likewise, inter-institutional contests never disappeared from the exclusively or predominately white college landscape, but they took on new forms during the anticompetitive era, most notably as play days, sports days, and telegraphic meets. Historians have described play days as a "model of democratic sport" because they gathered together students from many different colleges and universities, divided them into temporary teams, and did not differentiate among the participants' various skill levels. The national physical education societies endorsed these play days for these same reasons, because they allowed for numerous women to participate in a variety of sports without representing their institutions even for just one day. This arrangement prevented the creation of real team allegiances and passions for winning championships; the women could concentrate instead on the joy of playing for play's sake.[6]

Athletic officials designed their play days so that the events would work with other college athletic activities to socialize the athletes in specific ways. Foremost, of course, the plays days reinforced by their very structure the profession's disdain for highly competitive, highly trained athletes who prioritized winning and championships over the spirit of joyous participation. By involving large numbers of athletes of varying skill levels, the play days also prevented the isolation and adulation of highly skilled female athletes over their less able colleagues. Moreover, the ideal play day taught the participants other valuable social lessons and skills through the associated non-athletic events as well. For example, in 1929 Wellesley College (Massachusetts) hosted the first New England College Play Day, with 250 women from Wheaton College, Simmons College, Radcliffe College, Boston University, and Wellesley participating. The day began with a "mixer" and continued throughout the day with "every sort of activity popular with girls and women" offered. The day's grand conclusion was a buffet dinner, complete with "singing, novelty dances, and announcement of scores and the awards." Even the award ceremony adhered to the profession's beliefs about the undesirability of awards with intrinsic value; the awards were "original gumdrop animals and dolls made by some of the girls." By stressing a sense of sisterhood and shared purposes, and by including culinary and domestic skills in the festivities, this play day reinforced many of the explicit and implicit goals of the national physical education associations.[7]

In its interactions with Stanford University and Mills College, the University of California epitomized the types of changes that most

US colleges underwent as a result of the profound professional shift of the early 1920s. California women had a long history of competitions against women from nearby colleges and universities, and they continued that tradition throughout the 1920s and 1930s but in much different forms than before and with a great deal of discussion. During the 1910s and the early 1920s, California women competed against Stanford and Mills women in a variety of sports on an interclass-intercollegiate basis. This meant that the sophomores from California would battle for supremacy against the sophomores from Stanford or Mills, and the other classes would do likewise, often in conjunction with the "big game" between Stanford and California's football teams. Other times the three schools would meet together in "Triangular Sports Days" (TSDs) for the sole purpose of women's athletics. During the 1920s, however, officials at the three schools abandoned this popular arrangement in favor of a more traditional play day structure that adhered more closely with the Women's Division standards.[8]

Throughout the late 1920s and the 1930s representatives of these three colleges struggled to reconcile their different interpretations of what was acceptable for college sporting women. It was not always easy to make the TSDs meet the demands of all three. For example, in 1927 Mills College officials and students designed a play day that began by assigning registered students to their "color group" (team) for the day, but by 1929 the TSD had shifted to a more formal organization along class lines. This transformation to more standard teams was not enough to satisfy Stanford University's delegation, as the minutes of the University of California's WAA illustrate. They read, in part, "A letter from Stanford . . . indicates that they would like to change to intercollegiate competition. Mills apparently approves the present type of Play Day or something similar to it. Our own W.A.A. Council has expressed itself unqualifiedly in favor of the present plan or a similar plan and against intercollegiate competition."[9]

This debate over the proper format of the TSD continued into the following spring without a lessening of tensions. By the end of the spring term, Mills College had moved closer to the Stanford University position against the purely interclass format of the play days, favoring instead some sort of arrangement that would allow women from the different institutions to represent their institutions instead of merely their class. Louise S. Cobb, the faculty advisor to the University of California's WAA, reported that her "group has defended the present type of Sports Day with positively religious fervor" and that the California women could not "bear the thought of any compromise that involves whole teams from one college competing against whole teams from another." Cobb concluded that "unless some such compromise is effected we will have to drop out of the Triangle," the most prominent and important event in the California women's athletic schedule.[10] Clearly, the California contingent had found difficulty trying to reconcile their ideals with those of their colleagues at other schools.

Over the next several years these three schools continued their TSDs as well as their negotiations about what form these play days should have. In February 1931, the California WAA agreed to "try the new scheme of full teams from each class in each college" and to "do [its] best to satisfy Stanford and Mills"; but after hearing that the Women's C Society had mixed feelings about the proposal, the WAA drafted guidelines that the new TSD must meet in order for the University of California to participate. These special conditions set by the California WAA made it very clear that California remained dedicated to promoting the program of the Women's Division and its sister organizations. Through these conditions the California WAA tried to ensure mass participation by demanding that each institution send at least eighty women to the event and that each woman play in only two games. The WAA also demanded that "as many games as possible be played at the same time, distributing interest," and they added additional conditions designed to lessen the amount of notoriety a team or individuals could garner. They asked that no game's score ever be made public and that no team hold "special practices in preparation for the Day."[11]

Once in operation the new triangular sports day arrangement satisfied the California WAA, but the question of how far the schools could move on the intercollegiate competition continuum remained as an issue. The fall 1931 report "Review of W.A.A." illustrates this very well with this description of a recent triangular sports day at Stanford University: "The principle of competition involved—whole team competition on an interclass but not intercollegiate basis—seems thoroughly satisfactory to Council. The question of further (i.e. more nearly intercollegiate competition) is to be decided by Council early next semester." In October 1932, the WAA agreed to participate in another TSD that would feature "interclass competition instead of intercollegiate competition" and that would stress that the "idea of the day is not winning for winning's sake but sociability and good play."[12]

By the fall of 1933, the regulations governing the TSDs had changed once more, again moving toward more focused competition. Contrary to the University of California's earlier policies, the schools agreed to hold the TSD later in the term so that Mills College and Stanford University could "organize teams and have sport practices."[13] Over the next few terms, the schools added more sports to the TSDs, and the women of the California WAA again altered their earlier position by voting for an "interclass intercollegiate" TSD, one with the scores announced. This time, it was the Mills delegation that refused to participate under this limited intercollegiate arrangement, so the TSD remained the same, on an interclass not intercollegiate basis.[14]

After this decision, the TSD remained on an interclass basis through the rest of the 1930s and through the mid-1940s; however, other aspects of the TSD changed, revealing the continuing tension between the stated philosophy of the WAA and the desires of the students for more competitive outlets. For example, the three schools continued to pack more sports into the TSDs, and they also began complementing the original mass play days with more focused, sport-specific events, inaugurating "Triangular Basketball Days" and "Triangular Tennis Days" by the 1935–36 school year. According to the faculty advisor's report, the students' "enthusiasm was very marked."[15] The TSDs also seemed to retain their popularity; the fall 1937 gathering at the University of California attracted almost two hundred athletes for the day. The attendees enjoyed both a full day and a new athlete-matching system. The sports program included competitions in field hockey, archery, swimming (six different categories), golf, fencing, tennis (singles and doubles), and diving. The matching system, proposed by the California WAA's president, required the ranking of athletes playing individual sports so that the "competition [would be] more interesting for those taking part."[16] This new ranking system furthered the gradual move away from a strict implementation of the "democratic" anticompetitive standards promoted by the physical education professional organizations by formally separating the highly skilled athletes from the less skilled in order to facilitate more competitive events. According to Dorris Berry, the general chairman of triangular sports days for the University of California, this sporting day, conducted with the new ranking system, "was the most successful" to date.[17]

Throughout the late 1930s and early 1940s the opportunities for University of California women to test their athletic abilities against outsiders continued to multiply as the numbers of individual TSDs kept increasing while the university's women also received numerous invitations to other events. Between 1938 and 1941, California women were able to compete in hockey, tennis, golf, archery, basketball, tennis, swimming, badminton, volleyball, riding, and riflery, either in TSDs or in special events hosted by other universities. While many students must have appreciated the diversity of athletic offerings, some faculty members and students were concerned about the proliferation of events and the diffusion of local control. In March of 1940, the California Women's Athletic Council expressed fear "that if many Triangular Sports Days were had the whole idea would be lost."[18]

Educators at other institutions recognized the difficulties the University of California experienced trying to marry beliefs and practices, and other institutions devised their own approaches to the problems. In 1930, Ohio State instructor of physical education Helen Schleman argued in the *Journal of Health and Physical Education* that the California women, along with their counterparts at Stanford University and Mills College, had erred when they shied away from interclass intercollegiate competition. Schleman's article carried the provocative title "Experimental Play Days: Experimental Intercollegiate Competition for Women," and it explained how Ohio State was seeking to avoid the same mistakes in interpretation that had damaged the programs and the women at the three California schools and across the nation. According to Schleman, the women running the triangular sports days had mistakenly associated interclass intercollegiate competition with the varsity athletic programs that the professional physical education associations opposed. Schleman argued pointedly that "as a matter of fact, of course, the two types of competition are neither the same nor similar, but the members of the [Athletic

Conference of American College Women] who refused to see this point were presidents of college athletic associations from all over the country who had been taught arbitrarily that anything that sounded like interscholastic competition for girls was bad."[19] Schleman assured her readers that it was not.

Schleman's article explaining the "experimental play days" offered by Ohio State highlights the fact that, despite an overwhelming official consensus about the proper types of women's competition expressed in the publications of national professional organizations, complete uniformity never existed in operation. The 1929 Ohio State play day that Schleman described sought to integrate the Women's Division's hopes for mass participation in a large number of sports with the interclass-intercollegiate arrangement that allowed for more practice, better skills, and greater competition. The Ohio State organizers also structured the play day so that it would maximize the social possibilities inherent in intercollegiate interactions. Several women's organizations at Ohio State worked together to plan the day, and each woman from Ohio Wesleyan University (the other participating school) received a personal invitation from her Ohio State host for a day. The participants also heard presentations from adult speakers invited to "[get] across some fundamental ideas about cooperation as individuals and as campus organizations and something definite about sportsmanship."[20]

The University of Michigan hosted a similar play day for 170 participants from four institutions in November 1929, one that also featured interclass intercollegiate competition and produced the same desired "social by-products." Pitting teams that had previously practiced together against each other produced "open and fairly fast" hockey games. Throughout the day, according to one correspondent, the women competed hard and fairly while managing to avoid "undue influence on winning or losing." The players seemed to enjoy the arrangement and managed to maintain a "happy, entirely 'crab-free' mood throughout" the day's events. In her account of the play day, the University of Michigan's Elizabeth Halsey acknowledged that the use of teams derived completely from one school, instead of teams combining players from all the schools, was controversial. Halsey reported that many high schools had discovered that real interscholastic competition could produce "a feeling of tense and even bitter rivalry which makes sportsmanlike conduct of games difficult if not impossible"; however, she also claimed that "the natural desire" of athletic women was to play their best against prepared and competent competition. Halsey concluded that this initial University of Michigan play day had successfully navigated between the poles of overemphasis and denial of competition, but even that success did not blind her and her colleagues to the pitfalls that lay ahead. Accordingly, she conceded, "Whether further Plays Days of the same sort would eventually produce more organized competition, more emphasis on winning, and therefore less spontaneous good fellowship" remained "an open question."[21]

Throughout the rest of the 1930s, educators began to call this type of play day, one that allowed teams from one institution to practice beforehand and then compete on a designated day, "sports days," to differentiate them from the traditional play days. For example, the University of Maryland's women moved during the 1930s toward the sports day model while also increasing the emphasis given to their women's intramural programs. During the 1933 homecoming weekend the Maryland WAA sponsored a series of interclass games, entertaining spectators with the members' athletic prowess. For the next year's homecoming celebration, the women took the next logical step and invited hockey teams from nearby Marjorie Webster School for Girls and the American University for "closely contested games." Significantly, this was not interclass- intercollegiate competition but instead was a contest between the Maryland women's team and single teams representing the other schools. That same year, the Maryland yearbook reported that Maryland women participated in the "annual intercollegiate swimming meet" and that the Maryland women's basketball team won its game against the American University squad.[22] By the 1935 homecoming weekend, the women's athletic contribution had expanded yet again, with teams from two additional universities competing. That day, the Maryland team won three hockey games and lost one, to Western Maryland College. Later that same season, the University of Maryland hockey team participated in another hockey play day, this one sponsored by the Washington Field Hockey Association and including eight local colleges and universities. The yearbook proudly reported that the Maryland team earned a tie for first place in the standings with its performance that day. These types of play days maintained their popularity in the Washington, D.C., area throughout the rest of the decade, with basketball also emerging as an intercollegiate sport, although one contested on an interclass basis.[23]

While the University of Maryland's hockey, swimming, and, eventually, basketball contests provide excellent examples of the proliferation of sports days and other variations of intercollegiate athletics, these teams still competed only on a single day, not over an extended schedule. That was not the case for the University of Maryland's women's rifle team. Although scholars have discussed the 1920s emergence of popular riflery, hiking, and camping in terms of "noncompetitive recreational clubs," in fact, many of the women's rifle clubs and teams defined themselves by their competitive records. With roots extending back into the 1920s, the University of Maryland women's rifle team often competed in more than twenty competitive matches a year, most sponsored by the National Rifle Association (NRA). In fact, based on the dozens of universities from across the nation that the University of Maryland competed against, it appears that rifle shooting was one of the most prominent sports open to college women during the 1930s. While most of these competitions were conducted on a "telegraph" basis, several were not, permitting the women from one university to stand shoulder-to-shoulder, competing with their rivals from other institutions and presumably caring about the results.[24]

Shooting sports offered college women welcome athletic opportunities to distinguish themselves in addition to significant publicity. Again, the University of Maryland provides one of the best examples of sustained public celebration of collegiate female athletes. Throughout the 1930s, Maryland yearbooks heap praise on the teams and individuals that brought national championships back to College Park. In 1930, for example, the yearbook recognized the "remarkable" shooting of Alice Orton, who won the Women's Individual Intercollegiate Rifle Championship, becoming the third consecutive individual champion from Maryland. The next year's yearbook hailed "a banner year for the Women's Rifle team," one that saw the team win the National Team Championship match in a National Rifle Association event. According to the article's author, this was Maryland's first Women's Intercollegiate Rifle Championship since 1926.[25]

University of Maryland women's rifle squad, 1930s. *Courtesy of Special Collections and University Archives, University of Maryland Libraries.*

The University of Maryland women continued their successful shooting streaks during the following years. In the 1931–32 academic year Irene Knox led the rifle team to a successful defense of its national title by shooting perfectly from all three shooting positions, a "feat unparalleled" in the NRA's history and unequalled in men's intercollegiate history as well. The next year, Knox slipped all the way to second in the individual intercollegiate championship. Over the next several years, the University of Maryland women's rifle team continued to win the vast majority of its matches and to feature individual sharpshooters who placed in the national individual standings, but the squad did not win another national championship during the decade's remaining years.[26]

The attention given to the individuals and the teams for winning championships should have unnerved the physical educators most committed to the concept of playing for play's sake. Judging from the many pictures of the confident women holding rifles that adorned the pages of the University of Maryland yearbook, the women enjoyed their shooting; but the articles about their activities stress winning percentages over fellowship and individual and team championships over social lessons. Moreover, the Maryland shooters also earned more official recognition for their accomplishments, receiving varsity letters for their participation and prowess. Finally, even though they usually avoided the pitfalls of extensive travel by using telegraph meets, the women won these championships and competed against other universities' teams with a man as a coach. Although their pictures always reveal the shooters to be well-dressed, usually in dresses covered by shooting jackets, the rifle team at Maryland successfully managed to flaunt many of the other restrictions on female athletes endorsed by the professional organizations of the day.[27]

This was not just an East Coast phenomenon. The University of California's female shooters also competed both nationally and locally during the 1930s. In fact, California appeared on four of the five printed schedules of the University of Maryland's rifle team during the decade, while at other times California women participated in matches against Drexel University, the University of Washington, Louisiana State University, and the University of Kansas. The WAA also occasionally organized Saturday morning "pleasure-shooting" sessions for women, in addition to including riflery in the high school sports days it hosted. In the late 1930s, the WAA approved a "riflery play day" with San Francisco State College with the understanding that the competition could be interclass, but not intercollegiate; and in 1940 the WAA split hairs, sanctioning another meet with San Francisco Junior College as long as individuals shot only for themselves and not for their schools.[28]

Although these pleasure-shooting sessions and competitions were among women, not all of the California women's shooting was sex-segregated. In fact, in December of 1935, the WAA rifle team challenged the men's Reserve Officers' Training Corps (ROTC) team to a meet. Only a few months later, and perhaps as a direct result of this competition, a California student, Betty Sutton, requested the opportunity to try out for the university's varsity riflery team. The WAA, the female physical education staff, and the men's coach all supported Sutton's petition, but they also set strict guidelines on female participation on the men's team. These rules included provisions that the WAA handle all health eligibility matters, that all females' shooting practices and matches occur during WAA hours at the range, that women could practice only two hours a week without special permission from the director of women's physical education, that women must meet predetermined high standards for shooting while standing up, in addition to the three traditional shooting positions, to even try out for the team, and that "all matches [were] to be telegraphic or by letter."[29]

Although the relevant female and male university officials agreed to grant Sutton's request and allow women to try out for places on the men's varsity rifle team, their action did not represent a complete break from the orthodoxy that continued to govern women's college athletics. In fact, their guidelines served to ensure that the consensus standards, though breached in one important respect, would prevail in all others. According to their rules, women could compete with a men's team only if female physical educators continued to have control over the athletes' health and as long as the shooters never traveled, infrequently practiced, and never shot with the men present. As it turned out, the codification of strict regulations was unnecessary, and those wishing to prevent the inclusion of women on the men's team actually got their way in Berkeley. In the end, according to Cobb, the requirement that women demonstrate proficiency shooting from a standing position disqualified all who tried out for the team.[30]

A few years later, in Columbus, a similar situation unfolded when an Ohio State female student petitioned for membership on the men's varsity rifle team, but while the final result was the same—she did not get on the team—the process followed a different path. In 1940, physical educator Gladys Palmer wrote to Ohio State's athletic director, Lynn St. John, on behalf of sophomore Helen Jenkins. Jenkins was an excellent target shooter whose "life ambition," according to Palmer, was to make the All-American rifle team. Unfortunately for Jenkins, selection to this honorary team was contingent on inclusion on a school's varsity team. Palmer argued that Jenkins "undoubtedly . . . would have no difficulty in qualifying for the team from the point of view of skill in the activity," but her argument based on merit did not sway the men on the OSU Athletic Board. The board denied Jenkins admission to the team despite the coach's and "the boys'" professed willingness to accept her.[31]

Palmer told St. John that Jenkins deserved a straight answer from the university's athletic board about why she was not allowed to shoot with the men. Palmer recognized that having women compete directly against men was "incompatible with the best thinking of the profession and the public," so she forwarded Jenkin's question of whether a women's varsity team might solve the problem. The "twenty-two enthusiastic members" of the recently established Women's Rifle Club might have provided enough members to make such a team viable, Palmer reasoned. Jenkins was, after all, but one of the "ever increasing number of highly skilled sportswomen found in colleges today" that wanted and needed opportunities to hone and use their skills.[32] They didn't get their team, but by the late 1930s and early 1940s, Palmer and her Ohio State colleagues were becoming increasingly determined to provide those opportunities for female students, even if Jenkins never got hers.

Ohio State physical educators were pioneers in the pursuit of more competitive athletic opportunities for female college students for several reasons. The confluence of specific individuals, ideas, and opportunities helped lead Gladys Palmer, Mary Yost, Dorothy Sumption, and others to reopen the public debate about the proper competitive limits for college women. The existence of national trends favoring increased participation by women in public life and leadership encouraged these women's initiatives, as did a shared, more youthful and open outlook than that of most of their colleagues. More importantly, they recognized that behind the veil of official consensus were hidden a host of deviations from the officially sanctioned standards, and they believed that professionally trained women could maintain control over more competitive activities. When they combined this knowledge and belief with the understanding that many students desired more opportunities and that their men's athletic leaders would support them, the Ohio State leaders decided to act.

It is important to note that these Ohio State educators were a part of a new generation maturing professionally in an era that offered more visible role models of female leadership in public life. Working more than a decade after the Nineteenth Amendment granted women in the United States the right to vote, these innovators sought to open new doors for the next generation of women leaders. Following the lead of First Lady Eleanor Roosevelt and the first female cabinet member, Francis Perkins, female educators often distinguished themselves through their political involvement and their leadership abilities.[33]

In 1938, Blanche Trilling, the University of Wisconsin's director of women's physical education and one of the nation's most prominent physical educators, spoke about the importance of continuing advances and leadership by American women. Trilling said, "In the last twenty-five years women have won the battle for freedom in all phases of community life, and with the changes in their status have come many new adjustments." She argued that women "must add to their ever-present domestic responsibilities civic and community interests which have now become a right and a duty."[34]

Because Trilling was addressing a meeting of university women, she was actually preaching to the choir, women who already were active leaders in public life. For example, Adele Stamp, the dean of women at the University of Maryland during the 1930s, nurtured close friendships with Maryland governor Albert Ritchie, worked in numerous service organizations, including the League of Nations Association and the Prince Georges County Federation of Women's Clubs, and had the gumption to challenge J. Edgar Hoover about the accuracy of the Federal Bureau of Investigation's list of radicals.[35] Similarly, Anna Hiss of the University of Texas helped create statewide athletic associations, worked with municipal leaders to initiate a city recreation program, and eventually served on the Austin Foreign Policy Association, chairing the Latin American subcommittee. Almost by definition, the women who earned and managed to maintain their positions within the academy had great ability and strong personalities. That said, not all of them were willing to lead their profession in the direction that the Ohio State contingent wanted to go.[36]

Although Gladys Palmer is the woman usually identified with the later revolt at Ohio State, her Ohio State colleagues shared her convictions and willingness to work for changes in women's intercollegiate athletics. These Ohio State officials, including Mary Yost and Dorothy Sumption, believed that they spoke for an entire generation of female physical educators who wanted more opportunities for skilled women athletes. In her study of Ohio State women's athletics from 1885 to 1975, Mary Daniels suggested that the early death of chairman of the Women's Physical Education Division, Lydia Clark Benedict, in 1933 allowed Palmer to take charge as "a younger replacement long before other schools were in a position" to hire someone new.[37]

This earlier than expected promotion helped provide a new generation of athletic leaders with a spokesperson. Two years earlier, the University of Arizona's Ina Gittings had exposed a generational divide. Gittings had reported that she had "repeatedly heard the younger generation of pupils and instructors exclaim, 'But why can't we have varsity games?'" Gittings asserted, "It does not appear very well for the present arguments of the opposers [of competition] that the young do not even think it worth while to enter a serious discussion, but only ask for the 'joker' meanwhile reserving their convictions for the day when they can act."[38] That day came to Ohio State earlier than at most other universities, thanks to Palmer's ascension. In an essay composed ten years after Gittings's, an Ohio State physical educator recognized the situation, noting, "The young women in the field would be glad to tackle the problem [of intercollegiate competition]. However, they are bound hand and foot by their directors. They don't dare express opinions of their own. Many, too, have been so indoctrinated that they either can't think or are confined in their thinking."[39]

Even under Benedict's leadership, the Ohio State women's physical education staff had not been timid about expressing their opposition to the Women's Division of the National Amateur Athletic Federation and, by implication, its standards. In a staff meeting in the early 1930s, Benedict asked for a motion authorizing the department to send in the membership fee of ten dollars to the NAAF, but not one of the twelve staff members would make the motion. Jeanette Stein remembered that the opposition was not based on finances, but instead on principles. As Stein recalled, one colleague put it bluntly, "we don't approve of belonging to that organization, and we don't want to send our membership fee." Benedict recognized that she would "take a beating" professionally, but in the face of a unanimous staff, she had no other option but to comply with their wishes.[40]

If the Ohio State staff took courage from their shared resolve, they also found inspiration in the fact that several women outside of Columbus periodically demonstrated their willingness to rethink the limits on competition. While dominant among white college officials, the Women's Division's view was never without challenges, both in practice and in print, among its ranks either. In 1931, Gittings addressed the entire litany of expressed concerns about competition. She argued in the *Journal of Health and Physical Education* that professionally trained college instructors should be able to moderate the negative effects of women's athletics and that these fearful educators should graciously accept "the inevitable—the return of intercollegiate competition for women."[41]

Using a rhetorical strategy that Ohio State officials would also later employ, Gittings tried to placate doubters by arguing that the Women's Division and other concerned physical educators had done such a fine job promoting their ideals and beliefs over the previous eight years that reviving women's intercollegiate competition could safely occur as long as women controlled the programs. In fact, Gittings argued that reinstituting varsity athletic programs would "violate" only the travel prohibition of the Women's Division platform. Properly supervised varsity athletics, her argument held, would help college women gain confidence, skills, exhilaration, and vigor while also teaching them to control their passions for winning. Varsity teams could be "laboratories" for the desired "lofty social virtues" athletic programs should create.[42]

In this 1931 essay, Gittings argued that the profession's reliance on play days was misguided for at least two reasons. First, although they allowed travel and social bonding, play days were not effective tools for a physical education program because they were too fleeting, were "extremely weak," and offered "little or none of the joy and values of real games played skillfully, willingly, intelligently, and eagerly by well-matched teams." Second, the concept of playing only for "play's sake" made as much sense to Gittings as did eating "food for food's sake" or creating "work for work's sake." She held that unless the events actually taught the participants something, they were worthless. Gittings, however, did believe that play days, despite their inanity, would eventually engender something beneficial: a return to varsity competition for women. She predicted that play days would "evolve into actual varsity competition or die from ennui," visualizing the "girls in a Play Day as sheep, huddled and bleating in their little Play meadow, whereas they should be young mustangs exultantly racing together across vast prairies."[43] This was, of course, the way events unfolded in many places, California among them.

Gittings concluded her essay with a condemnation of those educators who would postpone the unavoidable return of varsity athletics, hiding behind fears of male control and of women's programs following the path that men's intercollegiate athletics had blazed. She scolded her colleagues, "There is nothing wrong with the games, competition, the girls, or travel, but there is something wrong with the directors, who have phobias at the thought of making the same mistakes in intercollegiates as men have made." There was also something wrong, in Gittings's mind, with the physical educators who did not trust themselves to control properly the inevitable redevelopment of intercollegiate athletics for women.[44]

Most of Gittings's colleagues did not share her faith in this inevitability, nor were they swayed by her attempts to address their concerns. In fact, although they did not "wish to take up cudgels against Miss Gittings' viewpoint," two authors felt compelled to rebut Gittings's arguments in the *Journal of Health and Physical Education's* next issue. Grace B. Daviess, an assistant professor of physical education at the University of Cincinnati, believed that Gittings's utopian vision of varsity sport would never materialize in reality. In its place, a return to varsity women's athletics would result in a revival of the undemocratic privileging of the minority over the majority, of the few elite athletes over the rest of college women.[45]

The field secretary of the Women's Division of the NAAF, Anne Hodgkins, responded directly to the question Gittings had posed with her article's title, "Why Cramp Competition?" Hodgkins bluntly replied that it is "varsity teams [that] actually do cramp competition by giving only a handful of girls an opportunity to enjoy the zest and exhilaration of competition."[46] She claimed that all of the benefits that Gittings said women could derive from varsity competition were available in the play days, events "designed to provide the *best* of varsity competition" to all college women, not to create the bleating sheep that Gittings described. Like Daviess, she argued that varsity competition was undemocratic, exclaiming, "At last, in this great democracy, we are beginning to realize what democratic education is" and that to focus on the few elite athletes would be to fall "out of step with present trends." Moreover, both Daviess and Hodgkins agreed that the college athletic leaders had to consider the message their actions sent to those outside the ivory tower, particularly to US high schools. Although almost all colleges had adopted the Women's Division standards and abolished varsity competition, many high schools had not yet, and to send a signal reinforcing the continuation of undemocratic programs was unconscionable to these educators.[47]

Nonetheless, throughout the decade the professional press and other media outlets also carried the message across the country (and definitely to Columbus) that at least a few educators continued to question or circumvent the official stances against highly organized, elite competition for women. In April of 1930, University of California alumna and world-renowned tennis star Helen Jacobs issued a call for intercollegiate women's tennis tournaments, writing, "It is a fallacy to regard competition for women in the light of it being a detriment to the sport," and competition is the "only thing that [will] raise women's tennis in the colleges to the heights that it deserves."[48] Contrary to the prevailing professional standards, Jacobs argued that most women had to develop their competitive urges, and college tournaments would provide the ideal laboratory for that development. Like men, women would raise the level of their play if they were playing for something tangible, and women could overcome their inhibitions about entering public tournaments if they had a reason to play, for the pride of their school. Jacobs identified a 1929 Boston University tournament as the "first Women's Intercollegiate Tournament," and she regretted that more people did not note or support "one of the most progressive steps in the game." She hoped that a college would eventually take a principled stand and support women's intercollegiate tennis equally as much as colleges supported men's tennis; after all, according to Jacobs, the women would develop many of the same qualities through competition as the men. This explicit appeal to make women's tennis more like the men's, and by extension make the women themselves more competitive like the men, was unlikely to sway physical educators terrified of that very occurrence.[49]

While there is no evidence to suggest that the Ohio State educators read the University of California alumni magazine, enough articles appeared in the professional press to guarantee that they kept abreast of the simmering debate about the propriety of competition and the proper role of university physical educators. Besides the "Cramping Competition" exchange of the early 1930s, other relevant articles occasionally appeared in print. For example, the *Journal of Health and Physical Education* published an article, complete with several pictures, about the 1937 National Archery Meet. According to the article's author (and the tournament's fourth-place finisher), the most notable aspect of the women's competition was that women who had been physical education majors in college earned the top four spots; moreover, all of these four had continued their professional development as high school physical educators. Clearly, these physical educators would have known about the professional strictures against high-level competition for young women in high schools and colleges, but they all felt comfortable enough to compete on their own in a national tournament for individual honors and great publicity. During that same academic year, the University of California competed in twenty-five intercollegiate, telegraphic archery meets. The Ohio State leaders saw hypocrisy in this dissonance between official ideology and personal actions.[50]

This incongruity between stated ideals and actual practice was most notable in regards to the sport of field hockey, or just plain "hockey." As Cahn has explained, "the case of field hockey indicates that it was not competition per se that triggered reformers' anger, but rather breaches of professional control and cultural sensibility."[51] Cahn and others have advanced this argument because many professional physical educators supported high-level hockey competition for themselves and often for their college students, often echoing male athletic enthusiasts in their praise for the sport's vigorous competition and required physical rigor. They could do so because field hockey was never considered a "male" sport; and because it was dominated by females, its participants were never in danger of becoming "mannish" or of having males control their activities. The differentiation of hockey also revealed social-class prejudices. Most hockey players tended to be relatively well off financially, and by celebrating the virtues of hockey and condemning industrial league basketball and baseball leagues, educators maintained clear boundaries between themselves and their working-class counterparts.[52]

Historian Joan Hult has noted that hockey provided college women intercollegiate athletic opportunities during the 1920s and 1930s, although the teams usually were officially club teams, not varsity teams. For example, Hult identified an intercollegiate hockey tournament held in Virginia in 1930 as a "typical" event. The University of California's hockey experiences during the late 1920s and the 1930s corroborate Hult's larger point that many college women skirted the prohibitions against high-level competition by playing the one sport in which educators usually allowed it. After boasting of a competitive field hockey team in the early 1920s, California de-emphasized its women's team in accordance with the standards of the professional physical education organizations. By 1929, however, the WAA was again sponsoring games pitting a California team against a traveling all-American hockey team and against the Bay Counties Athletic Association. The next year, the WAA's members and advisors considered joining the United States Field Hockey Association, an organization that had hundreds of members, featured a large bureaucratic organization, and hosted a national tournament. While opposing all efforts to move the triangular sports day toward intercollegiate competition, the University of California's women's athletic leaders endorsed field hockey games against traveling teams that were not associated with universities. Clearly, a double standard existed.[53]

This double standard became more explicit within a year, when California's Louise Cobb promoted a particular organization to her WAA advisees. Cobb "explained that the Northern California Hockey Association was organized for women college graduates, and that any women graduates may play if they are not at the same time playing with a college group."[54] With this one statement, Cobb recognized both the validity of college groups playing competitive field hockey and that of an athletic organization that excluded all women, however interested or talented, who did not have the seemingly unrelated means or ability to graduate from college. Throughout the rest of the decade, California teams continued to represent the university in competition against Stanford University, Mills College, and other sundry all-star teams and local athletic organizations; never in the minutes of the WAA does an objection to hockey competition appear.[55] A plan to lessen the hypocrisy and to offer all college women greater opportunities to compete would materialize, instead, in the Ohio State proposals for change.

In November 1938, Ohio State's Gladys Palmer published a groundbreaking and provocative essay entitled "Policies in Women's Athletics." This article was the initial salvo in what became a civil war among physical educators, and it was the first major step toward the expansion of women's intercollegiate sports. In this brief essay, Palmer first voiced publicly the questions and proposals that would raise so much controversy over the next few years, culminating in a plan for a women's NCAA and the hosting of the first intercollegiate golf tournament for women.

The fact that the proposals she offered on behalf of herself and her Ohio State colleagues immediately raised clouds of controversy should not obscure the fact that Palmer and like-minded educators shared many of the same philosophies and beliefs with the establishment groups and individuals who felt they were under attack. Palmer and her colleagues agreed that unlimited competition was dangerous for women. The Ohio State educators shared the fears of their professional organizations that if men controlled women's athletics they would corrupt and commercialize sports and athletes, ruining them just as they had the men's programs. Palmer's proposed plan expressly denounced the formation of permanent leagues in which teams competed for championships as men did. Finally, Palmer stated that she desired that "women who participate in sports [should be able] to do so without losing any of their natural feminine charm," whatever form the competition took.[56] It is clear that not all aspects of Palmer's and her colleagues' proposals were radical; the upstarts actually shared most of the assumptions that the orthodoxy upheld.

Despite listing these consensus views, Palmer's essay publicly expressed the highly controversial notion that college women could be both highly competitive and also appropriately feminine. Working from that premise, the proposed diversions from the beaten path, though few, were significant. Encouraged by the belief that the profession had already made almost everyone aware of proper values connected to women's athletics, strengthened by the understanding that other professionals believed as they did and by the realization that many colleges and universities were already participating in intercollegiate and other extra-institutional competitions, inspired by the perceived desires of undergraduate women for increased opportunities, motivated by the belief that elite women athletes deserved the right to test their abilities against other elite athletes, and surrounded by male athletic leaders singing the praises of competition, Ohio State's female physical educators dared to challenge their profession's hard stance against all intercollegiate competition for women. By arguing for limited and female-controlled forms of intercollegiate competition, Palmer challenged the most fundamental of her profession's tenets, the one against elite competition for college women.

Using a wise and probably even sincere tactic, the Ohio State officials argued that they felt free to propose changes only because the professional organizations had thoroughly warned all educators about the pitfalls of unregulated competition. By suggesting that the anti-elite, egalitarian, and democratic message had successfully permeated all levels of college athletics, the Ohio State contingent could then argue that the time for the next developmental stage had come. Only with the safety and protection of women athletes ensured, the Ohio State educators agreed, could officials consider the expansion of opportunities. Palmer noted that in spite of the virtual unanimity expressed in public pronouncements, her profession lacked a true consensus on the value of competition for women. Daring to highlight deviance from the norm, Palmer demonstrated through numerous examples that intercollegiate competitions and tournaments already existed despite the best intentions and practices of the profession's leaders. Additionally, by highlighting grassroots pressure for opportunities for women, Palmer focused on the "incredible development of interest" of the "literally millions of our young women" who wanted to play organized sports and games.[57] The problem, according to Palmer, was that the very women who had trained and studied how to organize and oversee women's athletics prohibited themselves from doing so outside college campuses, leaving untrained and potentially unscrupulous people, most of them men, to operate the expanding number of public leagues and tournaments.

After the publication of "Policies in Women's Athletics," Palmer and her colleagues watched and waited for an honest and open discussion of its arguments, assumptions, and proposals. The silence was deafening and, most certainly, a little ominous to the Buckeye contingent. Even after two years of waiting in vain for organizational responses to her 1938 article, Palmer and her colleagues remained careful not to couch their next call for action in terms of open rebellion. In 1940 Dorothy Sumption, an Ohio State associate professor of physical education for women, advanced an argument similar to Palmer's in her book, *Sports for Women.* Sumption argued that "competition for college students outside school walls is needed to parallel competitive attractions in sports offered to women in local, state, sectional, national, and international meets and tournaments," and she concluded her chapter on intercollegiate competition with the controversial and confrontational assertion that "intercollegiate competition for women is definitely here to stay."[58]

Sumption's department chairperson certainly supported this position. As she had written in 1938, Palmer similarly wanted her professional colleagues to face reality and accept that "it is impossible to legislate out of an individual the instinctive urge to compete—'competition is the very soul of athletics.' It *is* possible to guide effectively organizations for the promotion of sports toward the sound administration of women's competition."[59] Palmer was explicitly challenging the notion that competitiveness drove only men, arguing that, if controlled, it could also be a proper feminine quality. By sanctioning and claiming dominion over limited competition in and outside of schools, Palmer agreed with Texas's Anna Hiss, who had argued that female physical educators would be able to dramatically increase their influence in the outside world, perhaps curbing some of the dangerous excesses there as well.[60]

Ultimately, at the heart of the disagreement were different definitions of "democratic" sport. Much like proponents of anticompetitive, anti-intercollegiate sports, Ohio State's women's athletic officials also wanted to offer equal opportunities to all female college athletes. The two groups, however, understood the democratic principle of "equality of opportunity" differently. Whereas spokeswomen for the professional organizations argued that democratic equality was achieved by offering all women exactly the same facilities and the same level and amount of instruction, Ohio State leaders contended that equality occurred only when all students had the same chances to play games with other athletes of their own skill level. According to this argument, most students would be able to find within their institutions plenty of fellow students who had similar talents. Athletes with rare elite athletic ability, however, would have to look to other colleges and universities for the opportunity to test their skills against true peers.[61]

The women's physical educators at Ohio State moved in the early 1940s to put their ideas into action. In a document entitled "Concerning Competition," the united "faculty members of the Department of Physical Education for Women at The Ohio State University" argued that "members of college and university faculties [could] create a pattern for women's intercollegiate sports competition which [would] place sports in their true relationship to other activities and which [would] make our physical education programs richer and broader."[62] The Ohio State physical educators wanted to create a women's NCAA, structured like the men's NCAA, to oversee this bold new step in women's athletics. Because it would include only female physical educators, the Buckeye letter reasoned, there would be no danger that a women's NCAA would come to stand for the same values, or lack thereof, that the men's NCAA did. As envisioned by the Ohio State faculty, a women's NCAA would oppose the selling of tickets to any women's intercollegiate activity, "any procedures which tend toward the exploitation of the individual for the enjoyment of spectators or for the athletic reputation of the college," all instruction that made students believe that in competition they defended the reputation of their coaches or their school, "any practices which over-emphasize the making or breaking of records or the winning of championships," any differentiation between amateur and professional women's athletes, and any violation of a very strict set of health guidelines.[63] Palmer, writing for the Ohio State staff, hoped that "such an organization would move rather slowly in developing this phase of the program but that it would move"; and she wanted Ohio State to demonstrate its leadership potential by hosting an openly conducted, national intercollegiate golf tournament for women.[64]

Ohio State female physical educators proposed a women's NCAA and the women's intercollegiate golf tournament in 1941 with the firm belief that they had many legitimate reasons for doing so and with the support of many female colleagues and male Ohio State officials. They needed only the endorsement of their governing professional organizations to inaugurate a program of expanded athletic opportunities for college women and to open new leadership opportunities for the credentialed professional educators in industrial and extra-collegiate recreation leagues. That endorsement did not come in 1941. As others have noted, a women's NCAA was not radical in its stated values or goals, only in its proposed existence; but, when coupled with the Ohio State golf tournament, that was enough to scuttle a women's NCAA before it ever got started.[65]

Ohio State's female athletic officials wanted to demonstrate that properly supervised, elite competition could provide the same benefits as lower-level events while at the same time sating the appetites of highly skilled collegiate athletes within the protective confines of college and universities themselves. They believed that a women's NCAA was the proper way to organize such competitions, but they could also read the professional landscape and tell that they had no hope of creating such an organization. In the spring of 1941, the Ohio State author of "Girls Athletics" assessed the possibility of forming a women's NCAA this way, "I personally don't think we will be able to form an organization. I think that confusion and bad practices will increase until the time will come when we can laugh and say 'We told you so.' But that is an empty satisfaction when you are honestly trying to do a job that you know needs to be done."[66]

Ohio State's disappointed leaders resigned themselves to the reality that their professional colleagues were not willing to take this necessary, in their eyes, organizational step, but they were committed to doing what they could. As they quickly came to realize, most physical educators were not willing even to endorse the idea of a national golf tournament as an individual event, much less the institutionalization of its underlying goals. The hostility of the profession's establishment to their plans shocked Palmer and her colleagues, especially when they experienced it firsthand at two professional meetings in early 1941.

Ohio State physical educators announced their plans for the golf tournament in March, mailing "Concerning Competition" along with an official "Invitation to College Women Who Play Golf," which contained statements of support from Ohio State's president, athletic director, and dean of women. Mailed to more than three hundred colleges and universities and intended to operate with the support of the physical education establishment, this invitation required potential participants to secure the signature of their schools' head of physical education for women.[67] Much like the planners' optimism, this provision would later fall.

Despite the efforts of Palmer, Yost, and others to make the tournament as unobjectionable as possible to their colleagues across the nation, they did not succeed: the idea of dozens of middle-class white women playing tournament golf while under constant supervision was simply too radical for the majority of their colleagues. Choosing a sport associated with upper-class leisure did not placate their opponents, nor did the requirement that all participants wear nice dresses when competing. The tea hosted by the university president and his wife might have smoothed a few ruffled feathers, but the "mixed swim" and dance with arranged escorts probably raised other concerns. Simply put, the Ohio State organizers could not obscure the fact that they were promoting a national tournament for college women, enticing them to travel from all around the nation, encouraging them to compete, and then recognizing the best with trophies.[68]

The first troubling indication that establishment organizations would not support the planned tournament came during the meeting of the Midwest Association of College Teachers of Physical Education for Women, held in Huntington, West Virginia, in early April 1941. There, the Ohio State delegation presented its plans for a national tournament and argued for the creation of a women's NCAA. Unable to attend the meeting, Palmer received an urgent update on the proceedings from her colleagues, a telegram that nicely captured the reception of their ideas, especially the reaction of an older generation: "Bombshell exploded. Shrapnel flew wildly. Old guard resented that group was not consulted first as organization to consider movement."[69] After this ominous response, and summoned by a telegrammed invitation, Palmer decided to attend the National Association of Directors of Physical Education for College Women in Atlantic City, New Jersey, later that month.[70]

The Atlantic City trip was no more pleasurable for Palmer and her colleagues than Huntington had been for Ohio State's other representatives. In fact, in 1975, Yost still recalled her visit to Atlantic City as "a very traumatic experience."[71] In 1966, at a banquet commemorating the twenty-fifth anniversary of the inaugural tournament, Yost outlined how the Ohio State delegation had been "very severely criticized by many of [their] professional colleagues." The criticism was both personal and painful. Yost later recalled, "Friends of many years stopped speaking to us. We were accused of being publicity seekers."[72]

The acrimony went both ways in Atlantic City. In a Saturday morning meeting, the Ohio State ideas were denounced as "untimely," and a committee decided to "squash [them] as this is a publicity stunt." At a Sunday morning meeting, the chair instructed Palmer to remain seated; meanwhile, Yost and another Ohio State representative were "first ignored, then jumped on." Finally, during the Monday evening meeting, the conference passed several disparaging resolutions, including some against national tournaments and others opposing any organization that "might tend to increase the numbers of competitive events for women." The attendees called for yet another committee discussion of competition for women sometime in the future, presumably the distant future. Frustrated by the complete and official dismissal of their ideas, and also by the fact that numerous people endorsed privately, but not publicly, some form of intercollegiate competition for women, Yost labeled one opponent a "louse" and another delegate a "jellyfish" for refusing to take a firm stand either way.[73]

Proud vertebrates themselves, the Ohio State women's physical education staff vowed to press on and organize the golf tournament with or without the support of their profession's majority. The majority noticed. During April, May, and June 1941, the Ohio State staff received numerous letters either congratulating them on their courageous stand or cautioning them about the Pandora's box of dangers they were threatening to open. One educator revealed to Palmer that she had "always been and [was] now in accordance with your own views concerning competition." Several others sent Palmer letters of support, with many expressing real regret that they could not afford to send golfers to the tournament. Some correspondents described their own experiences with intercollegiate competition. A representative of the Jackson College for Women, Tufts College, informed Yost that her school had "intercollegiate competition [there] with a few other colleges within a small radius. I believe that it can be controlled so that the evils which have been claimed for it are nil. We have found it to be stimulating, helpful, and fun."[74]

The Ohio State tournament proposal also received a very public endorsement from *New York Herald Tribune* columnist Janet Owen.[75] Referring to the Atlantic City meeting of the National Association of Directors of Physical Education, Owen wrote, "This august body, matriarch of girls' sports on the college level, boxed the ears of a plan" that this reporter commended. Owen agreed that, in the past, the existence of women's varsity athletics had reduced the number and quality of athletic opportunities available to less-skilled women. She asserted, however, "In the last decade, the set-up changed into a sort of Communism wherein the skilled and unskilled were all given equal attention and training." The association's stated "democratic" goals of a "game for every girl, and a girl in every game" seemed practically socialistic to this columnist, a label of extreme significance in the era of the House Un-American Activities Committee and fervent anti-communism. According to Owen, the Ohio State plan giving athletes the chance to excel and match their skills at the highest level was a step in the proper "democratic direction."[76]

In many ways the debate over how much competition to allow was also a debate over what constituted "democratic" collegiate athletic programs. While most male athletic leaders used intercollegiate athletics as a "democratic" bulwark against socialism and radicalism, most female athletic leaders embraced in the name of democracy the very egalitarian system that the men loathed. While it is easy to see the extremes of both sides as representative, that creates a somewhat false dichotomy. As the Ohio State women were prodding their colleagues toward a version of democratic sport that allowed a greater accommodation of elite athletes' desire to compete against each other, many male athletic leaders were arguing for an increased emphasis in men's college athletics programs on mass participation as a way to spread democratic values, though they defined these values differently for men.[77]

Judging from their correspondence, the Ohio State officials had failed to convince most of their professional counterparts that the tournament plans were not precisely as threatening or dangerous as the women feared. The small number of entry forms that had arrived as the May 31 deadline approached indicated that the Columbus educators might have unnecessarily stirred up controversy and sacrificed personal relationships for nothing. After all of the controversy and strife, it looked like they would not have enough golfers to hold a tournament anyway. They decided, then, to alter the registration process and to allow interested athletes to register *without* the signature of their disapproving professors. This bypassing of antagonistic professional gatekeepers worked wonders, and soon there were plenty of completed entry forms to make the tournament viable. Eventually thirty-eight golfers representing twenty-one colleges and universities signed up for the first intercollegiate golf tournament for women.[78]

The old guard did not let the tournament proceed without voicing their dissent and giving their standard reasons for disapproval. While some suggested that a gathering of elite athletes without a tournament, and thus without winners, losers, and championships on the line, would be acceptable, the Ohio State format certainly was not that. Others offered the traditional argument that the trail Ohio State was blazing would lead to diminished opportunities for most collegiate women, commercialize women's sports, and put the emphasis exactly where it did not belong. This improper emphasis was, according to Iowa State physical educator, Elizabeth Halsey, to "determine winners and make money." Halsey compiled for Palmer a long list of Iowa State's objections to the plan, including one based on a notion of democracy that would have seemed absolutely alien to Ohio State's male athletic officials, much less its female leaders. Again connecting athletic policy with national politics, she offered perhaps the clearest distillation of the feminine definition of "democratic athletics." She wrote, "Democracy can adapt to rapidly changing economic and social conditions. It must, however, move away from the cutthroat competition and unregulated individualism and toward acceptance of disciplined self-regulation and cooperative planning." Athletics, in Halsey's mind, should contribute to this shift, and Ohio State was not doing its part.[79]

The major organizations sent representatives to monitor the tournament, look for ethical improprieties, and report on everything that happened in Columbus. Yost remembered years later that "for a while it looked as though there were more faculty members from other schools coming to investigate us than there were contestants."[80] Despite the overwhelming agreement between the Ohio State educators and their professional organizations on most issues, and despite the efforts of Palmer, Yost, Sumption, and others to make the tournament as unobjectionable as possible, these investigators saw much to concern them. The presence and endorsement of the men's athletic director at the opening ceremony surely gave the disapproving observers in attendance serious pause, as must have his statement, "I think that far too often our women do not have the benefits of keen competition in a sport of this kind."[81] The efforts of Ohio State's publicity director to attract media attention to the tournament and to the individual golfers certainly alarmed the observers. The use of a professional golfer, Patty Berg, as a referee and as the host of a golf clinic also increased concerns among many in the crowd. Finally, having a representative of the NCAA—the very organization most women physical educators felt had helped create commercialized, corrupt, and elitist athletic policies for men—speak to the assembled golfers and audience at the opening banquet must have reassured the tournament's opponents that their stance was correct. His hope that "some day this tournament will develop into a tournament similar to the [men's] held here last week" neatly articulated the precise fears many physical educators felt about this experiment.[82]

So, with the support of the Ohio State female leaders, the school's student body, the men's athletics staff, and many outsiders, and with the inquiring eyes of the establishment's representatives scrutinizing every move and function, the golfers teed off. The athletes proved that college women could play at an extremely high level, with the winner carding a 75 on the same course that college men had used to determine their national champion a week earlier. Despite almost unanimous professional strictures and Ohio State's own departmental policies against presenting awards to winners, the champions all received trophies or medals because the organizers "couldn't quite see [them] selves having a national tournament without following the custom of tournament awards." Yost later explained that the tournament organizers tried to negate the elite status associated with trophies by giving medals to almost every participant and by including on the medals the

Participants of the first intercollegiate golf tournament for women, 1941. *Courtesy of The Ohio State University Archives.*

innocuous words, "Those who strive for merit shall attain success." To those skeptical about the tournament, the presentation of awards was just more evidence that it celebrated and promoted the wrong values for proper American women.[83]

Not everyone left Columbus with a negative view of the tournament and its organizers; the college golfers clearly relished the experience. In fact, one athlete claimed that she should have "managed to flunk something this year at Michigan State" to have another year of college so she could compete again the following year. Despite enduring months of criticism and vocal challenges, the Ohio State organizers remained committed to their ideas, especially after seeing them in action. Encouraged by the success of the tournament and the enthusiasm of the golfers, Palmer made a final pitch for a women's

NCAA, announced the date of the next year's tournament, and boldly proclaimed that the "only thing that would interfere with the [tournament] date would be should our country be at war."[84]

Five months later, Japanese airplanes attacked the US fleet at Pearl Harbor, and World War II accomplished what determined organizations of physical educators could not—it stopped Ohio State from hosting a national intercollegiate golf tournament for women. The next tournament would not occur until 1946, again at Ohio State and again under the leadership of Palmer and Yost. The annual tournament remained at Ohio State until 1953, after which it traveled to all parts of the country. In 1966, Yost could look back with pride and recall, "The organization that we proposed in 1941 has come into being slowly. In 1956 three of our professional organizations . . . appointed members to a committee to 'draft plans for the continuation of the National Collegiate Golf Tournament for Women.'" This meeting led to the creation of the National Joint Committee on Extramural Sports for College Women and then to another organization that would ensure that the tournament continued.[85]

The year 1956 witnessed the wide acceptance of the ideas most female physical educators had rejected sixteen years earlier. Between 1941 and 1956, women's recreational softball and baseball leagues had gained enormous popularity, epitomized by the All-American Girls Softball (later Baseball) League's success during its existence from 1943 to 1954. This league also illustrated that the age-old questions about the possibility for feminine competition did not end with the athletes in nice dresses at the Ohio State golf tournament. Professional baseball players had to attend finishing school before playing and avoid "masculine" dress and hair styles, all to reinforce the belief that a league publication spelled out: "The more feminine the appearance of the performer, the more dramatic the performance."[86] Not coincidently, another professional athletic organization, created in 1946 as the Women's Professional Golf Association, by 1950 had changed its name to the Ladies Professional Golf Association, incorporating code language for class and femininity into its new and permanent title.[87]

It was not until the 1960s, in response to the growing women's movement and the urge to keep up with the Soviets, that the number of women's intercollegiate opportunities really began to increase. As Hult has pointed out, arguments over women's intercollegiate sports after the 1940s shifted to debates about what kind of competition was preferable instead of whether elite athletes should have the opportunity to compete.[88] In short, the belief that it was possible to preserve femininity while promoting elite athletic skill through controlled competition, the belief that Palmer, Yost, Sumption, and others had articulated in the late 1930s and early 1940s—the core idea that they had based their tournament around—was becoming the new orthodoxy by the mid-1950s.

The highly controversial and widely discussed inaugural national intercollegiate golf tournament for women was the first major step toward more equal collegiate athletic opportunities for men and women. The Ohio State organizers of the 1941 tournament were not radicals; in fact, they shared many more points of agreement with their professional colleagues than they did points of disagreement. Professors Palmer, Yost, Sumption, and the other Ohio State physical educators would not have celebrated the rise of a women's jock culture, just as they would probably have opposed the current commercialization and wide press coverage of women's college sports. They would have, however, applauded the fact that talented women now get a chance to test their athletic abilities against talented women from other institutions without sanction or censure.

CHAPTER 6

★ ★ ★ ★ ★

Commercialized Sport and Imagined Communities

The Buying and Selling of University Connections

Why does the California or Stanford alumnus, even in a remote corner of the world though he may be, forego comfortable slippers and warm fireside to attend a banquet whenever Big Game time rolls around? . . . He is seeking something more, seeking to recapture some of the spirit of undergraduate days, to feel once more the influence of university life, which unifies greater numbers of men and women, more permanently, than any other factor in American life.

—*THE CALIFORNIA MONTHLY*, NOVEMBER 1931

And football is not played for the benefit of school boys. It is for the alumni, the stadium fun, good will between Tennessee and California governors who have dates with movie stars, coaches who are gray-eyed men of destiny, receipts at the gate, receipts at the ticket office of the railroads and airlines.

—EDITORIAL, KNOXVILLE, TENNESSEE, 1939

During the tough times of the 1930s Americans sought community and common bonds, searching for elements and experiences that united them while economic, social, and political currents threatened to divide the nation. They often found these ties through participation in a consumer culture that increasingly influenced most aspects of American life. As Warren Susman put it, the 1930s witnessed a "determined struggle for the attainment of identity of an American Way of Life, a definition of culture in America and for Americans with an increased emphasis on strengthening basic cultural institutions seriously threatened by newer cultural forms . . . and the profound experiences of depression and war."[1] By the late 1920s, intercollegiate athletics had become one of these sacred cultural institutions worthy of protection, and university officials worked in concert with students, alumni groups, public officials, and the general population to preserve its standing. Ultimately, their strategy of using athletics as a means to create and sustain communities of interest in and concern for their universities largely succeeded. Through the practice of commercializing and commodifying college athletics, the universities not only protected and preserved intercollegiate athletics' place in American cultural and social life, but they also helped ensure the institutional survival of the public universities themselves.

Despite numerous areas of disagreement, throughout the 1930s US college officials could agree on at least one essential point: alumni groups and the taxpaying public paid more attention to universities' athletic teams than to their academic programs. Some lamented the fact; others accepted and tried to take advantage of it, but none denied it. This interest among the general population was not coincidental, nor was it entirely detrimental; in fact, in many ways it worked to the advantage of the universities. They were glad that they offered at least one product that could hold consumers' interests. During that decade, university officials, state leaders, and alumni groups all used intercollegiate athletic programs and the ideals the athletes represented to create and strengthen bonds, both real and imagined, between US public universities and their various vital constituencies.

University athletic programs created tangible links between the institutions and their alumni groups in two important ways. First, the universities legitimized and codified alumni interest in men's athletics by providing alumni representation on athletic governing committees and by listening closely to alumni concerns about the success and direction of intercollegiate teams. Secondly, by coordinating alumni events with sporting events, especially homecoming or big football games, the universities officially linked returning to one's alma mater, either in body or spirit, with athletics. By doing this, American university leaders consciously used athletic events to reinvigorate their alumni's school spirit and restore their affinity for their alma maters, all during a decade when universities needed this interest and support most urgently. While these approaches were not original to the Great Depression, they became much more focused and important during that time.

Equally as importantly, intercollegiate athletic programs, and football in particular, helped the universities forge vital links with citizens who had not attended their classes but whose support and goodwill were essential to public universities' continued survival. Despite the desires of reformers, US universities continued the commercialization of college sports, offering for consumption not only an entertainment product but also membership in a community of athletic supporters. This community creation was bilateral, with the universities vigorously publicizing and promoting their athletic teams and with the general public and alumni groups consistently demanding more information about and access to the teams. Relatively homogeneous official alumni groups, complete with membership rosters and game-day gatherings, constituted one form of interested community, while groups as diverse as citizens, tax-payers, and Californians also interested and involved themselves in university affairs through their vicarious participation in athletic programs. By hoping that "we" would beat "them" on the athletic fields and courts, these communities strengthened their ties to the public universities.

The decade of the 1930s was a time of real and perceived crisis for intercollegiate athletics, with financial and ideological challenges seemingly threatening their continued existence. Like most other US institutions, however, this one survived the Depression, modified but even stronger than before. The conscious and effective cultivation of athletics-centered communities helped to insulate intercollegiate athletics from the financial dangers that threatened the programs, and the increased use of radio broadcasts and other media to strengthen these bonds ensured that American intercollegiate athletic programs would continue along their path of creeping commercialism, not abandon it.

The prominent anthropologist Benedict Anderson used the term "imagined communities" to explain the formation of nationalist sentiments, not collegiate affiliations, but this concept also helps explain these later connections. Nationalism, Anderson posited, is a cultural form, not an ideology; it is more of a body of feelings and beliefs, sentiments and ideas than anything else. He explained, "It would . . . make things easier if one treated [nationalism] as if it belonged with 'kinship' and 'religion,' rather than with 'liberalism' or 'fascism.'"[2]

Anderson defined a nation as "an imagined political community . . . imagined as both inherently limited and sovereign." The relationships among the members of the nation are imagined because all of the members will never be able to know each other personally; in fact, most likely never even see each other, much less develop close relationships. The same applies to university supporters, especially during the 1920s and 1930s when an emerging era of radio broadcasts allowed fans to hear the games isolated in their own living rooms instead of as part of a crowd-packed stadium. Additionally, the national community is limited, in Anderson's formulation, because even if nations contain millions of members, outsiders always exist, in the form of other nations and rivals. Again, this also applies to university communities, particularly those formed around athletic teams. Thousands of Ohioans could listen to the Ohio State University football games on the radio, but the community of "Ohioans," by definition, could easily identify their opponents' fan as outsiders with opposing interests, especially if that opponent was the University of Michigan.[3]

The communities of university and athletic supporters generally also conceived of themselves as superior to their rivals, if not necessarily "sovereign," as Anderson wrote about national communities. During the 1930s, seemingly every US university noticed inequalities and misbehavior in its rivals' actions, but only rarely did a school identify serious misconduct in its own operations. Moreover, members of alumni groups and university publicity agents never tired of discussing either the unsurpassed athletic heritage of their own institution or the unparalleled athletic facilities on their campus. Finally, Anderson's definition of a nation applies to this discussion of university communities precisely because the various university constituencies understood themselves as real communities. Anderson argued, "The nation is always conceived as a deep, horizontal comradeship," as a large "fraternity" able to inspire great loyalty. During the Depression, large public universities dealt with at least two, often overlapping, groups that matched this description: the body of people who had attended the university (the alumni) and the body of citizens and taxpayers who financed the university and whose state the university's team represented.[4]

In his analysis of the growth of nationalism, Anderson focused on the importance of language and mass communication, especially what he called "print capitalism," and the shared notion of a literally timeless community. By way of example, he notes how moveable print in the 1600s enabled the rapid diffusion of ideas, allowing people to share information and beliefs much more easily than they could before and helping fuel the Protestant Reformation and the growth of various national and administrative vernacular languages. Similarly, in the 1930s, the availability of mass media fostered the creation of the university communities that revolved around athletics; for when newspapers, alumni publications, and radio broadcasts focused the public's attention on the athletic components of universities, the media helped create and reinforce the message that this was the most important product the universities produced. Nationalism also involves a sense of timeliness, as if national communities had always existed. Just as Americans in the 1930s could refer to how "we" won the American Revolution, a twenty-five-year-old athletic enthusiast of the same time could salute "our" decades of success on the gridiron. The supporters of college athletic teams during the 1930s imagined themselves to be part of a community, and they drew strength from their sense of belonging. In turn, these communities' interest and enthusiasm greatly strengthened the universities as well, helping to ensure the survival of the athletic programs and, in some cases, the schools themselves.[5]

Seeking to protect their institutions, during the 1930s public university officials sought to demonstrate their relevance to their host states and communities in a variety of ways that did not always involve athletics; in various ways they tried to prove that their essential nature or "character" mattered.[6] Increasingly, university leaders conformed to the norms of the burgeoning consumer culture, trying to "sell" the state university to the state's population by depicting it as a commodity:

new, improved, and useful to all. As the institutions negotiated their way through the funding crises of the era, they continuously advertised their utility to the general population. One way in which they did this was to prepare a detailed catalog of all the ways the universities' programs and people contributed to the state's prosperity and welfare, such as it existed. For example, in 1936, the president of Ohio State presented his annual report to the governor, opening with the argument "that probably there is no single citizen of Ohio who does not benefit indirectly from the explicit services of the University to the people and communities in every section of the state." Sixty pages later, the report concluded, none too subtly, with President George Rightmire's argument, "It is impossible ... to think of the Ohio State University as 'above, beyond, and separate' from the daily life of all kinds and classes of men, women and children, or all citizens and taxpayers of Ohio."[7] Between the forceful introduction and conclusion lay a detailed documentation of every university department's contributions to the state. Rightmire declared that even the History Department, despite "not render[ing] so conspicuously the type of public services which the more practical and scientific departments, such as Chemistry or Engineering can perform," was vital to Ohio and its citizens.[8]

Countless other universities deployed this same utility-based tactic across the nation. Throughout the 1930s the University of Maryland's leaders prepared documents that demonstrated the types of value the university added to the state. The compilers believed that these documents would "be for the benefit of the Governor, members of the Legislature, editors and others who are likely to discuss the University of Maryland and its relation to the state" and would be a "valuable contribution to the welfare of the university as a whole, and therefore to each branch of the institutions."[9]

In a political climate that required pragmatism and measureable results, most universities sought to defend their operations on practical grounds, but the response of the University of California's leaders indicates that some leaders of public higher education still felt comfortable discussing the less practical, and they would argue, more vital products of academic life. Robert G. Sproul, president of the university, reported in December 1932 that more than one million Californians benefited directly from the University of California's classroom and extension services, making it clear that the University of California "serve[d] the youth of the entire State." All service, however, was not direct or quantifiable. Sproul maintained that "there must be research and 'useless research' if there is to be progress" and that "any attempt to shackle [faculty members] with bureaucratic rules and regulations, or to force upon them studies assumed to be of practical value, would result in the destruction of the University as a seat of higher learning." After making the case for "useless research," however, Sproul explained how abstract research in political science, engineering, science, economic, household management, and other areas did, in fact, contribute to the advances that benefited ordinary Californians.[10] Throughout the decade, Sproul and other university presidents contended that public universities were successfully addressing their states' and the nation's major public concerns.[11]

Throughout the 1930s, public universities' administrators also made calculated efforts to strengthen their schools' positions by creating closer institutional and personal relationships with state government officials and members of the general population. In 1929, an Ohio State University supporter had financed visits to the Universities of Michigan and Illinois by important government and university officials. This excursion, and its resulting increased legislative awareness of Ohio State's existing operations and the support given to its rivals, led directly to increased appropriations. Similarly, cultivating personal relationships with governors and leading legislators helped Harry Byrd climb the University of Maryland's administrative ladder and then protect his university from budgetary devastation during the 1930s. Under President Byrd's tenure the University of Maryland continued to try to accommodate the general public and important guests, requiring professors and staff members to make time for visitors whenever they were on campus.[12]

Likewise, in 1938, the University of California appropriated $2,500 for an "educational fund" to pay for trips by small groups of state legislators to campus, where they could meet personally with student leaders and learn more about the "problems and interests of the student body and the University."[13] Public university leaders were willing to do almost anything to attract the interest of the public and its elected officials, yet virtually all of them realized that arguments based on the character and quality of their academic programs or on personal contact would not be enough to protect the universities and their interests. Therefore, these universities used athletics extensively during the 1930s to market positive images of themselves to outsiders and to create communities of interested and sympathetic observers.

As university leaders tried to build community support for their institutions and their actions, they always relied upon both rational arguments and emotional appeals. In particular, university officials pointed out that the universities directly benefited and educated many more people than the relative few that attended their classes. For example, of the 1,099,000 people that Sproul claimed his institution had helped in the 1931–32 academic year, almost 820,000 interacted with the university through agricultural extension services. This pattern was duplicated across the country, and during an era when most Americans did not have access to a college education and the nation's farmers were facing truly hard times, the extension efforts of universities generated a great deal of public goodwill. In order to understand the significance of college athletics to the creation of college-centered communities, one must first recognize that college athletics operated in many ways as an extension service, bringing the university, its people, its passion, and all that these things came to symbolize to the public that the university existed to serve.[14]

American educators had long recognized that intercollegiate athletics served as the single best extension arm of the university, as a division able to attract interest and inspire loyalty far better than its corresponding, campus-bound academic departments. With their youth, vitality, vigor, physical prowess, and optimism, athletes often offered the most attractive and appealing public faces of the universities, serving as perfect advertisements for beleaguered institutions. In 1920, in a call for donations for athletic facilities construction, the president of the University of Maryland captured this idea, writing, "Athletics is the strongest tie by which to bind Alumni, Students, and Faculty into a single unity for furthering building up the institution."[15] While this sentiment was neither novel nor widely challenged by the 1920s, many educators still did not like the reality it revealed.

When compiling *American College Athletics* during the late 1920s, Howard Savage recognized the wide appeal that college athletics had developed, writing that their "financial and public aspects, the reputation which they confer upon the institution, and a thousand other forces have united to make them not so much activities of undergraduate life as joint cooperative enterprises involving presidents, trustees, faculties, alumni, and townsmen, and the vast publics of the radio and the press."[16] Many other reports and editorials argued precisely the same point: that intercollegiate athletic programs, particularly football, were indeed "joint cooperative enterprises," dependent upon the support and enthusiasm of a wide range of interested groups for their financial and competitive successes, in this way serving as a microcosm of the universities that the athletes represented.

During the late 1920s and the 1930s, US public university leaders consciously cultivated and took advantage of this diverse array of interested groups to build a larger, university-based support community with a strong interest in athletics, a community composed of public officials, university alumni, and the general population. One telling example from the University of Tennessee student newspaper reveals how effective athletics could be in selling a university and an image to its constituencies and in fostering institutional, state, and even national goodwill toward a university. The columnist presented many reasons for the University of Tennessee to do everything in its power to prevent its football coach, Robert Neyland, from decamping to its rival, the University of Florida, deftly combining the rhetoric of commercialism and community within one argument:

> Through [Neyland's] amazing leadership and on the gridiron, Tennessee has become nationally known as a great and progressive institution. He has brought it more national advertising than half a dozen new buildings, the addition of a score of competent professors, and the constant plugging of ten thousand uninspired students could have ever brought.
>
> He has done more to sell Tennessee to the country than any other individual connected with the university in any manner.
>
> He has done more to see Tennessee to Tennesseans than any other Tennessean, native or "furriner."
>
> He has brought more pride to Tennessee's students than all the material development it can amass in ten years of consistent advancement. And why?
>
> Because: Football today is the great outlet of collegiate

> emotion; the great source of loyalty, inspiration, pride, and reverence.[17]

As they fought for money, attention, and affection, university officials recognized that their athletic programs constituted some of the best weapons available to them in this struggle. Therefore, university presidents and public relation officers worked diligently to get local, state, and sometimes even national leaders to attend their games, trying to use athletics to secure these officials' interest and loyalty. In 1930, the Associated Students of the University of California's manager of athletics encouraged Sproul to send tickets to "influential friend[s] of the University" whenever he thought it could help the school; and the University of California indeed made it policy during the 1930s to provide football season passes to all levels of state government officials, including assessors, state senators, and members of executive committees.[18] On the other coast, in 1939, one alumnus encouraged University of Maryland officials to persuade the governor to attend a Maryland football game, working under the assumption that "the support of the University of Maryland by your State officials and the whole hearted support of other citizens of your State would be of primary importance in increasing the attendance at the University of Maryland games." Because of its unique location, the University of Maryland did not cater only to state officials; instead, its athletic director sought to attract the national spotlight by cordially inviting President Franklin Delano Roosevelt, his wife, Eleanor, and their friends to attend the 1936 Maryland–Georgetown University game in College Park.[19]

Across the nation, when the public universities succeeded in attracting the interest of state political leaders, trouble often followed. For example, after the Pacific Coast Conference passed a rule limiting the number of games conference teams could play against nonconference teams, the University of California football teams from Berkeley and Los Angeles could no longer play as many local rivals as they had before, including the College of the Pacific, Santa Clara University, and St. Mary's University. State legislators, believing that this rule would reduce the revenue potential and the number of entertainment opportunities in their home areas, favored retaliation. Their explicit threats prompted a letter from a San Francisco city official to Sproul, warning of a "possible attack on your budget in the Legislature." The author wanted to "forewarn" Sproul of the possibility, writing that this "in my opinion is a 'hell of a way' to mix football and university budgets."[20] Other public university officials learned during the 1930s that increased interest from legislators, while necessary for funding purposes, could be undesirable in other respects.

Public universities could not afford to offend their states' political power brokers or alienate their alumni, the one segment of the population that had already developed emotional ties to the campus. In many ways, the masses of university alumni did not compose an imagined community of "Texas Exes" but an actual one of friendships and common experiences. A fair percentage of alumni probably had met each other during a shared college class or during an alumni gathering, and, therefore, many shared a genuine sense of communal ties. Most, however, did not; instead they acted as citizens in the University of Tennessee, Texas, or Nebraska *nation*, complete with sentiments of superiority and patriotism but with those emotions sparked by their alma mater instead of their nation. Recognizing this, universities intentionally utilized athletics as a tool to construct and maintain this most vital community structure. They did so in a variety of ways. These universities used homecoming games, athletics-centered alumni gatherings and publications, and formal alumni representation on athletic boards to recognize the importance of the alumni to the universities and to regenerate their interest in each other and in the fate of their alma maters.

Most universities by this decade enjoyed the support of well-organized alumni associations, complete with official membership rosters, dues, and publications. These groups composed the official bodies of the alumni, and they spoke with that group's recognized voice. Even with these common characteristics, their size and strength varied widely. For example, in 1932, UC president Sproul boasted that the 20,000 members of the University of California Alumni Association made it the nation's largest and that the *California Monthly* was the most widely circulating alumni publication in the United States. That year more than 10,000 California alumni gathered at more than fifty meetings "to renew their contract with the University." In contrast, the University of Maryland had only 413 paid alumni association members as late as 1941.[21]

Regardless of the size of these official alumni associations, they all employed athletics in a number of common ways to maintain the alumni members' interest in and passion for their alma maters, working to create imagined communities of mutual interest. First, by focusing much, and often most, of their attention on the athletic activities of their alma maters, the alumni associations reinforced the idea that the alumni population should care almost exclusively about the universities' athletic successes. During the 1930s, the *Maryland Alumni News* often discussed the university's athletic teams on every page, including feature stories, summaries of games, and numerous pictures of athletes representing the institution and of fans watching them do so. Almost all alumni publications similarly emphasized athletics, if not on every page, then on a sizable portion of them. For example, in the 1936–37 school year, the *Ohio State University Monthly* featured athletes on the cover of six out of ten editions; and the 1938–39 year included covers depicting cheerleaders, champion swimmers, a javelin thrower, another cheerleader with the homecoming queen, and two covers about alumni days and class reunions that featured athletics prominently in their activities. That year, only the January cover focused on the educational mission of the university.[22]

Some universities resisted catering to public's and their alumni's preoccupation with intercollegiate athletics, but during the Depression most institutions eventually yielded to the demands for more information about the one topic that always commanded the interest of outside observers: athletics. The University of California's experience with its alumni publication, the *California Monthly*, highlights the fact that even at academically elite universities, the drama and decisiveness of sports trumped all other topics in terms of interest. The pages of the *California Monthly* in the early 1930s represented the University of California's leaders' and alumni's belief that their institution was one of the nation's best and most comprehensive universities, offering readers articles and information on a great variety of academic and cultural topics. In 1933, the *California Monthly* editor politely explained to a disgruntled reader why the magazine did not publish more information about the university's sports team, pointing out that the magazine already published numerous articles about athletics and that early deadlines prevented more detailed accounts of some events. Still, as the decade progressed, the amount of coverage increased. Catering to continued alumni interest in California athletics, the alumni editors published "seven weekly news sheets," complete with postgame interviews, analysis of the games, and "locker room chit-chat," during the 1937 football season. A dispute with the postal service about sending a "football weekly" under the imprint of a "monthly" caused the termination of this service to the alumni, but the editors assured their readers that the *California Monthly* would continue to offer athletic coverage "unique among publications of America in its timeliness of last-minute news."[23]

The University of California editors recognized what their counterparts across the nation and their university president had long known: athletics kept the alumni interested, unlike any other topic. According to his close friend, colleague, and biographer, Sproul was very interested in intercollegiate athletics both personally and professionally. George Pettitt wrote, "No alumnus was more interested in attending intercollegiate competition than the President himself, and none could wave his arms more wildly or cheer more loudly." More importantly, Sproul "was well aware that many alumni were more familiar with the roster of the varsity football squad than with the catalog of the Academic Senate." But Sproul thought it better "that an alumnus should know the football players than not know anyone at the University, and alternating praise or criticism following victory or defeat in athletics seemed preferable to apathy." The editorial decisions of the *California Monthly's* editors, then, reflected the sentiments and strategies of the university's president as well.[24]

In addition to publicizing the events in alumni publications, universities cultivated alumni interest in the schools' athletic exploits in many other ways, including organizing alumni gatherings and activities around athletic events, usually football games. Throughout the 1930s, universities advertised the joys of returning to campus for homecoming games, and some institutions tried to transform all football contests into alumni affairs. For example, the University of Texas Ex-Student Association offered an alumni registry at most Texas away games. The announcement explained, "Oldtimers have a good time when they gather around Texas Exes' registration table at an out-of-Austin game. They sign the registry then look through all the pages to see if any of their campus cronies have come to the game—and usually some have—then they meet some other Ex standing at the table, and a big session follows." By registering, the Texas Ex got a free ribbon and also "inform[ed] all other Exes who register later that he is in town and ready to whoop." More than any other university program did, everyone recognized that football got the alumni ready to whoop.[25]

While the Texas alumni communities gathered in Oklahoma and Dallas to identify with each other and their alma mater's teams, the University of California alumni let the dates of the big game against Stanford University determine when alumni groups would meet in Philadelphia, Boston, Chicago, Shanghai, Honolulu, London, Paris, Constantinople, Buenos Aries, and elsewhere. This tradition continued throughout the decade, as the president's office periodically invited the "sons and daughters of California" to "celebrate the Big Game and pledge anew their loyalty to the University." Through mass telegrams, Sproul expressed his hope that the meetings would "bring joy in renewed memories of the campus and bright prospects of a victory over our friendly enemy."[26] After all, these scattered alumni shared more than memories of Berkeley classes; they still had a common enemy, albeit a "friendly" one.

Through these types of gatherings the universities marketed an idyllic university experience and traded on fond memories of the old campus home. The University of California sought to rekindle the flames of nostalgia with advertisements like this: "The Tang of Football Is in the Air and the Thrill of College Days Is Once Again with Us."[27] When explaining the appeal of these alumni gatherings coordinated with the university's important football games, the editor of the *California Monthly* explained that the alumni were "seeking to recapture some of the spirit of undergraduate days, to feel once more the influence of university life, which unifies greater numbers of men and women, more permanently, than any other factor of American life."[28] If the alumni association could help its member feel younger, more confident, and more connected by helping them recapture the excitement of their undergraduate days, then it was doing its job. Perhaps, especially during the dark days of the Depression, the possibility of reliving the excitement, rekindling the "spirit of university life," and participating, even vicariously, in great victories was even more appealing.

Moreover, even those alumni meetings that took place in less exotic locations and at times not coordinated with specific games often focused on the fortunes of the athletic teams. In January 1936, the *Maryland Alumni News* reported that the university had film footage of almost every Maryland football game from the recently completed season, and it offered these films as an "attraction for alumni get-togethers to follow the Terrapins in action of the gridiron."[29] The Big Ten Conference also allowed the use of film footage to serve as an attraction for community gatherings. According to a 1937 committee report, conference members could show films to "high school banquets, luncheon clubs, and other similar groups," with the provision that "detailed description, minute study, and frequent repetition of certain parts of a film" would not occur and that the projector operator would not focus on replays of referees' mistakes. The conference committee saw the value of using football films to stir up interest, but it did not want to use them to stir up controversy.[30]

Athletic officials also attended events as ambassadors of the universities. In 1937, the secretary of the Baltimore chapter of the Maryland Alumni Association invited athletic director Geary Eppley to an upcoming meeting to answer questions about the football team, a meeting that university president (and former football coach) Byrd also attended. The chapter's secretary informed Eppley, "The whole meeting has been planned with one object in view, that of stirring up enthusiasm among the Alumni for their Alma Mater." It is revealing that even with the president of the university attending their meeting, the Baltimore chapter's leaders thought that only a "bull session" about football could enthuse their membership.[31]

US universities also tried to reenergize and reaffirm their ties to their alumni communities by asking them directly for advice or assistance in athletic matters. They did this most formally through granting the alumni powerful seats on athletic-governing bodies. For example, the Athletic Board created at the University of Tennessee in 1935 included five alumni representatives out of fifteen total members, making the alumni superior numerically to the two student members. The administrative board at Ohio State was very similar. Under the Athletic Association's constitution approved in 1930, the alumni held two of ten seats, and this percentage held steady throughout the decade, never falling below the number of seats allocated to current students.[32]

In their efforts to maintain an interested community of alumni friends, university leaders frequently solicited the input of influential alumni about all sorts of athletic issues, but the officials often got more interest and feedback than they had bargained for. At the University of Texas, the alumni had a great deal of influence in the hiring of football coach Dana Bible, providing a $5,000 bonus for Bible when he signed his contract. Shortly thereafter, Bible validated the legitimacy of alumni assistance by sending a letter to the alumni associations, asking the alumni to help his program recruit players, employ partners, and perform other tasks designed to generate positive sentiment toward the university and its athletic teams. Specifically, Bible asked the Texas alumni to send money to the Athletic Department so that the school could fund jobs for its athletes. Bible explained, "No football team is made up of eleven men. The team that wears Orange and White consists of the entire squad, the entire student body, the faculty and the great group of Texas Exes and friends." He continued, "*So I invite you to get into the Longhorn football huddle* with hopes that it may be a close huddle and we all come out with the *same signal*."[33]

These types of exhortations and sentiments were common throughout the nation, and they only encouraged universities' alumni members to act outside the rules in order to help their alma maters. In 1931, University of California coach Bill Ingram received great attention when he publically turned down $15,000–20,000, with which he could have "bought" better athletes. Others were not so scrupulous. By encouraging the alumni to care about athletics, the universities also ran the risk of having them care so much that they became implicated in the resulting corruption and commercialism. Nevertheless, while university leaders could see the downside of alumni preoccupation with intercollegiate athletics, they still continued to use athletics as a tool to keep the alumni community intact and interested in at least one aspect of their alma mater's continued activities.[34]

Universities' leaders recognized that they could not survive on the goodwill of legislators and their alumni alone; they knew that they had to create feelings of community within their host state's general population as well. US public universities created their diverse communities of supporters by continuing the commercialization that had attracted increased criticism during the 1920s. Savage's was but only one of many voices decrying the commercialization of college sports during the late 1920s and early 1930s; however, with the onset of the Depression and the related decline in athletic revenues, university officials did not decrease their commercial orientation but rather increased it. This increased commercialism occurred in several ways. First, the universities tried to schedule games that would make the public care about the fate of the state's representative team. Second, the universities allowed more companies to associate their products directly with the universities and their athletic teams through advertisements and game-day merchandising. Finally, the universities increasingly began delivering their products to their customers' homes in the form of educational radio programs and, especially, through wildly popular broadcasts of football games and other sporting events.[35]

Officials had long known that traditional games against traditional rivals could generate tremendous amounts of interest in (and income for) a state's main public university, and administrators recognized that more novel intersectional games and intrastate games could do the same. In 1932, for example, the president of Western Maryland College wrote to then University of Maryland vice president Byrd, hoping to inaugurate a series of football games between the two schools. He acknowledged the important role athletics could play in building ties to the state's populations, writing, "I am sure you have in mind the creation of college and university rivalries that will mean much for our state institutions in appealing to the people of our own state." As cited earlier, University of Tennessee football coach Neyland received credit for creating a situation where "Tennesseans are proud of Tennessee . . . [and are] proud the nation now looks toward Tennessee with deepest respect. Proud to call [the University of] Tennessee THEIR Tennessee."[36] Neyland continued to satisfy his university and his adopted state when his team beat a New York University squad in 1931, a victory that, as a headline read, "Gain[ed] Vols Nation-Wide Fame," while also contributing to statewide pride. Beating a nationally prominent team could galvanize an entire state, but to build a true community of interested citizens, the universities would have to find yet other ways to connect with them.[37]

The University of California provided the most extreme example of universities using athletics to create more unity within their host states, utilizing the football games between the Los Angeles and Berkeley campuses of the University of California to further Sproul's ambitious "One University" agenda. Sproul was president of the entire University of California system, including both the Berkeley and Los Angeles campuses as well as other outposts at Riverside, Davis, San Francisco, and Mount Hamilton; and during the 1930s, as UCLA, in particular, grew in size and reputation, maintaining peace among the branches became more difficult. After UCLA got permission and financing for graduate programs in the early 1930s, it became clearer that the University of California system included two full-fledged, ambitious universities, not just the one in Berkeley. Sproul was determined to prevent regional jealousies from tearing down the great university system that he helped build, and he reminded UCLA's students in 1932 that the state was "building one great university in California" and that the students should "let no small mind direct you along the paths of suspicion, distrust or jealousy."[38]

The historian of the University of California, Verne Stadtman, argued that "the danger of ill-feeling between the two campuses increased in 1933" when the Los Angeles and Berkeley campuses met for the first time on the football field. Sproul recognized this peril and worked to ensure that these contests strengthened and did not undermine the one-university ideal. This result seemed plausible because the different branches had already begun playing each other in minor sports and basketball, not just football, without great difficulty or controversy. Trying to jumpstart the football series, the general manager of the UCLA associated students organization, S. W. Cunningham, argued that if any sport would cause ill will, basketball would have done so, with its close proximity of fans and the roughness of play. Teams representing the two campuses, however, had met four times in the 1931–32 academic year without any difficulty or animus involved. Citing this example, Cunningham argued, "The alumni of the University are not likely to divide in any way over a football game that would cause them to lose sight of their allegiance to the 'One University' idea that now appears to be pretty firmly grounded." Cunningham also noted that having the Berkeley officials continue to refuse to play the Los Angeles football team, when they would schedule games with the private, Los Angeles–based University of Southern

Program for California vs. UCLA football game, 1933. *Courtesy of the Bancroft Library, University of California, Berkeley.*

California, might create the very hostility that University of California leaders wanted to avoid.[39]

After authorizing football competitions between the two branches, University of California officials carefully scripted a ceremony designed to communicate the "One University" ideal through the games pitting the Berkeley and Los Angles teams against each other. Before the inaugural contest, held on November 4, 1933, the two universities' bands marched into the stadium together, playing the national anthem with the US flag and the respective campuses' flags flying together. Just before kickoff, representatives of the two institutions met in the middle of the field to approve a trophy that would go to the winner and to give each other "best wishes for a friendly rivalry for the future."[40] Then, Sproul spoke on behalf of both universities, declaring this a unique game for several reasons, including the fact that both institutions shared the exact same academic standards and that it was "the first game ever held at which every spectator could rightly claim both teams as his own." Sproul expounded on this theme of communal values and shared interests as represented by the football contest:

> The State University is the university of each of us as student, official, parent, or taxpayer, and both these teams represent the State University. You may prefer one team to the other, but they are both your teams. As President of the University in all its parts, I cannot even have a real preference, and so this perpetual trophy is delivered to me as a neutral judge. I accept it with that understanding and dedicate it through the long years to clean sport and fair play, to generous rivalry, and to the unity of the University of California.[41]

Not everyone agreed that the game fostered intra-institutional unity, however important it was, and community building had never been the sole reason for the contests. Supporters of the proposed football rivalry between the schools contended that the series would do much more for the universities than build the one-university sentiment; it would also help pay both universities' athletic bills. This was a persuasive argument in the 1932–33 school year, especially at UCLA, where athletic finances were not as sound as they were in Berkeley. For example, in 1932 Sproul cited the costs of the enterprise when he wrote against the formation of a UCLA crew team; this was in spite of the fact that Sproul considered "crew racing" to be "the best of college sports."[42] In his March 1932 letter to Sproul, UCLA's Cunningham devoted most of his letter to extolling the unifying benefits of the potential rivalry, but he also noted that the "financial returns" would not be bad either. He anticipated that the profits from the game "would go a long way toward pulling us out of [UCLA's] present difficulties."[43] While the financial potential of the rivalry remained less important than the potential unifying power of the games, the money remained tempting to many on both ends of the state and on both sides of the issue. It was in such big games, popular and crowd-pleasing, that the community-building and commercial interests of the universities overlapped the most.

Many critics argued that the popular "big" and intersectional games, with their large press contingents and lucrative gate totals, epitomized the commercialization of college athletics. In 1929, Howard Savage had lambasted American intercollegiate athletics, particularly football, as being overly commercial, but by 1931 when he reevaluated the collegiate landscape, Savage had seen a remarkable and, to him, desirable change. He observed, "The most recent development in the relation of the public to college sports is a growing resistance on the part of the college to the further commercialization of athletics." Much to his delight, Savage concluded, "Many groups have found the commercialization of college sports to their interest. Theirs is the influence that the colleges in general have begun to resist."[44]

Over the course of the next decade, it became clear that Savage's optimism was misplaced, that the commercialism of intercollegiate athletics had, in fact, increased during the 1930s. Others saw this to be the case, as when a mother wrote to the University of California president to complain that her son had not gotten into the university when less-qualified athletes had been admitted. She saw the disparity as evidence of a moral crisis, asking, "Is not education defeating itself when such things occur? The whole thing to me seems to be a money making scheme—the way foot ball is being commercialized and especially so if management allows such to continue."[45] Throughout the decade many others raised the same questions.

While some criticized what they perceived as the general commercial orientation and the related, misplaced priorities of the universities and their athletic programs, others focused on what they saw as specific, egregious examples of improper institutional commercial emphasis. When criticizing the University of Tennessee for leaving twelve football players behind on its 1940 Rose Bowl trip and taking sports writers in their stead, one columnist sarcastically congratulated the university because "when it makes its drive for fame and filthy lucre in the football world, it is open and aboveboard about its purposes."[46] In California, an outraged citizen, H. L. Ferguson, argued that "a great institution should have a great soul" and that when the University of California football program featured a cigarette advertisement inside its front cover, the university revealed that it did not possess such a soul. In fact, according to Ferguson, "a parent or school that places cigarettes in the hands of youth are morally criminal," and by accepting this advertisement the university "not only place[d] the stamp of approval on pupils smoking but [lent] its influence to a nefarious business." President Sproul's reply that the university did not try to encourage or prevent its students from legal activities probably did not persuade his correspondent that using cigarette money to finance sports was proper.[47]

Others protested the blatant commercialism in practice, not in theory. At Ohio State, the University of Michigan band aroused criticism by spelling out "Buick" on the Ohio stadium field with its marching members. At the University of Texas, the commercialism appeared in the stands, not on the field. In 1931, the Texas Athletic Council allowed the Universal Brokerage and Distribution Company of Durham, North Carolina, to distribute two thousand advertising seat cushions, and the next year the council approved letting students sell "miniatures of Longhorn Steers or Bevos [the mascot's name]" as long as the sales did not occur within the stadium itself and, significantly, as long as the council received 15 percent of the gross sales total.[48]

The direct linking of commerce and college athletics was repeated all across the nation. One University of Maryland alumnus who had been harassed by vendors and merchants hawking paraphernalia asked a Maryland official, "Doesn't it seem to you even in these days when commercialized football is the rule of the day that some regard should be paid to the alumni and student body who after all are the backbone of the Maryland team's support?"[49] A few years later, the university gratefully accepted donated shipments of Wrigley's gum for its football team members; and, within a few years, its representatives

University of Maryland president Harry Byrd and athletic director Geary Eppley watch a Terrapin game in the 1930s. *Courtesy of Special Collections and University Archives, University of Maryland Libraries.*

were soliciting free chewing gum for the university basketball teams. During the Great Depression, asking for handouts from large corporations did not bother the Maryland officials as much as the advertisement and sale of some of these corporations' products bothered many in the university's crowds, but the universities could logically argue that the advertisers supported the games that the crowds traveled to witness.[50] Although regrettable to most observers inside and outside the academy, commercialized sport was firmly established by the 1930s, and the Depression conditions did not inspire leaders to abandon the commercialized path. In fact, in their quest to satisfy their constituents and customers, the universities dramatically increased their commercial orientation, and the acceptance of radio broadcasts is just one example of this.

During the 1930s US universities increasingly took advantage of a new commercial enterprise and a new form of mass communication to build their vital communities of support; they turned to the radio. In the past, universities had used official publications, press releases, and personal appearances to disseminate information about their activities, and they continued to do so after the emergence of radio as a powerful communication force. For example, university officials continued visiting Rotary clubs and other civic organizations, attempting to incorporate the clubs into the wider university community.[51] The universities also tried to draw people of the surrounding towns onto campus, and many justified the numerous stadium expansion projects in these terms, often lowering ticket prices to keep the games within the price ranges of the surrounding population. Increasingly, they supplemented these efforts with radio broadcasts to bring the university to the masses that were not coming to the university.

This was especially true after some university officials recognized that their price adjustments would not do enough to draw capacity crowds to their recently expanded stadiums. At the University of Tennessee, trustees advocated selling football tickets to all of the state's high school students at the same price as to university students. Their reasoning was simple: the university had "practically no use for the recent additions to the Stadium." The trustees hoped that selling high school students cheap tickets would increase their interest "both in sport and in respect to their state institution." Trustee Paul Kruesi noted that the university's "principal patronage" came from "a comparatively narrow radius of perhaps fifty miles" and that the additional thousand or more high school students might help fill a cavernous stadium that was too often too empty. This would be especially useful because, as Kruesi saw it, "the new Stadium is detrimental to our cause most of the time, because there is no possibility of filling it under normal circumstances, and the psychological effect on those who do attend is awfully bad when they see thousands of unoccupied seats." Kruesi concluded, "Any artificial measures we can take to give the semblance of success will be justified."[52] For Kruesi, reducing prices for high schoolers' tickets would accomplish two important tasks: it would help generate new communities of supporters while also helping convince those that already attended Tennessee games that a community of supporters indeed existed.

This desire to fill the recently expanded stadiums across the nation was one reason many university officials initially lobbied against football game broadcasts, as many university officials preferred to cultivate the traditional sort of community that gathered together and bought tickets over the imagined communities of loyal supporters that did not make pilgrimages to the campuses for football games. In contrast, the argument for radio broadcasts was not based on the tremendous profits that the broadcast contracts offered; in fact, many feared that broadcasts would lead to a net loss for the universities' athletic programs. They reasoned that allowing radio broadcasts would remove the incentive for fans to pay to attend games by allowing them access to the excitement of the games for free over the airwaves. In one representative statement, in 1931 the Executive Committee of the Southern Conference agreed that "broadcasting was detrimental to gate receipts and that broadcasts should have the approval of the two contending institutions." The Southern Conference later approved a ban on all broadcasts of conference games, based on this belief. During the early 1930s, the University of Texas followed a slightly different path, trying to attract paying customers and also satisfy those who could not attend the games. The Texas Athletic Council allowed broadcasts of some games, but in many cases it did not permit the radio stations to reveal before the game day, or even before noon of the game day, that they would broadcast the game.[53]

The Southern Conference ban on radio broadcasts of football games, and other bans like it, did not last for long, however, as they fell victim to the argument that such broadcasts could do more good than ill in terms of creating communities of loyal and dedicated university supporters. One radio executive wrote, "We cannot conceive of anyone, able to go to a football game, having the time and the money, staying away to listen to the broadcast of same." He continued, "College spirit and loyalty and the love of seeing the game, do not run that way. Those, that can possibly go, go, and those that cannot, follow the broadcast, regretting all the while that they are unable to be at the field and actually be one of the crowd that hear cheering, during the broadcast." But, he reasoned, if the universities really wanted to increase the numbers of people who cared about the universities and their teams, then they would cater to those that wanted to be in the crowd but who could not. These included those confined to sickbeds and those who could not afford to attend the games. Moreover, broadcasts could also teach people about the game of football, bringing ever more people into the potential spectator pool.[54]

While some might dismiss these claimed benefits of broadcasting as the biased boasts of an interested party, the alumni publications of US universities teemed with statements that suggested the claims were genuine. One University of California alumnus wrote in 1935, "Many of 'our group' (California graduates 1930–34) cannot afford to attend more than a game or two a season . . . and the broadcasts hold an important place in maintaining their interest in California activities."[55] Other California correspondents wrote to Sproul to tell him about the "most unexplainable thrills imaginable" they had experienced while listening to the 1935 California–Stanford University game. Mr. and Mrs. C. C. Crampton described their emotions in this way: "Play by play the game went on, our hearts tense and spirits winging their love to 'Our Boys,' and finally at the conclusion, when the physical victors marched in front of the U.C. section; we heard only a great hubbub, then a great song burst forth as if from a mighty army; Hail to California, Hail All Hail. What power, what spirit what great Spiritual Victory; nothing I have ever heard over the air equaled it."[56]

Clearly, the broadcasts of football games could do exactly what university leaders hoped that the games themselves would do: bind more closely the interests and feelings of the alumni to their alma mater. During the 1930s it became clear that game broadcasts could also make those who never had attended the schools feel more attached to the universities as well. The best-known example of this phenomenon comes from University of Notre Dame. Notre Dame recruited its legions of "subway alumni"—primarily urban, working-class

Catholics who had never attended the university but who felt intense loyalty to it—with its national football schedule and its policy encouraging radio broadcasts of Notre Dame football games. By allowing free broadcasts of its games and playing a difficult and glamorous schedule, Notre Dame ensured that the radio waves would carry news of its successes across the nation throughout the 1930s. For example, in 1933, CBS broadcast five Notre Dame games on its national network, allowing millions to listen to and identify with the team.[57]

During the 1930s, many public universities discovered that they too could follow this model and use radio broadcasts to build allegiances and communities of supporters. According to at least one observer, radio broadcasts could even help to diversify the crowds that attended college football games, adding a new group of "self-appointed alumni" to the alumni and students who had previously attended the contests. These "self-appointed alumni" were "those who [had] followed the battles of the teams via radio and [had] come out to see the playing of ['their'] college."[58]

Many of these self-appointed alumni already had reasons to support the public universities' teams before the advent of radio broadcasts; after all, the teams represented their states and the universities existed because of their tax dollars. With their dollars came a vested interest and the basis for a claim that the tax-paying citizens deserved a voice in setting athletic broadcast policies. In 1931, after the University of Tennessee followed its policy by denying permission to radio stations wanting to broadcast Tennessee football games because the university feared drops in revenue, a public outcry ensued. The general public's dissatisfaction with the university's stance led directly to House Resolution Number 2, adopted by the Tennessee House of Representatives. The resolution pointed out that the University of Tennessee existed only at "enormous expense to the tax-payers of the state" and that the football team represented that institution and its host state. The resolution detailed how the university's "great games [had] been brought to the rural people through the radio" and how "thousands [had] enjoyed them who could not do so otherwise." These broadcasts had helped the school become "closer to the people, and . . . come to occupy a position in the life of the state enjoyed by no other tax-supported school in Tennessee." The resolution concluded with a call to the university's administration to reevaluate its stance against broadcasts and to, "if possible, allow all games played at the State University to be broadcasted to the people of the State."[59] Eight years later, Neyland was giving live radio interviews, by the side of the train, as his team arrived in Miami for an Orange Bowl game against the University of Oklahoma.[60]

The argument for access to athletic broadcasts based on a sense of taxpayers' rights indicated that the universities had successfully made their cases that they and, most especially, their athletes represented and served their entire state's population. The citizens of Tennessee were not alone in their demands for broadcasts. By the mid-1930s, South Carolina, among other states, had passed a law *requiring* broadcasts of all football games played by the main branch of the state university.[61] In California, J. E. Gurich wrote to Sproul as "a former student" and as a "tax payer of this state," arguing that "the tax payers of California are the people who keep up the University, and they should get a little consideration in return."[62] The desired consideration was, of course, continued radio broadcasts of University of California football games.

In April of 1937, the *California Monthly* announced that the time for "thoughtful discussions and comments" on the past football season had come; and the editors concluded that "no single activity ha[d] brought in wider or more favorable comment from alumni of the University of California, distributed throughout the cities of California, as well as in far away rural districts of the state, than the broadcasting of the football games participated in by the students of the University." Intercollegiate athletics and the broadcasts thereof had helped create and maintain vibrant communities of alumni and "self-appointed alumni" and had kept these communities interested in the welfare of the university. As *California Monthly* editors realized, the football broadcasts made "possible explanation[s] of non-athletic activities, which, in a State University performing manifold services, are exceedingly important." The broadcasts provided "a better understanding of the University of California to the people of the state, and at the same time carrie[d] to them an interpretation of the University in a manner that the man in the street [could] best absorb."[63]

This was the vital point. Broadcasts of athletic games gave US public universities access not only to alumni but also to the "man in the street." Ideally, these audiences became impassioned enough by students' athletic achievements to support the universities in their non-athletic endeavors. Building communities of loyal athletic supporters through extension programs, community outreach, and radio broadcasts was a means for universities to draw fans to other aspects of the institution. Although most alumni and other supporters would continue to care more about the football team than about the Forensics Department, university officials worked to capitalize on this interest for the benefit of the athletic programs themselves, but also to benefit the entire university.

In the fall of 1940, universities got their first glimpse of the future when the University of Maryland football team played the University of Pennsylvania in front of two relatively small audiences: the crowd in the stands and the people sitting in front of their televisions at home or in demonstration sites. In one of the very first (if not the actual inaugural) televised football games with commercial sponsors, the Quakers destroyed the Terrapins, 51–0. Maryland's players could take some solace in the fact that only a few hundred people could have watched the game on television because of the technology's novelty, but administrators certainly took note of the event and its potential significance for the future of college athletics as a tool to reach larger audiences more effectively.[64]

Epilogue

The defects of American college athletics are two: commercialism, and a negligent attitude toward the educational opportunity for which college exists.

—HOWARD SAVAGE,
IN *AMERICAN COLLEGE ATHLETICS*, 1929

To be sure, big-time college sports has entertained the American public, but it has all too frequently done so at the expense of our colleges and universities, their students, faculty, and staff, and the communities they were created to serve. They have infected our academic culture with the commercial values of the entertainment industry. They have distorted our priorities through the disproportionate resources and attention given to intercollegiate athletics. . . . Most significantly, big-time college sports have threatened the integrity and reputation of our universities, exposing us to the hypocrisy, corruption, and scandal that all too frequently accompany activities driven primarily by commercial value and public visibility.

—JAMES DUDERSTADT, *INTERCOLLEGIATE ATHLETICS AND THE AMERICAN UNIVERSITY*, 2000

If the "big-time" label that was so prominent during the Great Depression still applies to US college athletics, the scale and, in many ways, the character of the operations to which it refers have changed dramatically. Whereas in the 1930s most universities hoped to make a few thousand dollars from their new radio-broadcasting contracts, in 2010 CBS and the Turner Broadcasting System paid more than $10.8 *billion* for the right to broadcast the annual NCAA men's college basketball tournament for eleven years. In 2012, it became public that contracts for the newly announced college football playoff system should generate more than $400 million a year, starting in 2014.

If the scale of the finances involved has changed dramatically, so has the racial and gender makeup of modern college athletes. One could easily argue that the most significant changes in the nature of intercollegiate athletics in the United States have been the gradual opening of opportunities to previously excluded racial groups and the growth in women's varsity athletic programs and opportunities since the 1972 passage of Title IX. As an indicator of the successes of this legislation, and also of the continuing disparity between women's and men's college athletics, in 2001 ESPN purchased the women's basketball tournament broadcast rights for the same period for a relatively paltry $200 million. Many women's varsity programs have become exactly what the physical education professional leaders feared in the 1930s: competitive, commercialized, and constantly publicized. In short, women's athletics are also big-time now.

If the core characteristics of intercollegiate athletic programs would be familiar to a time-traveler from the 1930s, so too would the central criticisms voiced about these programs. Over the last couple of years, many significant critiques of the conduct and emphasis placed on intercollegiate athletics appeared in print. Through extensive coverage in the national press, including the *Washington Post, the New York Times,* the *Los Angeles Times*, and *the New Yorker*, these works sparked a wide-spread, public, and long-running discussion about the issues central to this study: How do universities finance their intercollegiate programs? How do they connect their athletic programs to educational missions and character building? How do big-time athletics affect the formation and operation of communities?

The current list of critics' concerns would sound distressingly familiar to Howard Savage and other authors of 1929's *American College Athletics*, as would many of the responses to the criticisms. This is not to imply that nothing has changed; much has. College athletics are unquestionably "cleaner" now than they were in the 1930s. Coaches do not gain national acclaim simply for refusing to buy players, and universities interested in maintaining their eligibility must do more than simply discourage their alumni from creating slush funds. Now, thanks to a much stronger—many would argue too strong—NCAA, observers can rest assured that all student athletes are at least enrolled in the universities they represent. That was simply not the case in the early decades of the 1900s.

Old arguments in support of college athletics die hard, and many continue to laud intercollegiate athletic programs for their education value. At least many praise the educational *potential* of athletic programs. For example, James Duderstadt, the former president of University of Michigan, explained his views in his largely critical *Intercollegiate Athletics and the American University*: "As a former student-athlete, as a faculty member, as an academic administrator, and, quite frankly, as a fan at the University of Michigan, I have long held the view that sports can contribute to the educational mission of the university." He did not, however, provide details about how this advancing of the educational mission occurs, stating only that it can. Duderstadt was much more specific when he echoed legions of other observers, both present and past, noting, "Varsity sports can provide unifying events that pull together the extraordinary complex and diverse communities that make up the contemporary university." Still, despite the potential educational benefits and the real community-building benefits of varsity athletics, Duderstadt recognized that unreformed intercollegiate athletics have the "potential to do great harm to the university."[1]

Other studies posit that athletics already are doing great harm to US colleges and their students and raise questions about the types of communities athletics are creating on US campuses. Indiana University's Murray Sperber entitled his 2000 critique *Beer and Circus: How Big-Time College Sports Is Crippling Undergraduate Education*, while, in 2001, James Shulman and William Bowen chose a more restrained title: *The Game of Life: College Sports and Educational Values*. With detailed descriptions of the connections between university students' binge drinking, gambling, excessive partying, and big-time athletics, and with chapter titles such as "Rally Round the Team—As Long as It Wins and Covers the Spread," Sperber argued that college sports certainly help create communities, but in doing so they foster values that undermine, not support, the educational core of US universities.[2]

With a different set of evidence and writing from different perspectives, Shulman and Bowen present an equally scathing, if more measured, critique of the ways intercollegiate athletics affect campus communities. As statisticians and officers of the Andrew W. Mellon Foundation (Bowen is the former president of Princeton University), these two authors put more than forty years of data from the nation's elite universities to good use. Since these authors focused on the most selective of US colleges and universities, some might expect that they would not find the same sorts of athletics-related problems that large, less selective, public universities face. Instead, they discovered that the problems are more pronounced and more troubling at their examined institutions. Shulman and Bowen argued, "*Athletics is a much more serious business, in terms of its direct impact on admissions and the composition and ethos of the student body, at an Ivy League school or coed liberal arts college than at a Division I university*" (emphasis in original). In schools with small student populations and numerous athletic programs, athletes can constitute almost 40 percent of the student body. These athletes enter these elite institutions with test scores and grade point averages well below the general student average; once matriculated, as a group they fail to do even as well as they had been projected to do. Moreover, the athletes, male and female, generally eschew traditional liberal arts majors in favor of more "practical" business and social science programs and insulate themselves within "jock" communities, thus further limiting their contact with their fellow students. By doing this, they fail to take advantage of the opportunities that their athletic abilities have provided for them and have, in real terms, taken from others. Shulman and Bowen concluded that the schools that allow this to happen, simply put, concentrate too much on athletics and "are not focused on fulfilling their educational mission."[3]

All of these studies highlight the problems associated with the hyper-commercialism in intercollegiate athletics, the root of most evil they associate with college sports, and they all offer suggestions about how to address the problems. The Knight Foundation Commission on Intercollegiate Athletics' 2001 report, entitled *A Call to Action: Reconnecting College Sports and Higher Education*, tries to rally the troops for reform with rhetoric that recalls the Cold War: "The athletics arms race continues only on the strength of the widespread belief that nothing can be done about it. Expenditures roar out of control only because administrators have become more concerned with financing what is in place than rethinking what they are doing." The report continues, arguing that "the market is able to invade the academy both because it is eager to do so and because overloaded administrators rarely take the time to think about the consequences" and offering a wide array of actions that would help them align more appropriately the influence and importance of athletics on US college campuses.[4] Finally, we are sure to soon have numerous scholarly studies adding to the countless journalistic critiques of the ways that Penn State University's football-first culture and the lack of leadership at several levels led to a crisis of criminal and moral scandal unparalleled in US sports history.

Despite the enormous number of positive changes in the operations of college athletics, those interested in changing the existing balance between the athletic and academic sides of US universities are still confronting the same problems and proposing the same types of solutions as did their predecessors many decades ago. If, however, the ideological and financial challenges of the 1930s could not force substantive changes, then the current reformers should not be too optimistic. After all, the same conditions that saved intercollegiate athletics during the Depression exist in more pronounced forms today: the universities have invested too much money on athletic infrastructure to drop the programs completely; their leaders feel that they must continue escalating the commercialization of the programs in order to pay for facilities and salaries and to keep up with their rivals; and through a wide variety of mass media, colleges can still gain much more attention and create deeper allegiances through college athletics than through any other tool at their disposal. Appropriately enough, while writing this epilogue I received a letter from the University of Tennessee Alumni Association announcing that my area's Volunteers will gather every week throughout the fall at a local restaurant to watch the football team play. I'm sure the turnout will be strong and the crowd enthusiastic. I might go myself.

NOTES

Introduction

1. *Ohio State University Monthly* 22 (October 1930): 2.

2. *Ohio State University Monthly* 23 (December 1931): 93; *Ohio State University Monthly* 24 (February 1933): 145.

3. "The Ohio State University Athletic Department Consolidated Statement of Receipts and Expenditures," 1–2; and "Detail of Football Receipts," 1–2, both in "The Ohio State University Athletic Department, Financial Statements," April 27, 1936 ("Athletic Board: Minutes: September 1934–June 1940," 9/e-1/1), Director of Athletics, The Ohio State University Archives, Columbus (hereafter cited as TOSUA).

4. There is an entire body of scholarship dedicated to explaining the importance of corporations to the direction of the New Deal and the essential conservatism of its reforms. See, in particular, Barton J. Bernstein, "The New Deal: The Conservative Achievements of Liberal Reform," in *Towards a New Past: Dissenting Essays in American History*, ed. Barton Berstein (London: Chatto and Windus, 1970); Howard Zinn, ed., *New Deal Thought* (Indianapolis: Bobbs-Merrill, 1966).

5. Lawrence W. Levine, "American Culture and the Great Depression," *Yale Review* 74 (January 1971): 196.

6. Warren I. Susman, *Culture as History: The Transformation of American Society in the Twentieth Century* (New York: Pantheon Books, 1984), 192–94. Susman correctly noted that this insecurity had more causes than the onset of the Depression, citing the instability caused by the characteristic American mobility, both social and physical, as another root.

7. Susman, *Culture as History,* 192.

8. See, in particular, Howard J. Savage, Harold W. Bentley, John T. McGovern, and Dean F. Smiley, *American College Athletics* (New York: Carnegie Foundation for the Advancement of Teaching, 1929); John R. Thelin, *Games Colleges Play: Scandal and Reform in Intercollegiate Athletics* (Baltimore: The Johns Hopkins University Press, 1994); John S. Watterson, *College Football: History, Spectacle, Controversy* (Baltimore: The Johns Hopkins University Press, 2000), chapters 9 and 10 in particular. Ronald Smith argued convincingly in his *Sports and Freedom* that no golden age of "pure" college sports ever existed. See Ronald A. Smith, *Sports and Freedom: The Rise of Big-Time College Athletics* (New York: Oxford University Press, 1988).

9. For more on the "progressive" view of sport, see R. Smith, *Sports and Freedom;* Donald J. Mrozek, *Sport and the American Mentality, 1880–1910* (Knoxville, University of Tennessee Press, 1983); Mark Dyreson, *Making the American Team: Sport, Culture, and the Olympic Experience* (Urbana: University of Illinois Press, 1998); Stephen Hardy, *How Boston Played: Sport, Recreation, and Community, 1865–1915* (Boston: Northeastern University Press, 1982); Steven A. Reiss, *City Games: The Evolution of American Urban Society and the Rise of Sports* (Urbana: University of

Illinois Press, 1989); Dominick Cavallo, *Muscles and Morals: Organized Playgrounds and Urban Reform, 1880–1920* (Philadelphia: University of Pennsylvania Press, 1981); Mark Dyerson, "Regulating the Body and the Body Politic: American Sport, Bourgeois Culture, and the Language of Progress, 1880–1920," in ,*The New American Sport History: Recent Approaches and Perspectives*, ed. Steven W. Pope (Urbana: University of Illinois Press, 1997), 121–45; Mark Dyerson, "The Emergence of Consumer Culture and the Transformation of Physical Culture: American Sport in the 1920s," *Journal of Sport History* 16 (1989): 261–81; Marc Horger, "Play by the Rules: The Creation of Basketball and the Progressive Era, 1891–1917" (PhD diss., Ohio State University, 2000).

10. See Helen L. Horowitz, *Campus Life: Undergraduate Cultures from the End of the Eighteenth Century to the Present* (New York: Alfred A. Knopf, 1987), 160–66; Frederick Rudolph, *The American College and University: A History* (New York: Vintage Books, 1965), 465–88; David O. Levine, *The American College and the Culture of Aspiration, 1915–1940* (Ithaca, NY: Cornell University Press, 1986), 204–7.

11. See, especially, Stephanie J. Shaw, *What a Woman Ought to Be and to Do: Black Professional Women Workers during the Jim Crow Era* (Chicago: University of Chicago Press, 1996); Susan K. Cahn, *Coming on Strong: Gender and Sexuality in Twentieth-Century Women's Sport* (New York: Free Press, 1994).

12. See, especially, Cahn, *Coming on Strong;* Ellen Gerber, "The Controlled Development of Collegiate Sport for Women, 1923–1936," *Journal of Sport History* 2 (1975):1–28; Joan S. Hult, "The Governance of Athletics for Girls and Women: Leadership by Women Physical Educators, 1899–1949," *Research Quarterly* (Centennial Issue, 1985): 64–77; Ronald Smith, "Women's Control of American College Sport: The Good of Those Who Played or an Exploitation by Those Who Controlled It?," *Sport History Review* 29 (May 1988): 103–20.

CHAPTER 1. In the "Trough of a Depression"

1. David O. Levine wrote, "American higher education fared better than most social institutions during the Depression. The value of higher education was rarely questioned. . . . In the face of adversity, then, American higher education consolidated and even strengthened its position in modern American society." See Levine, *The American College and the Culture of Aspiration*, 185. Levine also noted that the Depression shook "the confidence of American higher education"; he continued, "Though few colleges closed their doors in the 1930s, many were plagued by the constant fear of impending financial disaster" (186).

2. Harvey Green, *The Uncertainty of Everyday Life, 1915–1945*, Everyday Life in America ser., ed. Richard Balkin (New York: HarperCollins, 1992), 127.

3. "Analysis of Attendance at the Main University, Long Session, 1910–11 to 1929–30," Harry Y. Benedict Papers, Literary Production: History of University of Texas, Research Material, General Faculty Information, 1928–1937, Center for American History (CAH), University of Texas Archives (UTXA), Austin (hereafter cited as Benedict Papers, CAH, UTXA); Verne A. Stadtman, ed., *The Centennial Record of the University of California* (Berkeley: University of California Press, 1967), 219–20.

4. James Riley Montgomery, *Threshold of a New Day: The University of*

Tennessee, 1919–1946 (Knoxville: University of Tennessee, 1971), 272; James E. Pollard, *History of the Ohio State University: The Story of Its First Seventy-Five Years, 1873–1948* (Columbus: Ohio State University Press, 1952), 256 and 293.

5. Donald W. Whisenhunt, *The Depression in Texas: The Hoover Years* (New York: Garland Publishing, 1983), 105. John A. Douglass advanced an argument similar to Whisenhunt's. Discussing the University of California's enrollment trends, Douglass noted, "State government experienced a significant decline in revenues and proceeded to make massive cuts in public education funding. At the same time, a weak employment market for high school graduates increased the attractiveness of a college education." John A. Douglass, "Californians and Public Higher Education: Political Culture, Educational Opportunity, and State Policymaking," *History of Higher Education Annual* (16) 1996: 82; H. Y. Benedict to E. A. Burnett, December 17, 1936 ("Questionnaires, Sept 1, 1936—," VF 18/A.a*)*, University of Texas President's Office Records, 1907–1968, CAH, UTXA. University of Texas president Harry Benedict responded to a 1935 letter from a friend looking for a job in this way: "Such a swarm of job applications surround me all the time that I am forced to urge almost anybody to hold on like grim death to any job they happen to have." H. Y. Benedict to Jonnie Fay Ashby, March 26, 1935 ("'A' Correspondence," 2B59), Benedict Papers, CAH, UTXA.

6. Stadtman, *The Centennial Record of the University of California*, 221–22.

7. Montgomery, *Threshold of a New Day*, 272.

8. A poor old Country Boy, unknown, to H. Y. Benedict, E. J. Matthews, and Dr. Parlin, September 18, 1931 ("Office of President, 1929–1932," VF 4/D.a,), President's Office Records, 1907–1968, CAH, UTXA.

9. "Press Release: 'For Release to Morning Papers of Sunday, November, 1936'" ("Correspondence, Addresses, October, 1934–April, 1936," 2B59), Benedict Papers, Office of the President, CAH, UTXA.

10. Ibid.; "Comptroller's Report for the Year 1929–30" ("Comptroller," VF 11/D), President's Office Records, 1907–1968, CAH, UTXA; Copy of "President Benedict's Speech over Station KRLD, Dallas, 8:30–8:45 P.M., March 2, 1935" ("Addresses Oct. 1934–April 1936," Correspondence, 2B59), Benedict Papers, U.T. Files, Office of President, CAH, UTXA.

11. "Commencement Address," August 26, 1935 ("Correspondence, Addresses, Oct., 1934–April, 1936," 2B59), Benedict Papers, CAH, UTXA.

12. "Summary of General Budgets, The University of Texas, Distributed to Faculty at Budge Meeting, June 17, 1931" ("Office of the President-Miscellaneous, 1932–34," VF 4/D.a), President's Office Records, 1907–1968, CAH, UTXA. The cost-of-living calculations were done using the website http://www.westegg.com/inflation/. It explains its methodology by writing that "the pre-1975 data are the Consumer Price Index statistics from *Historical Statistics of the United States* (USGPO, 1975). All data since then are from the annual *Statistical Abstracts of the United States*." See S. Morgan Friedman, *The Inflation Calculator,* available online at http://www.westegg.com/inflation/, accessed October 4, 2014.

13. Verne A. Stadtman, *The University of California, 1868–1968* (New York: McGraw-Hill, 1970), 257–58.

14. Ibid., 258.

15. University of California (System), Office of the President, *Report of the*

President of the University of California, 1930–1932 University of California Bulletin, 3rd ser., 25, no. 7 (December 1932) (Berkley: University of California Press, 1932): 7–8.

16. Ibid., 8.

17. *University of California Budget for 1929–30*, 3; *University of California Budget for 1930–31*, 3; *University of California Budget for 1931–32*, 3; *University of California Budget for 1932–32*, 3; quotes from Office of the President, *Report of the President of the University of California, 1930–32, 36; University of California Budget for 1933–34*, 3; *University of California Budget for 1934–35*, 3; *University of California Budget for 1935–36, 3; University of California Budget for 1936–37*; 3; *University of California Budget for 1937–38*, 1; *University of California Budget for 1938–39*, 1; and *University of California Budget for 1939–40*, 1.

18. University of California (System), Office of the President, *Report of the President of the University of California, 1936–38, University of California Bulletin*, 3rd ser., 30) (Berkeley: University of California Press, 1938): 1, 3, 5; University of California (System), Office of the President, *Report of the President of the University of California, 1938–1940, University of California Bulletin*, 3rd ser., 32 (Berkeley: University of California Press, 1940): 1.

19. Montgomery, *Threshold of a New Day*, 90, 92, 94.

20. J. J. Walker to Dr. H. A. Morgan, February 21, 1933 ("X. Budget and Finances—C. Annual Budgets—9. 1931–31, AR-l, box 3), President's Papers, 1867–1954, University of Tennessee Special Collections, Hoskins Library, Knoxville (hereafter cited as SC, UTNK); *Orange and White* (Knoxville, TN), November 3, 1931

21. Montgomery, *Threshold of a New Day*, 95, 97.

22. J. J. Walker to Roy C. Wallace, January 16, 1933 ("X. Budget and Finances—C. Annual Budgets—9. 1931–31," AR-l, box 3), President's Papers, 1867–1954, SC, UTNK.

23. Minutes of the Annual Meeting, Board of Trustees, the University of Tennessee, July 31, 1933, 280–81, SC, UTNK.

24. Examples of these letters abound in the President's Papers files related to budgets. For specific examples, see J. J. Walker to C. M. Preston, Knoxville, December 20, 1932, and J. J. Walker to H. A. Morgan, April 10, 1933 ("X. Budget and Finances—C. Annual Budgets—9. 1931–31," AR-l, box 3), President's Papers, 1867–1954, SC, UTNK.

25. Montgomery, *Threshold of a New Day*, 116–17.

26. Paul H. Bergeron, Stephen V. Ash, and Jeanette Keith, *Tennesseans and Their History* (Knoxville: University of Tennessee Press, 1999), 276–77; Montgomery, *Threshold of a New Day*, 117.

27. Minutes of the Annual Meeting, Board of Trustees, the University of Tennessee, December 3, 1938; Budget director Henry Burke's quote is found in Montgomery, *Threshold of a New Day*, 119.

28. Montgomery, *Threshold of a New Day*, 120–21. In the segregated South of the 1930s, the Democratic Party was often the only political party of real significance and power; therefore, winning the Democratic primary was tantamount to winning the general election because few serious challenges arose from outside the Democratic Party. However, in Tennessee the situation was slightly different because East Tennessee has traditionally been predominantly Republican. Nonetheless, as one scholar has noted about 1930s Tennessee politics, "The

Republican vote, concentrated in east Tennessee, was insufficient to threaten Democratic control of the governorship. The candidate who amassed the approximately 150,000 votes necessary to win the Democratic primary became governor of Tennessee." Candidates with the support of Memphis's political boss, Edward Crump, needed only 100,000 additional votes because Crump could guarantee 50,000. Bergeron, Ash, and Keith, *Tennesseans and Their History*, 273.

29. Hoskins, quoted in "Education Will Solve South's Problem says President," *Tennessee Alumnus* 19 (August 1939): 3.

30. Ibid.

31. Montgomery, *Threshold of a New Day*, 120–21.

32. George Callcott, *A History of the University of Maryland* (Baltimore: Maryland Historical Society, 1966), 282.

33. Callcott, *History of the University of Maryland*, 299–304, also 284. Callcott wrote that Pearson "lack[ed] an educational philosophy" and that he did not want to do anything "with a university besides keep it running, and such an attitude on the part of an academic administrator is likely to be disastrous." See Callcott, *History of the University of Maryland*, 299.

34. Callcott, *History of the University of Maryland*, 299.

35. "Annual Income for Educational Purposes from State and Federal Appropriations and Other Sources" ("Statement of Income by Years 1920–21 to 1935–36 Inclusive, University of Maryland and State Board of Agriculture, Office of Comptroller, November 17, 1936," ser. 8, box S1), ACC 94–85, Records of the President's Office, Unprocessed, Special Collections, University of Maryland Library (hereafter cited as SC, UML); Callcott, *History of the University of Maryland*, 300; "Annual Income for Educational Purposes from State and Federal Appropriations and Other Sources"; "Annual Income from State and Federal Appropriations and Other Sources for Educational Purposes Based on a One Hundred Dollar Unit" ("Statement of Income by Years 1920–21 to 1935–36 Inclusive, University of Maryland and State Board of Agriculture, Office of Comptroller, November 17, 1936," ser. 8, box Sl), ACC 94–85, Records of the President's Office, Unprocessed, SC, UML; "Average Annual Income per Student from State and Federal Appropriations and Other Sources for Educational Purposes" ("Statement of Income by Years 1920–21 to 1935–36 Inclusive, University of Maryland and State Board of Agriculture, Office of Comptroller, November 17, 1936," ser. 8, box S1), ACC 94–85, Records of the President's Office, Unprocessed, SC, UML.

36. Callcott, *History of the University of Maryland*, 300. Some professors complained publicly about the state of the state's university, arguing that "a building program is a laudable thing, and highly to be commended, but it should always be strictly secondary to the real university, the association of faculty and students in enthusiastic devotion to learning." See Callcott, *History of the University of Maryland*, 303; A. E. Zucker, "The Real Issue at the University of Maryland," *Washington Post*, May 16, 1935; "Terrapins in Scholarship," *Washington Post*, May 7, 1935; Callcott, *History of the University of Maryland*, 311.

37. Callcott, *History of the University of Maryland*, 313–19. As Callcott explained, it would be hard to overemphasize the importance of Byrd to the University of Maryland. He helped found the intramural program and the Southern Intercollegiate Athletic Conference. He picked and named the university mascot,

lent his own name to the football stadium, and helped create the alumni board. See Callcott, *History of the University of Maryland*, 321, for more details.

38. Callcott, *History of the University of Maryland*, 323–24.

39. "Meeting of the Board of Regents, 19 May 1933" (Book 3, ser. 4, box 1); "Meeting of the Board of Regents, 22 April 1935" (Book 3, ser. 4, box 1); "Meeting of the Board of Regents, 19 March 1937" (Book 4, ser. 4, box 2); "Meeting of the Board of Regents, 29 September 1937," (Book 4, ser. 4, box 2), all from Records of the Board of Regents, SC, UML; Callcott, *History of the University of Maryland*, 328.

40. H. C. Byrd to Charles T. Woolent, November 16, 1937 ("H. C. Byrd, 1937–44," ser. 1, box 1), Papers of Geary Eppley, SC, UML.

41. "Meeting of the Board of Regents, 21 May 1939" (Book 5, ser. 4, box 2); "Meeting of the Board of Regents, 26 May 1939" (Book 5, ser. 4, box 2); "Meeting of the Board of Regents, 20 October 1939" (Book 5, ser. 4, box 2); "Meeting of the Board of Regents, 21 June 1940" (Book 5, ser. 4, box 2), all from Records of the Board of Regents, SC, UML.

42. "Exhibit A: General Salary Reduction Rule Adopted by the Legislature in Preparing the 1933–35 Appropriation Bill" ("Office of the President—Miscellaneous, 1932–34," VF 4/D.a), President's Office Records, 1907–1968, CAH, UTXA; "Table Number Two" ("Special Committee on the Budget," VF 5/C.B), President's Office Records, 1907–1968, CAH, UTXA; "Exhibit A: General Salary Reduction Rule Adopted by the Legislature in Preparing the 1933–35 Appropriation Bill," CAH, UTXA; E. C. Barker et al. to the President and the Honorable Board of Regents of The University of Texas, June 2, 1933 ("Office of the President—Miscellaneous, 1932–34," VF 4/D.a), President's Office Records, 1907–1968, CAH, UTXA.

43. Judging from one table attached to the above-cited "Exhibit A," many, if not all, of the exemptions went to professors working in the medical sciences.

44. Again, even after taking considerable deflation into account, the cuts were damaging. According to http://westegg.com/inflation/, $100.00 in 1935 was worth $129.45 in 1928. So, although the real value of money had increased almost 30 percent, that still did not offset the almost 60 percent in decline in per student spending. See again, Friedman, *The Inflation Calculator*, available online at http://www.westegg.com/inflation/, accessed October 4, 2014.

45. H. Y. Benedict et al. to James V. Allred et al., January 26, 1937 ("Office of the President, 1936–37," VF 4/D.a), President's Office Records, 1907–1968, CAH, UTXA.

46. "Reasons for Salary Changes" ("Office of the President, 1936–37," VF 4/D.a), President's Office Records, 1907–1968, CAH, UTXA.

47. *Ohio State University Monthly* 22 (October 1930): 2.

48. *Ohio State University Monthly* 24 (February 1933): 145.

49. "University History ser.: Decade of 1930–1940—Weathering the Depression," *Ohio State University Monthly* 40 (April 1949): 28; George Rightmire, "Annual Report of the President," *Sixty-Second Annual Report of the Board of Trustees of the Ohio State University to the Governor of Ohio, for the Year Ending June 30, 1931* (Columbus: Ohio State University, 1931), 22; "University History ser.: Decade of 1930–1940—Weathering the Depression," 28; quotes from pages 22 and 23, respectively, in Rightmire, "Annual Report of the President."

50. *Ohio State University Monthly* 23 (December 1931): 93.

51. Ibid.

52. "University History ser.: Decade of 1930–1940—Weathering the Depression," 29.

53. Academic year 1933–34 statistics are from *Sixty-Fourth Annual Report of the Board of Trustees of the Ohio State University to the Governor of Ohio, for the Year Ending June 30, 1934* (Columbus: Ohio State University, 1934), 39–42; John B. Fullen,"University Trims Sails," *Ohio State University Monthly* 25 (October 1931): 3–4.

54. Pollard, *History of the Ohio State University*, 309; quote from *Ohio State University Monthly* 24 (February 1933): 145.

55. George Rightmire "Annual Report of the President," *Sixty-Third Annual Report of the Board of Trustees of the Ohio State University to the Governor of Ohio, for the Year Ending June 30, 1933* (Columbus: Ohio State University, 1933), 9.

56. *Sixty-Fourth Annual Report of the Board of Trustees of the Ohio State University to the Governor of Ohio, for the Year Ending June 30, 1934*, 37–38.

57. Richard O. Davies, *American Obsession: Sports and Society since 1945* (Forth Worth: Harcourt Brace College Publishers, 1994), 20–21, quote on 21.

58. Quote from *Sixty-Eighth Annual Report of the Board of Trustees of the Ohio State University to the Governor of Ohio, for the Year Ending June 30, 1938* (Columbus: Ohio State University, 1938), 10.

59. Budget information from fiscal year 1936–37 is from *Sixty-Seventh Annual Report of the Board of Trustees of the Ohio State University to the Governor of Ohio, for the Year Ending June 30, 1937* (Columbus: Ohio State University, 1937), 122–25; budget information from 1939–40 is from *Seventieth Annual Report of the Board of Trustees of the Ohio State University to the Governor of Ohio, for the Year Ending June 30, 1940*, (Columbus: Ohio State University, 1940), 14–18; both quotes and all information are from "University History ser.: Decade of 1930–1940—Weathering the Depression," 31.

60. Callcott, *History of the University of Maryland*, 302 and 303; "Report of Committee Appointed by President of the Senate of Maryland to Investigate the Affairs of the University of Maryland," February 16, 1933, 9–10, quote on 9 ("Legislative Investigation [1933]," ser. 7, box 20), ACC 94–85, Records of the President's Office, SC, UML.

61. "American Association of University Professors Committee on Effect of Depression and Recovery on Higher Education, Salaries Appointment, and Promotion Policies," 1935 ("Questionnaires, [1 of 3]," ser. 8, box 32) ACC 94–85, Records of the President's Office, SC, UML; "Report of Committee Appointed by President of the Senate," 14.

62. Callcott, *History of the University of Maryland*, 303.

63. "Comparison of Enrollment and State Support, University of California—All Campuses," *Report of the President of the University of California, 1936–38* (Berkeley: University of California Press, 1939), 16.

64. *Report of the President of the University o/California, 1930–32*, 8; *Report of the President of the University of California, 1932–34*, 16 *University of California Bulletin*, 3rd ser., 28, no. 10(December 1934) Berkeley: University of California Press, 1934), 16; Stadtman, *The University of California*, 259; *Report of the President of the University of California, 1932–34*, 16.

65. Stadtman, *Centennial Record of the University of California*, 264.

66. Quotes from *Report of the President of the University of California, 1936–38*, 14.

67. *Ohio State University Monthly* 25 (February 1934): 155; George Rightmire, "Annual Report of the President," *Sixty-Fourth Annual Report of the Board of Trustees of the Ohio State University to the Governor of Ohio, for the Year Ending June 30, 1934*, 31–33; quote from George Rightmire, "Annual Report of the President," *Sixty-Fifth Annual Report of the Board of Trustees of the Ohio State University to the Governor of Ohio, for the Year Ending June 30, 1935* (Columbus: Ohio State University, 1935), 9.

68. *Report of the President of the University of California, 1936–38*, 18.

69. Ibid.; *California Monthly* 36 (June 1936).

70. H. Y. Benedict to C. D. Simmons, November 28, 1932 ("UT Buildings Erected with Federal Aid," VF 15/D.B), President's Office Records, 1907–1968, CAH, UTXA.

71. C. D. Simmons to H. Y. Benedict, December 2, 1932 ("UT Buildings Erected with Federal Aid," VF 15/D.B), President's Office Records, 1907–1968, CAH, UTXA; H. Y. Benedict to Burnett, December 17, 1936. President's Office Records, 1907–1968, CAH, UTXA.

72. Montgomery, *Threshold of a New Day*, 104–8; Bergeron, Ash, and Keith, *Tennesseans and Their History*, 260.

73. Montgomery, *Threshold of a New Day*, 128–30.

74. Ibid., 129.

75. List of Committee of Women's Athletics (CWA) projects ("XII. Civil Works Administration (1933–1935)," AR–1, box 4), President's Papers, 1867–1954, SC, UTNK; Montgomery, *Threshold of a New Day*, 130.

76. F. M. Massey to James D. Hoskins, January 17, 1938 (Folder "No. 12 [2], Stadium project, 1938–40," box 2), Tennessee "Business Manager . . . , 1932–52," University Papers, SC, UTNK.

77. Callcott, *History of the University of Maryland*, 325; Geary Eppley to Ryland N. Dempster, May 7, 1936 ("National Youth Administration, 1936," ser. 1, box 7), Papers of Geary Eppley, SC, UML; Callcott, *History of the University of Maryland*, 325.

78. Callcott, *History of the University of Maryland*, 325–26.

CHAPTER 2. Financed by Football

1. Benjamin Rader, *American Sports: From the Age of Folk Games to the Age of Televised Sports*, 3rd ed. (Englewood Cliffs, NJ: Prentice Hall, 1996), 182; Savage et al., *American College Athletics*, 87. See Raymond Schmidt's *Shaping College Football: The Transformation of an American Sport, 1919–1930* (Syracuse, NY: Syracuse University Press, 2007) for a comprehensive examination of the expansion and successes of college football during the 1920s.

2. K. L. Wilson, "Present-Day Financial Problems in University Athletics," *College Physical Education Association Proceedings* 27–28 (December 1933): 14; Clarence Robert Barnett, "College Athletics and Physical Education in Ohio During the Depression" (PhD diss., Ohio State University, 1972), 85.

3. Information on seating is from "Stadium Scrip," *California Monthly* (July

1930): 15; information on the dedication of the stadium is from Stadtman, *The University of California, 288.*

4. Savage et al., *American College Athletics,* 87; W. W. Campbell to W. W. Monahan and L. A. Nichols, January 25, 1930 ("1930:730," CU-5, ser. 2), Office of the President Papers, University of California, Berkley (hereafter cited as UCB); J. A. Nichols, "Statement Regarding Southwest Athletic Area," October 2, 1930 ("1930:730," CU-5, ser. 2), Office of the President Papers, UCB.

5. W. W. Monahan to W. W. Campbell, February 3, 1930 ("1930:730," CU-5, ser. 2), Office of the President Papers, UCB.

6. Savage et al.'s *American College Athletics* argued that the University of California and Ohio State University had something else in common; Savage contended that they both belonged in the group of universities that decided "to erect stadiums for football and other branches before providing adequate indoor facilities." See Savage et al., *American College Athletics,* 91.

7. James E. Pollard, *Ohio State Athletics, 1879–1959 (Columbus: Ohio State University Athletic Department, 1959),* 117–22.

8. Ibid., 117–29. See also "A History of the Major Capital Obligations and Expenditures," 2–3 ("Budget: Athletic Department: Financial History of: 1922–1935; 1937–1942," 9/e–1/5), Director of Athletics, TOSUA.

9. "A History of the Major Capital Obligations and Expenditures," 1 and 3.

10. Pollard, *Ohio State Athletics,* 220.

11. Savage et al.'s *American College Athletics* reports on some of the lesser athletic revenue totals as well. For example, Baylor University made only $10,000 a year in athletic profits, while Cornell University netted only $19,000. Southern Methodist University athletic programs produced $117,000 in gross revenue and a profit of $27,000. As the text will demonstrate, the Universities of Texas, Tennessee, and Maryland invite more appropriate comparisons with these institutions than with the biggest of the big-time programs, such as at the University of California and Ohio State. See Savage et al., *American College Athletics,* 87. Athletic Council Minutes, February 6, 1929, 212; Athletic Council Minutes, February 12, 1929, 214; Athletic Council Minutes, October 22, 1929, 227; Athletic Council Minutes, November 25, 1929, 229, all located in the conference room of the University of Texas athletic director's office; response to *Chicago Daily News* Almanac Questionnaire, July 15, 1936 ("Questionnaires, September 1, 1936–," VF 18/lLa), President's Office Records, 1907–1968, CAH, UTXA; Brad Austin, "'College Would Be a Dead Old Dump without It': Intercollegiate Athletics in East Tennessee during the Depression Era," *Journal of East Tennessee History* 69 (1997): 46–47.

12. W. H. Hottell, "Many Improvements in Athletic Plant," *Maryland Alumni News* (June 1930): 3.

13. February 21, 1930, Minutes, Book 2, 300–301 (box 1, ser. IV), Records of the Board of Regents, UML; May 25, 1931, Minutes, Book 2, 354 (box 1, ser. IV), Records of the Board of Regents, UML; "Athletic Building to Be Dedicated," *Maryland Alumni News* (January 1932): 1.

14. For the best example of a school that did choose to abandon its "big-time" program, see Robin Lester, *Stagg's University: The Rise, Decline, and Fall of Football at the University of Chicago* (Urbana: University of Illinois Press, 1994).

15. "Football Viewed as Facing Crisis," *New York Times,* January 3, 1931, 13.

16. Ibid.

17. "Reports Football Wanes in Colleges," *New York Times*, June 15, 1931, 12.

18. Meeting of the Board of Regents, May 10, 1929 (Book 2, box 1, ser. 4), Records of the Board of Regents, SC, UML; H. C. Byrd to Craig Taylor, December 28, 1932 ("Correspondence, 1932, October–December," box 3, ser. 1), Papers of Harry C. Byrd, SC, UML; "Spring Sport Hope at Maryland Dimmed by Banking Problem," *Washington News*, March 7, 1933; H. C. Byrd to S. V. Sanford, March 2, 1933 ("Southern Conference, 1933," box 10, ser. 2), Papers of Geary Eppley, SC, UML.

19. W. H. Hottel, "Taking a Glimpse at Athletics in Maryland," *Maryland Alumni News* 4 (June 1933): 4.

20. "Appendix C (To Docket for [Board of Regents] Meeting of January 5, 1931)" ("Intercollegiate Athletic Council, 1929–1933," VF 5 *EIB)*, President's Office Records, 1907–1968, CAH, UTXA.

21. "Summary of Net Football Receipts 1928 to 1937" ("Intercollegiate Athletics, 1936–1937," VF 5/E.B), President's Office Records, 1907–1968, CAH, UTXA. The net football receipts fell from roughly $104,000 in the 1930–31 fiscal year to $85,000 in 1931–32 and to $69,000 in 1932–33, bottoming out at $45,000 in 1933–34. This last total was a mere 43 percent of the 1930–31 total. According to the website for the American Institute for Economic Research (AIER), the 1933–34 total was worth $57,807 in 1930 dollars. See American Institute for Economic Research, *A.I.E.R. Inflation Calculator,* available online at http://www.aier.orglcgi-bin/colcalculator.cgi, accessed August 15, 2001.

22. "Intercollegiate Athletics: Net Gain or Loss by Sports, Years Ending August 31" ("Intercollegiate Athletics, 1932–1934," VF 5/E.B*)*UTXA; and "Comparison of Gain and Loss by Sports: For the Fiscal Years Ended August 31, 1932, 1933, 1934, 1935–36," October 6, 1936 ("Intercollegiate Athletics, 1936–37," VF 5/E.B.), both in President's Office Records, 1907–1968, CAH, UTXA.

23. J. W. Coombs to Thomas S. Shibe, November 28, 1932 ("Southern Conference, 1932 March–December," box 10, ser. 2), Papers of Geary Eppley, SC, UML.

24. See "Excerpts from Minutes of Meeting of the Directors of Athletics of the Intercollegiate Conference, Friday December 4, 1931 at the Sheraton Hotel in Chicago" ("Intercollegiate Conference—Athletic Director's Correspondence, 1930–1938" 9/e-1/9), Director of Athletics, TOSUA; Ralph W. Aigler, "Financial Aspects of the University's Athletic Program" ("Addresses and Articles: 1931–1941," 9/e–111), Director of Athletics, TOSUA. Again, according to the ALER, deflation made the $152,000 the equivalent of $189,722 in 1929 dollars.

25. "The Ohio State University Athletic Department Consolidated Statement of Receipts and Expenditures," 1–2; "Detail of Football Receipts," 1–2; and ""Projected Budget," 1, all in "The Ohio State University Athletic Department, Financial Statements," April 27, 1936 ("Athletic Board: Minutes: September 1934–June 1940," 9/e–1/1), Director of Athletics, TOSUA.

26. Ibid. The $129,000 in the 1932–33 fiscal year, according to the ALER, was equal to $169,839 in 1928. Even with this adjusted figure, the total drop was more than 60 percent from the 1927–28 and the 1929–30 totals.

27. "Associated Students—University of California, Income and Expense by Departments—Jan. 1 to Dec. 31, 1919" ("1930:730," ser. 2, CU-5), Office of the President Papers, UCB; "Associated Students University of California Statement

of Financial Conditions, December 31, 1933," ("1933:100," ser. 2, CU-5), Office of the President Papers, UCB.

28. Herbert Simons, "Football Dollars Pay the Freight for Other Sports at Illinois," *Chicago Times* January 29, 1939 ("Intercollegiate Conference: *Chicago Times* Articles (Big Ten Articles): 1939," RG 9/e- 119), Director of Athletics, SC, TOSUA.

29. "Is Football Interest Waning?," *Journal of Health and Physical Education* 2 (December 1931): 22; see also Thelin, *Games Colleges Play, 26–27.*

30. Thelin, *Games Colleges Play,* 77–78; Edward Crane to H. Y. Benedict, October 20, 1932 ("Intercollegiate Athletic Council, 1930–1932," VF 5/E.b), President's Office Records, 1907–1968, CAH, UTXA; "Summary of Receipts and Disbursements for the Period September 1931 to Apri11, 1932," 2 ("Intercollegiate Athletic Council," VF 5 E/B.b), President's Office Records, 1907–1968, CAH, UTXA.

31. Edward Randall to H. Y. Benedict, October 20, 1931, and Leslie Waggener to R. Y. Benedict, October 20, 1931 ("Intercollegiate Athletic Council, 1930–1932," VF 5/E.b), President's Office Records, 1907–1968, CAH, UTXA.

32. Robert G. Sproul to W. W. Monahan, March 4, 1935 ("1935: 500," CU-5, ser. 2), Office of the President Papers, UCB; Thelin, *Games Colleges Play,* 55–56. The University of California was only one of many institutions that looked to Harvard and Yale Universities for leadership or guidance. In this letter, UC president Robert G. Sproul asked his director of men's physical education to explain in more detail a recent Harvard, Yale, and Princeton agreement regarding intercollegiate athletics. Sproul wrote, "It would aid me greatly if you could find time in the near future to draft a set of rules and regulations for the U of California, similar to those set forth in the Harvard U. booklet, for instance. The whole question of our athletic policy is to be up for discussion and determination in the near future, as we go out to select a new football coach, and I should like to have your ideas in definite and concrete form and to put as many of them as possible into effect in our future athletic program." Robert G. Sproul to Frank Kleeberger, November 26, 1930 (1930:371, ser. 2, CU-5), Office of the President Papers, UCB. In 1935, Sproul tried to help negotiate a crew competition with a joint UCB and UCLA team rowing against a combined Harvard-Yale or Oxford-Cambridge team. When it was clear that this would not occur, Sproul encouraged the ASUC general manager to find two other "first-class universities" against which the combined California teams could compete.

33. Thomas E. Putnam to Robert G. Sproul, March 23, 1931 ("1931:504," CU-5, ser. 2), Office of President Papers, UCB.

34. Information for this paragraph and the following graph comes from the "Summary of Receipts and Disbursements" for the 1930–31, 1931–32, 1932–33, 1933–34, and 1935–36 school years. The information for 1934–35 came from a similar document with a different name, "Receipts and Disbursements." The statements covering the years 1930–34 are located in "Intercollegiate Athletics, 1932–34" (VF *5/E.B),* President's Office Records, 1907–1968, CAH, UTXA. The remaining documents are located in "Intercollegiate Athletics, 1934–35" and "Intercollegiate Athletics, 1935–36" (VF *5/E.B),* President's Office Records, 1907–1968, CAH, UTXA.

35. "Detail of Football Receipts," in "The Ohio State University Athletic Department: Financial Statements," April 27, 1936 ("Athletic Board: Minutes: Sept. 1934–June 1940," 9/e–111), Director of Athletics, TOSUA. In 1931 when the OSU Athletic Board was discussing the possibility of playing a game against the

University of Notre Dame and donating the proceeds to charity, a guest argued that such a game in Cleveland would attract 100,000 fans willing to pay three dollars each for tickets. Although the game never materialized, surely the members of the OSU Athletic Board did not forget the revenue potential such a game offered. See OSU Athletic Board Minutes, November 2, 1931, 170–71, Director of Athletics, TOSUA.

36. The OSU Athletic Board agreed to play the two games with the University of Notre Dame in its January 17, 1933, meeting. Only one member, Justin Morrill, voted against the two-game series. Although neither the board of trustees' minutes nor the athletic board minutes indicate why Ohio State was interested in inaugurating a series then, one can speculate that the drawing power of Notre Dame and the potential revenue the games would generate must have seemed particularly attractive in early 1933. Detail of football receipts, Ohio State University Athletic Department Financial Statements; Murray Sperber, *Shake Down the Thunder: The Creation of Notre Dame Football* (New York: Henry Holt, 1993), 436–37; OSU Athletic Board Minutes, June 3, 1936 ("Athletic Board: Minutes: 1934–1940," RG 9e–1/1, 1), Director of Athletics, TOSUA.

37. Pollard, *Ohio State Athletics,* 281.

38. "Klandestine Klan Created to Further Stadium Drive," *Ohio State Lantern,* October 25, 1925, 1; Sperber, *Shake Down the Thunder,* 158–62.

39. *Columbus Dispatch,* October 31, 1935; *Columbus Dispatch,* November 1, 1935; Sperber, *Shake Down the Thunder,* 435.

40. Charles T. Forster to L. W. St. John, January 15, 1940, Notre Dame University —Resumption of the OSU–Notre Dame Football Relations—1940 (RG 9/e–1/14), Director of Athletics, TOSUA; Rader, *American Sports,* 187.

41. L. W. St. John to Charles T. Forster, January 31, 1940, Notre Dame University —Resumption of the OSU–Notre Dame Football Relations—1940, 1–3. For information on Ohio State's students' religious affiliations during these years, see Annual Report of the Registrar—1935–36 (Book I), Office of the Registrar (RG 6/f–3/3), TOSUA; Annual Report of the Registrar—1936–37, Office of the Registrar (RG 6/f–3/4), TOSUA.

42. John Griffith to L. W. St. John, November 15, 1938, Intercollegiate Conference—Commissioner Correspondence (Griffith) 1938–Mar. 1939 (RG 9/e–1/10), Director of Athletics, TOSUA; L. W. St. John to John Griffith, November 21, 1938, Intercollegiate Conference—Commissioner Correspondence (Griffith) 1938–Mar. 1939, TOSUA.

43. "Numbers of Tickets Sold" and (for information from chart) "Detail of Football Receipts," both in "The Ohio State University Athletic Department: Financial Statements," April 27, 1936 ("Athletic Board: Minutes: Sept. 1934–June 1940," 9/e–1/1), Director of Athletics, TOSUA.

44. OSU Athletic Board Minutes, February 22, 1932, 191 ("Athletic Board: Minutes: 1927–1934," 9/e–l/l).

45. "Number of Tickets Sold," April 27, 1936.

46. Ibid.

47. L. W. St. John to Edward H. Laurer, May 6, 1932 ("Intercollegiate Conference —Athletic Director's Correspondence, 1930–1938," 9/e–1/9), Director of Athletics, TOSUA.

48. University of Texas Athletic Council Minutes, June 7, 1933, 333, and June 12, 1934, 358. University of Maryland president H. C. Byrd maintained his interest in athletics long after he left the sidelines. In 1938, Byrd wrote to the University of Michigan's athletic director, Geary Eppley, explaining why he thought some upcoming games deserved higher ticket prices than others. As Byrd saw it, "the idea of charging $1.65 and $1.10 for the Western Maryland game, with the situation that now exists up there, and $1.50 and .75 for the games with Virginia and V. M. I., and $1.65 and $1.10 for the Georgetown and W. & L. games, cannot be sustained by any reasonable measure. . . . [I]t seems to me that if the Georgetown game is going to be worth anything, it should be a $2.00 game. Furthermore, it would seem to me that the Homecoming Game could well be a $2.00 game." See H. C. Byrd to Geary Eppley, August 24, 1938 ("Football, 1937–39," ser. 2, box 5), Papers of Geary Eppley, SC, UML.

49. Meeting of the Board of Regents, May 10, 1929 (Book 2, ser. 4, box 1), Records of the Board of Regents, SC, UML; "Contract with Naval Academy," ("Contracts, 1930–1935," ser. 2, box 3), Papers of Geary Eppley, SC, UML.

50. "Maryland-Navy Football Game," November 12, 1932 ("Ticket Sales, 1932–47," ser. 2, box 15), Papers of Geary Eppley, SC, UML; "Maryland vs. Washington and Lee," November 19, 1932 ("Ticket Sales, 1932–47," ser. 2, box 15), Papers of Geary Eppley, SC, UML.

51. For the specific reference to the amount necessary for football to support itself, see Geary Eppley to Jamison Swarts, December 1937 ("Contract, 1939," ser. 2, box 3), Papers of Geary Eppley, SC, UML. To get a sense of the range of contracts, see the entire contents of "Contracts" folders in the same collection. During the 1930s, most the University of Maryland's football contracts offered guarantees of $1,000 to $5,000 and carried the provision that the teams would split the net proceeds if they exceeded the guaranteed amount. J. P. Hess to Paul J. Kruesi, Folder 12, box 2, University of Tennessee Board of Trustees Business Manager Papers, University of Tennessee Archives (hereafter cited as UTNA); Montgomery, *Threshold of a New Day*, 360–61.

52. "Some Observations Submitted by John L. Griffith on the Paper Presented by Mr. Ross and on the Proposed Questionnaire to Be Sent to Members of Governing Boards of Universities," 4 and 5 ("Intercollegiate Conference: Board of Regents: Questionnaire: 1931," 9/e–1/9), Director of Athletics, TOSUA.

53. Pollard, *History of Ohio State*, 302, 305. For a fuller discussion of the wrangling over the budget cuts demanded by the OSU Board of Trustees and resisted by the OSU Athletic Board, see the Athletic Board Minutes, August 4, 1931, August 20, 1931, and November 23, 1931 (RG 9/e–l/l), Director of Athletics, TOSUA. See also "Record of Proceedings of the Board of Trustees of the Ohio State University," August 6, 1931, and October 9, 1931 (Board of Trustees Minutes, 1/a), TOSUA. The November 9, 1931, minutes (Board of Trustees Minutes, 1/a, TOSUA) contain the trustees' acceptance of the athletic board's proposal to follow university salary reduction guidelines only with money derived directly from the university. For example, OSU athletic director St. John was originally budgeted to make $9,000 in the 1931–32 school year, with $5,500 coming from his salary as a university professor and $3,500 coming from the Athletic Board for his service as athletic director. Under the accepted salary cuts, the $3,500 remained untouched, but St. John forfeited 10

percent of his university salary, leaving him with a total salary of $8,450. *Ohio State University Monthly* 23 (1932): 367.

54. "The Ohio State University Athletic Department Consolidated Statement of Receipts and Expenditures," 1–2.

55. Wilson, "Present-Day Financial Problems in University Athletics," 16.

56. Savage et al., *American College Athletics,* 189.

57. Ibid., 171–73.

58. University of Texas Athletic Council Minutes, January 22, 1931, 265; Minutes of Executive Session, January 30, 1929 ("1:6," CU-282), University of California, Berkeley, Associated Students Records, UCB; Minutes of Finance Committee Meeting, May 5, 1930 ("2:5," CU-282), Associated Students Records, UCB; Minutes of Finance Committee Meeting, March 4, 1931 ("2:5," CU-282), Associated Students Records, UCB.

59. Minutes of Executive Session, May 12, 1933 ("1:6," CU-282), Associated Students Records, UCB.

60. For the references to Price's salary adjustments, see "Minutes of Executive Session," December 3, 1930, April 8, 1931, and March 1932 ("1:6," CU-282), Associated Students Records, UCB; for the assistant football coaches' salaries, see the same record group, "Minutes of Executive Session," February 11, 1931 and March 28, 1932.

61. "Minutes of Executive Session," April 21, 1937, and April 24, 1939 ("1:7," CU-282), Associated Students Records, UCB.

62. "1932–33 Athletic Salaries (Total from All University Sources)" ("Intercollegiate Conference: Salary Comparisons: 1929–1933," 9/e–l/12), Director of Athletics, TOSUA. These averages are slightly inflated because some of the salaries reflect money received as compensation for serving as an assistant coach in another sport. For example, at Indiana University, the head football coach was also the head track coach, but his entire $5,000 salary was reported in the football coach salary table. "Ohio State University, Salaries of Intercollegiate Athletic Staff" ("Intercollegiate Conference: Salary Comparisons: 1929–1933," 9/e–l/l), Director of Athletics, TOSUA; Pollard, *Ohio State Athletics,* 152.

63. Montgomery, *Threshold of a New Day,* 347–50; Austin, "College Would be a Dead Old Dump without It," 50.

64. Robert G. Sproul, "Report of the President of the University, Dec. 31, 1932," *Report of the President of the University of California, 1930–1932* (Berkeley: University of California Press, 1932), 24–25; W. H. Hottel, "Lacrosse Team Is Gaining Maryland National Recognition," *Maryland Alumni News* (May 1932): 3.

65. Wilson, "Present-Day Financial Problems in University Athletics," 16.

66. Al Toombs, "Spring Sport Hope at Maryland Dimmed by Banking Problem," *Washington News,* March 7, 1933, found in "Scrapbook" (box 5, ser. 4), Papers of Harry C. Byrd, SC, UML; University of Texas Athletic Council Minutes, December 7, 1932, 320.

67. Pollard, *Ohio State Athletics,* 179; *Ohio State University Monthly* 24 (1933): 122–23.

68. Pollard, *Ohio State Athletics,* 194, 208, and 245; Athletic Board Minutes, November 23, 1936, 4 ("Athletic Board: Minutes: September 1934–June 1940," 9/e–l/l), Director of Athletics, TOSUA.

69. University of Texas Athletic Council Minutes, May 23, 1933, 332; October 5, 1936; January 29, 1935, 366; and October 19, 1936, 421.

70. Minutes of Finance Committee Meeting, September 28, 1931 ("2:6," CU-282), Associated Students Records, UCB; Frank L. Kleeberger to Robert G. Sproul, January 15, 1934 ("1934:500," CU-5, ser. 2), Office of the President Papers, UCB; J. H. Corley to D. G. Maclise, April 10, 1934 ("1934:500," CU-5, ser. 2), Office of the President Papers, UCB.

71. Geary Eppley to Norton Pritchett, June 30, 1939 ("Correspondence, 1937–1942," ser. 2, box 2), Papers of Geary Eppley, SC, UML. In 1938, Eppley had written to Pritchett, the athletic director at the University of Virginia: "We have been considering the whole question of minor sports here at Maryland, and, in order to give more students an opportunity to represent the Institution in intercollegiate athletics, I have been thinking about recognizing soccer, golf, wrestling, fencing, etc. as minor sports." See Geary Eppley to Norton Pritchett, June 7, 1938 ("Football, 1937–1939," ser. 2, box 5), Papers of Geary Eppley, SC, UML; "Outstanding Contributions of the Men's Department of Physical Education for the Biennium 1938–1940" ("Correspondence, 1937–1942," ser. 2, box 2), Papers of Geary Eppley, SC, UML.

72. Pollard, *Ohio State Athletics*, 152–53.

73. Sperber, *Shake Down the Thunder*, 285–86, 326, 384.

74. Richard Whittingham, *Saturday Afternoon: College Football and the Men Who Made the Day* (New York: Workman Publishing, 1985), 50; Rader, *American Sports*, 185.

75. For example, by 1935 the University of Texas Athletic Council was recording its dissatisfaction with Chevigny's financial management in the official council minutes. See May 24, 1935, 374; University of Texas Athletic Council Minutes, January 10, 1937, 427–28 (quote on 428). Whittingham reported that the state legislature had to approve Bible's salary and raised the university president's salary so that it would be proportional to Bible's. Whittingham, *Saturday Afternoon*, 53.

76. For example, the University of Texas earned $4,500 from its broadcast contract for the 1938–39 football season; whereas, that same year, the University of Tennessee earned only $2,500 from radio broadcasts of its games. Even as late as 1943, the University of California was to receive only $8,500 for the broadcasts of its games, despite wanting as much as $85,000 in 1935 for the broadcast rights. See University of Texas Athletic Council Minutes, March 31, 1938, 450; University of Tennessee Athletic Board Minutes, April 22, 1938, AR-8, UTNA; ASUC Finance Committee Minutes, August 13, 1943 ("2:9," CU-282), Associated Students Records, UCB; and ASUC Finance Committee Minutes, February 25, 1935 ("2:6," CU-282).

77. University of Texas Athletic Council Minutes, February 21, 1935; October 24, 1938; January 4, 1937.

78. "The Ohio State University Athletic Department: Financial Statements."

CHAPTER 3. Competitive Democratic Athletics for Men

1. Watterson, *College Football*, 78–79.

2. Rudolph, *The American College and University*, 463. For more on how the universities tried to serve their host population as a way of creating a sense of community, see chapter 6.

3. Chapters 4 and 5 of this book address the use of sports and the curtailment of competition to teach "traditional" gender roles for women.

4. Pollard, *History of Ohio State*, 299, 300 (quote on 299); Robert G. Sproul,

"Statements by Presidents of Universities and Colleges on the Educational Value of Military Training" (Washington, DC, 1935), 4 ("Military Department, July 1, 1935–Dec. 31, 1936, no. 1," ser. 8, box 32), Records of the President's Office, ACC–94–85, SC, UML.

5. Sproul, "Statements by Presidents of Universities and Colleges on the Educational Value of Military Training," 4; Stadtman, *The University of California*, 302–3. Helen L. Horowitz argued that, during the Depression, although some students became radicalized and many outsiders believed most students had become more radical politically, "in numbers the political rebels were few. They led with little following among their own kind." See Horowitz, *Campus Life*, 161, and see pages 162–68 for profiles of selected "radicals" and for explanations of the connections between individuals' campus activism and larger political movements.

6. *Report of the President of the University of California, 1932–34*, 20. On page 21 of this report, Sproul told the governor and other readers of the report that "the best permanent answer to radicalism in America is a more equitable distribution of work and wealth; the best temporary answers are the barbs of ridicule and the thunders of silence."

7. Stadtman, *The University of California*, 303.

8. Callcott, *History of the University of Maryland*, 307.

9. Ibid., 307–8; Montgomery, *Threshold of a New Day*, 288; James D. Hoskins in "Statements by Presidents of Universities and Colleges on the Educational Value of Military Training" (Washington, DC, 1935), 4 ("Military Department, July 1, 1935–Dec. 31, 1936, no. 1," ser. 8, box 32), Records of the President's Office, 94–85, SC, UML.

10. Montgomery, *Threshold of a New Day*, 289.

11. Pollard, *History of the Ohio State University*, 300; George E. Deatherage to Robert G. Sproul, October 13, 1937 ("1937:390," CU-5, ser. 2), Office of the President Papers, UCB.

12. George W. Rightmire to A. [H] C. Byrd, March 29, 1933 ("Negro Education, 1933–35," ser. 1, box 8), Papers of Harry C. Byrd, SC, UML. For examples of these and other articles, see "Anti-War and Anti-Communism. Newspaper Clippings on College Life, Communism and Pacifist Movement, 1926–1932" (ser. 7, box 2), Records of the President's Office, SC, UML; "Alleged Radical Drift of Y.M.C.A. to Come to Fore," *Baltimore Sun*, September 13, 1926, in "Anti-War and Anti-Communism. Newspaper Clippings on College Life, Communism and Pacifist Movement"; H. C. Byrd to J. S. Eichelberger, October 14, 1932 ("Correspondence, Oct. –Dec., 1932," ser. 1, box 3), Papers of H. C. Byrd, SC, UML; Francis R. Welsh to H. C. Byrd, March 22, 1935 ("Anti-War and Anti-Communist [Misc. Correspondence: Anti-War, Communism, Lees and Coale vs. Pearson, 1932–34]," ser. 7, box 1), Records of the President's Office, SC, UML. In 1938, a local newspaper reported, "The University of Maryland apparently has put its finger on all the organized groups of native-born Americans and foreigners who for several years have been conducting these partly camouflaged Communist drives in schools and universities throughout the country. The roster of these propagandists is said to be more complete at College Park than at any other seat of learning and their appearances on University of Maryland platforms are now things of the past." See "Maryland U. Aims to Crush Reds," 1938 ("Scrapbook [Byrd Book]," ser. 4, box 4), Papers of H. C. Byrd, SC, UML.

13. Stadtman, *The University of California*, 294.

14. Ibid., 294–96.

15. Ibid., 297–300. This defiance of public opinion would continue into the war years. In April of 1942, the *California Monthly* published an article by UC political science assistant professor Eric C. Bellquist entitled "Tolerance Needed." In this extended essay, Bellquist cautioned his readers that "certainly few things are ever quite so dangerous to civil liberties as a patterned patriotism on the loose, no matter how high and pure the aims and motives of those who shape it" (see page 8).

16. Minutes of Executive Session, November 15, 1939 ("1:8," CU-282), Associated Students Records, UCB.

17. Minutes of Executive Session, March 27, 1940 ("1.8," CU-282), Associated Students Records, UCB.

18. *The Spark*, June 1932 ("National Student League [Spark], 1932," V.F. 18/C.B.), President's Office Records, CAH, UTXA.

19. R. L. Batts to the Regents, June 14, 1932 ("National Student League [Spark], 1932, V.F. 18/C.B.), President's Office Records, CAH, UTXA.

20. Chester H. Bryan to H. Y. Benedict, June 17, 1932 ("National Student League [Spark], 1932, V.F. 18/C.B.), President's Office Records, CAH, UTXA.

21. H. Y. Benedict to Chester H. Bryan, June 22, 1932 ("National Student League [Spark], 1932, V.F. 18/C.B.), President's Office Records, CAH, UTXA.

22. Callcott, *History of the University of Maryland*, 306; H. C. Byrd to R. H. Wettach, March 21, 1933 ("Negro Education, 1933–35," ser. 1, box 8), Papers of Harry C. Byrd, SC, UML.

23. W. M. Hillegeist to P. A. Pearson, June 16, 1935 ("Negro Education, 1933–35," ser. I, box 8), Papers of Harry C. Byrd, SC, UML. Marshall was assisted in this trial by his legal mentor, Charles Houston. During the trial, Marshall argued that the case dealt with broader issues than simple admission to a university's professional school; instead, on trial was the "moral commitment in our country's creed." See John Egerton, *Speak Now against the Day: The Generation before the Civil Rights Movement in the South* (New York: Alfred A. Knopf, 1994), 152.

24. H. C. Byrd to Roger Howell, July 16, 1935 ("Negro Students, July 1, 1935–June 1, 1937 [1 of 2]," ser. 8, box 39), Records of the President's Office, SC, UML.

25. Callcott, *History of the University of Maryland*, 306; Thurgood Marshall to H. C. Byrd, March 19, 1937 ("Negro Students [2 of 2]," ser. 8, box 37), Records of the President's Office, SC, UML.

26. Callcott, *History of the University of Maryland*, 307.

27. Pollard, *History of the Ohio State University*, 303–4. The minutes of the OSU Board of Trustees' meetings do not discuss Miller's firing.

28. For a detailed and unflattering description of race relations and discrimination at Ohio State during the 1930s see William J. Baker, *Jesse Owens: An American Life* (New York: Free Press, 1986), 33–42; "Black Students: Ohio Universities: Statistical Summary of Expressional and Factual Data: 1934" (3/f/37), George Washington Rightmire, TOSUA; flier ("Anti-Negro Guild: Correspondence and Fliers: 1917," 3/f/45), George Washington Rightmire, TOSUA; A. Park to George W. Rightmire, June 8, 1937 ("Anti-Negro' Guild: Correspondence and Fliers: 1937"); J. D. Morrill to George W. Rightmire, June 15, 1937 ("Anti-Negro Guild: Correspondence and Fliers: 1937"); Pollard, *History of the Ohio State University*, 346.

29. George Baker to the Director of Athletics, March 8, 1937 ("Intercollegiate Conference: Athletic Director's Correspondence, 1930–1938," 9/e–1/9), Director of Athletics, TOSUA; "Petition to the Meeting of Western Conference Officials in the City of Chicago, March 13, 1937" ("Intercollegiate Conference: Athletic Director's Correspondence, 1930–1938"); John Griffith to Lynn St. John, March 8, 1937 ("Intercollegiate Conference: Athletic Director's Correspondence, 1930–1938"); *Makio*, 1938–1948, the Ohio State yearbook.

30. In October 1929, the University of Texas's athletic director and mathematics professor, Dr. H. J. Ettlinger, reviewed Taft's article in the student newspaper, the *Daily Texan*, and found fault with the former president's argument. Ettlinger contended that the mere existence of popular football teams and expensive coaches and stadia did not prevent schools from attaining academic excellence. Ettlinger also argued that Taft overestimated the importance undergraduates placed on football, writing, "The average student on the campus pays no more attention to a championship football game than the average prosperous business man on the street pays to the World ser.." See "Ettlinger Reviews Taft Article on Business Football," *Daily Texan*, October 1929 ("Athletic Council, 1929–1930," VF 5E.B), President's Office Records, 1907–1968, CAH, UTXA.

31. For information about the Atherton report, see the *California Monthly* 44 (April 1940): 28. For more information about other critical reports on the conduct of college football during the 1930s, see Watterson, *College Football*, 177–90.

32. Thelin, *Games Colleges Play*, 22.

33. Ibid., 53–59.

34. Henry Pritchett, preface to *American College Athletics*, ed. Savage et al., xix.

35. Savage et al., *American College Athletics*, xxi.

36. Ibid., 166.

37. Ibid., 175.

38. "Benedict's Charge of Over-Emphasized College Sports Finds Refutation at Alabama University," *Austin American*, February 2, 1928; R. A. Pearson to Charles Hamilton, January 7, 1931 ("Correspondence, 1931, January–June," ser. 1, box 3), Papers of Harry C. Byrd, SC, UML.

39. Robert G. Sproul to Percy M. Whiteside, December 26, 1930 ("1930:371," CU-5, ser. 2), Office of the President's Papers, UCB; Statement by Robert G. Sproul, February 3, 1931 ("1931:79," CU-5, ser. 2), Office of the President's Papers, UCB; Robert G. Sproul to George L. Macdonald, January 19, 1932 ("1932: 209," CU-5, ser. 2), Office of the President's Papers, UCB.

40. Robert G. Sproul to A. B. Reading Jr., November 19, 1930 ("1930:371," CU-5, ser. 2), Office of the President Papers, UCB.

41. Robert G. Sproul to James A. Force, November 21, 1930 ("1930:371," CU-5, ser. 2), Office of the President Papers, UCB.

42. William W. Campbell to Susan Jane Dikeman, January 17, 1930 ("1930:371," CU-5, ser. 2), Office of the President Papers, UCB.

43. Thelin, *Games Colleges Play*, 53.

44. Ibid., 53–57.

45. Robert G. Sproul to T. M. Putnam, May 29, 1930 ("1930:183," CU-5, ser. 2), Office of the President Papers, UCB.

46. Dating the emergence of a Pacific Coast Conference commissioner is difficult. Thelin indicated on pages 54–55 of *Games Colleges Play* that the PCC had

a full-time commissioner by 1933, and the minutes of the December 31, 1931, PCC meeting record the presence of J. A. Butler, commissioner of the PCC. However, Putnam's report to Sproul of the meeting immediately after the above-quoted letter indicated that only California, UCLA, and Oregon State, out of ten universities, supported a commissioner; and a 1939 report by commissioner Edwin N. Atherton indicated that he had begun his two-year survey of conference conditions before becoming commissioner. He wrote that, after subtitling his report to the conference's faculty representatives, he "was named Commissioner for a three-year term, with [his] general duties being to ascertain, assemble, and report the facts regarding compliance or non-compliance of member colleges and individuals with the rules." See Edwin N. Atherton, "The Conference Rules," *California Monthly* 43–44 (March 1940): 12.

47. J. W. Bell to H. C. Byrd, December 29, 1931 ("Southern Conference, 1931," ser. 2, box 10), Papers of Geary Eppley, SC, UML; H. C. Byrd to Fielding H. Yost, January 15, 1932 ("Southern Conference, 1932, Jan.–Feb.," ser. 2, box 10), Papers of Geary Eppley, SC, UML.

48. Nathan W. Dougherty, "Review of Carnegie Foundation's Report on American College Athletics, Bulletin #23" ("Carnegie Foundation—Reports on Sports in American Colleges," MS-1376, box 21), Nathan Washington Dougherty Collection, SC, UTNK.

49. R. A. Fetzer and Howard W. Odum to Geary Eppley, January 25, 1938 ("Geary Eppley, 1937–1961," ser. 2, box 2), Papers of Geary Eppley, SC, UML.

50. "That Carnegie Report" and "The Texas Side of It," *Alcade* 18 (November 1929): 69 and 70, respectively.

51. H. Y. Benedict, "Benny Ventures a Peregrinusing: All Dedicated to Bill Ruggles, Sports Writers, Fans, Professors, and Carnegie Reporters, Possible Solutions of the Intercollegiate Athletic Problem, Pictured on One Gridiron," *Alcade* 3 (December 1929), 95 and 97.

52. Savage et al., *American College Athletics*, 291.

53. Ibid., 310, 311.

54. Mark Dyreson, "Regulating the Body and the Body Politic: American Sport, Bourgeois Culture, and the Language of Progress, 1880–1920," in *The New American Sport History*, ed. Pope, 123.

55. Dyreson, "Regulating the Body and the Body Politic," 131–37.

56. F. H. Yost to L. W. St. John, April 22, 1922 ("Intercollegiate Conference: Commissioner, Correspondence [Griffith], 1922–1929," 9/e-1/9), Director of Athletics, TOSUA; John Griffith, "Address before the State Teachers Association," November 29, 1929, 6, 15, 14 (quotes on 6 and 14).

57. Frederick Rudolph wrote that during the Depression "the educational outlook of John Dewey made headway in the colleges for the first time. Dewey's insistence that education and experience were one and the same thing, his concern over the disjunction between education and society, found new acceptance in a period when the failings of organized society pressed in upon individual experience." See Rudolph, *The American College and University*, 468. See also Callcott, *History of the University of Maryland*, 330–31. A 1932 student paper from Ohio State argued, "This concept of physical education lends itself to the progressive method of education. In this light physical education can become one of the most effective instruments for the relating and integrating of the various fields of academic

instruction and of life. . . . [P]hysical education becomes a way of living. The virtues of courage, endurance and strength, honesty, competence, imagination, joyousness, and pride are engendered—through it all a spirit of splendid living maintains." See Oscar L. Thomas, "The Educational Objectives in Athletics" ("Physical Education: 'Educational Objectives in Athletics': by Oscar L. Thomas: 1932," RG 9/e–1/17), Director of Athletics, TOSUA.

58. Minutes of Southern Conference, January 14, 1932 ("Southern Conference Minutes, 1932–33," ser. 2, box 14), Papers of Geary Eppley, SC, UML.

59. Clyde Littlefield, "The Functions of College Athletics and Some Things That Are a Menace," *Alcade*, vol. 18, 296, 297.

60. Frank Kleeberger to Robert G. Sproul, November 29, 1930 ("130:371," CU-5, ser. 2), Office of the President Papers, UCB; Robert G. Sproul to Clare M. Torrey, December 4, 1930 ("1930:371," CU-5, ser. 2), UCB.

61. Frank Kleeberger to Robert G. Sproul, November 29, 1930 ("130:371," CU-5, ser. 2), Office of the President Papers, UCB.

62. Historians have long understood the importance of this type of ideology to advocates of institutionalized sports. Ronald Smith's *Sports and Freedom: The Rise of Big-Time College Athletics* offers perhaps the best explanation of how many Americans defended their sporting ventures by claiming physical, social, and spiritual benefits. Smith highlights the attentions devoted to the amateur ideal, based on a British university model. That emphasis on amateurism still echoed during the Depression period examined here. More recently, Steven Pope's *Patriotic Games: Sporting Traditions in the American Imagination, 1876–1926* (New York: Oxford University Press, 1997) illustrates the conscious efforts many Americans made to link their sporting activities with their country's heritage, traditions, and values.

63. In the 1936 Republican Party platform, Republicans "pledge[d] [them]selves . . . to preserve the American system of free enterprise, private competition, and equality of opportunity, and to seek its constant betterment in the all." Likewise, in 1938, President Franklin D. Roosevelt wrote, "The promotion of wholesome sports is a constructive second to none in the work of upbuilding [*sic*] the youth of the land, of guaranteeing a sound mind in a sound body." The Republican quotation came from Kirk H. Porter and Donald Bruce Johnson, eds., *National Party Platforms, 1840–1956* (Urbana: University of Illinois Press, 1956), 366. The Roosevelt quotation comes from a letter, Franklin D. Roosevelt to Samuel E. Hoyt, November 23, 1938 (PPF 4508), Franklin D. Roosevelt Library, New York City, and is quoted in John Wong, "FDR and the New Deal on Sport and Recreation," *Sport History Review* 29 (1998): 184–85.

64. For one of the earliest examples of this argument, see Barton Bernstein's essay, "The New Deal: The Conservative Achievements of Liberal Reform." Bernstein wrote of the New Deal that it was "designed to maintain the American system, liberal activity was directed toward essentially conservative goals" and that Roosevelt "protected the established system: he sapped organizational radicalism of its waning strength and of its potential constituency among the unorganized and discontented" (ibid., 264, 265).

65. Bob Gilbert, *Neyland: The Gridiron General* (Savannah, GA: Golden Coast Publishing Company, 1990), 99. Gilbert quotes Neyland, but he does not provide a citation for the statement.

66. For an engaging study of college football during World War II and the Cold War period, see Kurt Edward Kemper's *College Football and American Culture in the Cold War Era* (Urbana: University of Illinois Press, 2009).

67. John Griffith recognized exactly what Dyerson argued, that during the 1920s and 1930s many Americans had abandoned their belief in the formative powers of athletics. Still, Griffith and his colleagues in the nation's universities did not follow this general trend and, in fact, worked against it. In 1941, Griffith wrote to the "Nation's Athletic Leaders" that "there is abundant evidence that our people generally like athletics but they think of sports in terms of entertainment and amusement and not as an essential part of education or of military training either. Can we not take the lead in trying to show them the real value of athletics?" See John Griffith to the Nation's Athletic Leaders, September 15, 1941 ("Intercollegiate Conference: Commissioner Correspondence [Griffith] 1941–1942 [Folder 2 of 2]," 9/e–1/10), Director of Athletics, TOSUA.

68. Hebert S. Atkinson to Lynn W. St. John, November 24, 1931 ("Intercollegiate Conference: Board of Regents: Questionnaire: 1931," 9/e–1/9), Director of Athletics, TOSUA; and David E. Ross, "Athletics," October 29, 1931, 2, 3, 4, ("Intercollegiate Conference: Board of Regents: Questionnaire: 1931," 9/e–l/9), Director of Athletics, TOSUA. Howard Savage discussed Ross's speech in his article, "The Carnegie Foundation's Study of American College Athletics—Three Years Later," *Research Quarterly of the American Physical Education Association* 4 (1933): 20–21.

69. Ross, "Athletics," 9.

70. Ibid., 9, 6, and 9. To read some contemporary and representative explanations of the role competitive athletics could play in building character, see, among others, Herbert E. Hawkes, "What Should the Physical Education and Athletic Departments Contribute to the Education of College Youth?," *College Physical Education Association Proceedings* 38 (1934); Charles D. Giaugue, "New Objectives to Meet Modern Trends," *Journal of Health and Physical Education* 8 (February 1937): 71–127; Frank S. Lloyd, "Liberal Cultural Values of Physical Education," *Journal of Health and Physical Education* 9 (February 1938): 69–117; and William L. Hughes, "The Role of Intercollegiate Athletics in National Preparedness," *College Physical Education Association Proceedings* 44 (1940): 21. The University of Texas's D. A. Penick, who also served as the president of the Southwest Conference, wrote about the values athletics could teach college students: "There is an incentive to right living, there is the development of the spirit of cooperation and team-work, body-building, character-building, development of courage, resourcefulness, initiative, fairness, courtesy, sportsmanship, determination, leadership, will power, quick thinking, perseverance, playing openly and honestly and generously, taking victories modestly and defeats quietly, cheerful obedience to rules and rulings of officials." D. A. Penick, "The Ideals of Intercollegiate Athletics—Are They Attainable?," *College Physical Education Association Proceedings* 36 (1932): 34.

71. If nothing else, Morrill's statements feature the buzzwords that captivate students of America's then maturing consumer culture. Morrill lauded the ability of group sports to provide outlets for individuals' personalities while also instilling character. Warren Susman has argued that the United States underwent a gradual shift in emphasis from inner-directed "character" stressing morality to outer-directed "personality" emphasizing popularity and admiration. Morrill's assertion

that athletics can instill character is significant because Susman's review of over two hundred sources reveals that around the tum of the century, the time of Morrill's education, certain words were most often associated with character. According to Susman, these words included *"citizenship, duty, democracy, work, building, golden deeds, outdoor life, conquest, honor, reputation, morals, manners, integrity,* and above all, *manhood"* (emphasis his). Throughout the 1930s, most of these words also found themselves offered as products of intercollegiate athletics. See Susman, *Culture as History*, xii, 273–74.

72. J. L. Morrill to L. W. St. John, December 11, 1931 ("Intercollegiate Conference: Board of Regents: Questionnaire: 1931"), 1.

73. Ibid., 2–4.

74. L. W. St. John to H. S. Atkinson, December 26, 1931 ("Intercollegiate Conference: Board of Regents: Questionnaire: 1931").

75. "Some Observations Submitted by John L. Griffith on the Paper Presented by Mr. Ross and on the Proposed Questionnaire to be Sent to Members of Governing Boards of Universities" ("Intercollegiate Conference: Board of Regents: Questionnaire: 1931"), 4, 5. There was still another response to this controversy instigated by Ross and the Carnegie report: a University of Minnesota survey claiming to "reflect the attitudes of 10,000 individuals toward athletics in a typical mid-western state university." The authors of the study, funded, not coincidentally, from football revenues, recommended only a few minor changes in athletic operations and largely endorsed the existing system. After selectively citing different groups' responses to different questions, the study ended by claiming that most university presidents "apparently believe in the social philosophy of education," meaning that the social values instilled into men during competition made the activities worthwhile. Not wanting anyone to misinterpret its advocacy of the social philosophy of education with the support of any socialist cause, the report concludes that the "Intercollegiate Conference exemplifies the true spirit of democratic and representative government."

76. For example, Griffith reported in October 1936 that most eastern schools' student bodies were supporting the Republican candidate for president, while the Ohio State students supported Roosevelt. Griffith could not understand why "the middle west still believes in the magic of government and thinks that Hoover ran 59 national trains in addition to ours into the ditch and that Roosevelt has pulled them all out." In his reply, St. John thanked Griffith for keeping him updated on the latest speeches and expressed his sorrow that he was "not in a position to do a more active piece of work in support of the things that you and I both believe." A few weeks later, Griffith discussed the presidential election with St. John: "Well, Saint, we took an awful licking yesterday, didn't we? I was reconciled to a Roosevelt victory but I never dreamed it would be a landslide. Apparently America wittingly or unwittingly sold her vote. Well, if things don't work out well the next four years they can't blame you and me because we did what we could to bring about a change." See John Griffith to Lynn St. John, October 20 1936; St. John to Griffith, October 22. 1936; and Griffith to St. John, November 4, 1936 ("Intercollegiate Conference: Commissioner Correspondence [Griffith] and St. John, May 1936–March 1937," 9/e–1/10), Director of Athletics, TOSUA. For other examples of the shared beliefs of Griffith and St. John, see especially Griffith to St. John, May 2, 1941, and St. John to Griffith, May 10, 1941 ("Intercollegiate Conference: Commissioner Correspondence [Griffith] 1940–1941 [Folder 1 of 2]," 9/e–1/10), Director of Athletics, TOSUA.

77. Memorandum to the Directors of Athletics of the Intercollegiate Conference, February 3, 1932 ("Intercollegiate Conference: Athletic Director's Correspondence: 1930–1938," 9/e-l/9), Director of Athletics, TOSUA.

78. John L. Griffith to L. W. St. John, February 3, 1932 ("Intercollegiate Conference: Athletic Director's Correspondence: 1930–1938," 9/e–119), Director of Athletics, TOSUA; Memorandum to the Directors of Athletics of the Intercollegiate Conference, February 3, 1932 ("Intercollegiate Conference: Athletic Director's Correspondence: 1930–1938"), 2 and 2–3.

79. John Griffith to Frank E. Richart, July 5, 1939 ("Intercollegiate Conference: Commissioner Correspondence [Griffith] 1939–1940 [Folder 2 of 2]," 9/e–1/l o), Director of Athletics, TOSUA; John L. Griffith to Colonel G. L. Townsend, March 8, 1938 ("Intercollegiate Conference: Commissioner, Correspondence [Griffith], 1937–38," 9/e–1/9), Director of Athletics, TOSUA. Townsend had been on active duty at Ohio State for twelve years as a professor of military science and tactics. After leading the "largest R.O.T.C. unit in the country," Townsend became professor emeritus of military science and tactics upon his retirement. See Board of Trustees Minutes, February 25, 1938 (Board of Trustees Minutes, 1/a), TOUSA

80. "Athletics Exemplify the American Way" ("Addresses and Articles: 1931–1941," 9/e–l/l), Director of Athletics, TOSUA; John L. Griffith to Newton Fuesske, August 10, 1922, 1 ("Intercollegiate Conference: Commissioner, Correspondence [Griffith], 1922–1929," 9/e–l/9), Director of Athletics, TOSUA; "Athletics Exemplify the American Way," 2.

81. "Addresses and Articles: 1931–1941," George Washington Robnett, ed., *News and Views*, no. 62, 1, 2. Judging from a letter to Robnett, this article appeared in 1939. See Griffith to Robnett, February 16, 1939 (Intercollegiate Conference: Commissioner Correspondence [Griffith] 1938-March 1939," 9/e–l/lo), Director of Athletics. See John Griffith to Directors of Athletics of the Conference, June 27, 1938 ("Intercollegiate Conference: Commissioner, Correspondence [Griffith], 1937–38," 9/e–1/9), Director of Athletics, TOSUA.

82. C. E. Bilheimer, "A Study of Athletic Finances in the Second District of the National Collegiate Athletic Association," *College Physical Education Association Proceedings* 37 (1933): 11.

83. Jesse F. Williams, "Physical Education and the Depression," *College Physical Education Association Proceedings* 36 (1932): 11.

84. Fielding H. Yost, "The Place of Varsity Athletics in a Program of 'Athletics for All,'" *Journal of Health and Physical Education* 2 (June 1931): 62; E. M. Sanders, "Builders of Character of Teachers of Activities?," *Journal of Health and Physical Education* 2 (November 1931): 25.

85. Alexander J. Stoddard, "The Relation of Physical Education to the Purposes of Democracy," *Journal of Health and Physical Education* 8 (November 1937): 520. See also Ohio State's D. Oberteuffer, "Physical Education and the Democratic Ideal," *College Physical Education Association Proceedings* 43 (1939).

86. Hughes, "The Role of Intercollegiate Athletics in National Preparedness," 21. See also Harry A. Scott, "The Ramparts We Watch," *College Physical Education Association Proceedings* (1940). The Maginot Line was a line of defensive fortifications constructed by the French along their eastern border between 1929 and 1936.

87. John Griffith to Lynn St. John, November 27, 1934 ("Intercollegiate Conference: Commissioner Correspondence [Griffith and St. John], 1934," 9e–1/10),

Director of Athletics, TOSUA; St. John to Griffith, December 6, 1934, TOSUA. The three groups that St. John identified were the National Student League, the League Against War and Fascism, and the "Social Problems Club." According to St. John, the National Student League and the League Against War and Fascism were the "communistic" ones. In another letter, Griffith asserted that the American Constitution was "based on the principle of private property ownership, inheritance rights, etc." He concluded this argument with the position that "those who believe in Communism are free to live in Russia and those who believe in the other isms can go where those isms are practiced." See John Griffith to George W. Robnett, February 16, 1939 ("Intercollegiate Conference: Commissioner Correspondence [Griffith] 1938–March 1939," RG 9/e–1/10), Director of Athletics, TOSUA.

88. The athletic directors of the Big Ten universities were more concerned with "socialism" when the effected revenues were large ones. Being human, they were not always consistent in their advocacy of absolute competition; after all, their universities already worked within conference confines. In the spring of 1935, Ohio State and seven other universities supported a motion to allow a conference-wide broadcasting contract. The June 7, 1935, minutes of the Ohio State Athletic Board include the report that "the Directors and Faculty Representatives went on record as favoring a cooperative broadcasting program for the Conference, although two of the college presidents were opposed to the idea." "Athletic Board Minutes, 1934–1940," June 7, 1935.

89. Glenn Frank, "Football in the American University," December 4, 1936, 1, 2–3, and 4, "Addresses and Articles—1931-1941" (RG 9/e-1/1), Director of Athletics, TOSUA.

90. L. W. St. John to T. Nelson Metcalf, March 26, 1934; and Frank G. McCormick to L. W. St. John, April 3, 1934, 1934 ("Intercollegiate Conference: Athletic Director's Correspondence: 1930–1938," 9/e–1/9), Director of Athletics, TOSUA.

91. John Griffith to Mark Sullivan, May 6, 1941 ("Intercollegiate Conference: Commissioner Correspondence [Griffith] 1940–1941 [folder 1 of 2]," 9/e–1/10), Director of Athletics, TOSUA.

CHAPTER 4. Communal Values and Women's Sport

1. Cahn, *Coming on Strong*, 18.

2. Debra A. Shattuck, "Bats, Balls, and Books: Baseball and Higher Education for Women at Three Eastern Women's Colleges, 1866–1891," *Journal of Sport History* 19 (Summer 1992): 94–95, 98–107 (quote on 98).

3. Cahn, *Coming on Strong*, 18; Joan Paul, "Clara Gregory Baer: Catalyst for Women's Basketball," in *A Century of Women's Basketball: From Frailty to Final Four*, ed. Joan S. Hult and Marianna Trekell (Reston, VA: American Alliance for Health, Physical Education, Recreation, and Dance, 1991), 45.

4. Betty Spears, "Sandra Berenson Abbot, New Woman: New Sport," in Paul and Trekell, *A Century of Women's Basketball*, 25; Robin Bell Markels, "Bloomer Basketball and Its Suspender Suppression: Women's Intercollegiate Competition at Ohio State, 1904–1907," *Journal of Sport History* 27 (Spring 2000): 34–36.

5. For a good overview of the "new woman" in the 1920s, see Sara M. Evans,

Born for Liberty: A History of Women in America (New York: Free Press, 1989), chapter 8, "Flappers, Freudians, and All That Jazz." See also Rader, *American Sports*, chapter 9, *passim*.

6. Rader, *American Sports*, 212–13.

7. Cahn, *Coming on Strong*, 56. See also Larry Engelmann, *The Goddess and the American Girl: The Story of Suzanne Lenglen and Helen Wills* (New York: Oxford University Press, 1988). To get a sense of the immense press interest in the first competition between these two athletes, see Englemann's third chapter, entitled "Ballyhoo."

8. Cahn, *Coming on Strong*, see 27–30.

9. For a discussion of how the workers and managers interacted to create the model Canadian industrial recreation program, see Susan L. Forbes, "Industrial Recreation for Females at the T. Eaton Company: Resistance and Transformation," paper presented at Women in the Zone: Women in Sport Symposium, Bowling Green, Ohio, Bowling Green State University, March 18, 2000; Rader, *American Sports*, 215; Roxanne M. Albertson, "Basketball Texas Style, 1910–1933: School to Industrial League Competition," in Hult and Trekell, *A Century of Women's Sport*, 115.

10. For a discussion of "welfare capitalism," see Lisabeth Cohen, *Making a New Deal: Industrial Workers in Chicago, 1919–1939* (New York: Cambridge University Press, 1990), 161–83. For information on the incorporation of recreation programs, see Cohen's charts on 164 and 176–79; Alice Kessler-Harris, *Out to Work: A History of Wage-Earning Women in the United States* (New York: Oxford University Press, 1982); Albertson, "Basketball Texas Style," 158–59; R. N. Blackwell to All Approved Basketball Officials, January 5, 1931 ("Southwest Athletic Conference, From 1930 Through_," VF 17/A.A), President's Office Records, 1907–1968, CAH, UTXA. Blackwell was writing on behalf of the Directors and Business Managers Association of the Southwest Conference.

11. Rader, *American Sports*, 216; Cahn, *Coming on Strong*, 44.

12. In 1922, the American Physical Education Association passed this resolution: "We regard the representation of America at the Women's International Athletic Games held in Paris in July, 1922, as inopportune and unauthorized by any national representative body and, in view of the present state of women's athletics in this country, we are not in favor of international competition at this time." See "Summary and Discussion on Athletics for Girls: Atlantic City Recreation Congress, October 9–12, 1922," *American Physical Education Review* 28 (January 1923): 69. Seven years later, in 1929, the same organization explicitly targeted the Olympics with its resolutions: "*Whereas*, training for formal spectator athletic events like the Olympic Games tends to restrict interest and limit the use of public facilities, such as schools, colleges, parks, playgrounds, and other civic recreational systems to those practicing for special events, and *Whereas*, the exploitation of individuals coincident with such contests tends to subordinate an interest in athletic activity and accomplishment in such activity to an interest in awards, such as public adulation, financial gain, or both *Resolved*, that the Section on Women's Athletics of the American Physical Education Association go on record as being opposed to girls and women entering the Olympic Games." See "Resolutions of the Section on Women's Athletics of the American Physical Education Association," *American Physical Education Review* 34 (May 1929): 310.

13. Cahn, *Coming on Strong,* 47; Englemann, *The Goddess and the American Girl,* 24–25.

14. Cahn, *Coming on Strong,* 48–49; quotation in Rader, *American Sports, 216.*

15. Helen N. Smith, "Evils of Sports for Women," *Journal of Health and Physical Education* 2 (January 1931): 8.

16. Cahn, *Coming on Strong*, chapter 2, passim, see especially page 54.

17. For Lenglen information, see Cahn, *Coming on Strong*, 48–50. For more information on how Lenglen kept innovating in athletic costume design, see also Englemann, *The Goddess and the American Girl,* 24–25 and 348. For more on the changing standards of sexual activity and body display among young American women in the 1920s, see Joan Jacobs Bromberg, *The Body Project: An Intimate History of American Girls* (New York: Vintage Books, 1998), xxx, xxix, 99, 104–7, and 156–58.

18. Rader, *American Sports,* 212–13.

19. Susan Cayleff argued that physicians often considered athletic women in the 1920s and the 1930s as "inverts," as lesbians. Babe's working-class roots, when considered with her demonstrated excellence in "masculine" sports such as track, javelin, baseball, and basketball, led many to question her sexuality. As Cayleff wrote, most "experts" believed that young women "ought to be training for heterosexual relations and popularity, not competing in sports." See Susan E. Cayleff, *Babe: The Life and Legend of Babe Didrikson Zaharias* (Urbana: University of Illinois Press, 1995), 19. In 1999, a panel of ESPN judges named Didrikson as the tenth-best athlete of the twentieth century, citing her excellence in "basketball, track, golf, baseball, tennis, swimming, diving, boxing, volleyball, handball, bowling, billiards, skating, and cycling." See http://espn.go.com/sportscentury/features/00014147.html, accessed October 4, 2014.

20. See Cayleff, *Babe,* 133–39; Rader, *American Sports,* 214–16; Cahn, *Coming on Strong,* 215–16. Both Cahn and Rader wrote about a famous 1947 *Life* article entitled "Babe Is a Lady Now: The World's Most Amazing Athlete Has Learned to Wear Nylons and Cook for Her Huge Husband." Cahn also described a *Saturday Evening Post* article that used Didrikson's "big breasts, a small waist, and thirty-seven inch hips" as proof that this former tomboy had become a woman. See Cahn, *Coming on Strong,* 216.

21. Markels's "Bloomer Basketball and Its Suspender Suppression" suggests that the history of the suppression of women's athletics at colleges is more complex than most accounts present. She argues that male athletic leaders played a much more significant role in the termination of the women's programs than most historians have acknowledged.

22. Rader describes the leadership of the National Amateur Athletic Foundation's Women's Division as national "leaders in women's education, the Girl Scouts, YWCAs, and women's clubs." Rader, *American Sports,* 215. R. Smith, "Women's Control of American College Sport," 103–20 (quotes from 103). Susan Cahn noted that other women's organizations had used similar tactics and agreed with Smith's assessment of motivations if not the label of exploitation. She wrote, "In hindsight, this strategy looks like a rearguard action to conserve professional educators' status and outdated standards of female propriety." See Cahn, *Coming on Strong,* 67.

23. Barbara J. Harris, *Beyond Her Sphere: Women and the Professions in American History* (Westport, CT: Greenwood Press, 1978), 141–42 (quote on 141).

24. See Hult, "The Governance of Athletics for Girls and Women," 64–66 (quote on 66).

25. Ibid., 66.

26. Rader, *American Sports,* 216. The sixteen resolutions adopted by the Women's Division included the following:

> "4. Resolved, in order to develop those qualities which shall fit girls and women to perform their functions as citizens,
>
> (a) That their athletics be conducted with that end definitely in view and be protected from exploitation for the enjoyment of the spectator or for the athletic reputation or commercial advantage of other organization.
>
> (b) That schools and other organization shall stress enjoyment of the sport and development of sportsmanship and minimize the emphasis which is at present laid upon individual accomplishment and the winning of championships . . .
>
> 5. Resolved, that for any given group we approve and recommend such selection and administration of athletic activities as makes participation possible for all, and strongly condemn the sacrifice of this object for intensive training (even though physiologically sound) of the few . . .
>
> 11. Resolved, that suitable costumes for universal use be adopted for the various athletic activities."

For a complete list of the resolutions, see the appendix to Agnes Wayman, "Women's Division of the National Amateur Athletic Federation," *Journal of Health and Physical Education* 3 (March 1932): 7, 53–54.

27. Gerber, "The Controlled Development of Collegiate Sport for Women," 10. These organizations included the Committee on Women's Athletics of the APEA, the Association of Directors of Physical Education for Women in Colleges and Universities, the Athletic Conference of American College Women, the American Association of University Women, and the National Association of Deans of Women, all of which endorsed the platform between 1923 and 1926.

28. Alice Allene Sefton, *The Women's Division National Amateur Athletic Federation: Sixteen Years of Progress in Athletics for Girls and Women, 1923–1939* (Stanford, CA: Stanford University Press, 1941), 12.

29. Ibid. In 1930 the WDNAAF had 650 total institutional and individual memberships, and in 1938 it had 768. Sefton, *The Women's Division National Amateur Athletic Federation,* 32. The organization was so important that Ohio State's Mary Yost wrote, in 1941, "I doubt if there is a woman in Physical Education who does not know what it was and what it stood for." "Girls Athletics," 2 ("Athletics: Girls: 1940s," 9/e-5/a/8), Accession 84/94, TOSUA.

30. For an extremely detailed discussion of the interaction among the various organizations concerned with "proper" women's athletics, see Hult's article, "The Governance of Athletics for Girls and Women." The information for this paragraph came from pages 66–67. For an in-depth discussion of the Women's Division of the National Amateur Athletic Federation, see Gerber, "The Controlled Development of Collegiate Sport for Women," 1–28.

31. See number five in the list of the 1923 Women's Division resolutions, available in footnote 26.

32. University of Texas Athletic Council Minutes, April 7, 1930, October 9, 1930, October 30, 1930, June 13, 1931, and June 23, 1932. In a May 1930 letter to Texas president H. Y. Benedict, Hiss noted that a tax decrease would lower her $1,708 budget an additional $200. Hiss expressed her profound disappointment to Benedict, informing him, "This 'disappointment' happens too regularly to encourage us to proceed with any hopes of a permanent program of work." See Anna Hiss to H. Y. Benedict, May 23, 1930 ("W.A.A. 1930," 3R237), University of Texas Physical Training for Women Records, CAH, UTXA.

33. University of Texas Athletic Council Minutes, May 22, 1939.

34. For a discussion of the intended character development associated with the early years of women's college basketball, see again, Paul, "Clara Gregory Baer," 45; Sefton, *The Women's Division National Amateur Athletic Federation*, 29.

35. Sefton, *The Women's Division National Amateur Athletic Federation*, 29.

36. H. Smith, "Evils of Sports for Women," 8.

37. Ibid., 8.

38. In 1940, Ohio State physical educator Dorothy Sumption described a telegraph meet: "A competitive event between two or more schools in which each team telegraphs the results of the competition to the other school, or to a central designated school or organization, is called a telegraphic meet. The teams do not actually meet each other. Only the results are compared, and the winner is this selected." Dorothy Sumption, *Sports for Women* (New York: Prentice-Hall, 1940), 224.

39. For details about the joining of beauty pageants and basketball tournaments, see Cahn, *Coming on Strong*, 94–96. See also Stephanie L. Twin, ed., *Out of the Bleachers: Writings on Women and Sport* (Old Westbury, NY: Feminist Press, 1979).

40. The University of Maryland yearbook, the *Reveille*, reported on the construction of a new women's dormitory and gymnasium in its 1932 edition. The author wrote, "These buildings fill a long-term need on our campus. Prior to this year Physical Education for women was of necessity a bit haphazard. The only place for intramural sports and games was the men's gymnasium. This year, with our own building, we have had a very successful program of intramural sports." The author continued, "At the present writing an athletic field for coeds is in the process of construction, and in a short time, women students at the University will have a rather complete physical education plant of their own" (195).

The University of Texas participated in the national educational building spree in the 1920s and early 1930s, erecting new men's and women's gymnasia, a new student union, and a new auditorium. The new women's gymnasium, completed in 1931, included 16 offices, three large gymnasia and one smaller one, a dancing studio, a library, shower and dressing rooms, a pool, and reception areas. The new outdoor complex included an archery range, twelve tennis courts, two hockey fields, a short, six-hole golf course, and some golf practice areas, among other areas. See "University of Texas" ("U.T.S.A. History," 3R244), University of Texas Physical Training for Women, CAH, UTXA.

41. Savage, *American College Athletics*, 91.

42. "Report on T.A.F.C.W. Convention—Waco," [1938] ("A.F.C. Materials,

Correspondence, etc.," 3R246), Physical Training for Women Records, CAH, UTXA. The proper way to display active female bodies had long been a concern of college officials. The University of California agreed to play the first women's intercollegiate basketball game on the West Coast against Stanford University only with the agreement that no men could watch the game; instead more than seven hundred women saw this inaugural match.

43. Cahn, *Coming on Strong*, 4.

44. The quote is attributed to one of the author's colleagues named Rogers in Ina Gittings, "Why Cramp Competition?," Journal of Health and Physical Education 2, no. 1 (January, 1930): 11. The quote comes from Frederick Rand Rogers, "Olympics for Girls?," *School and Society* 30 (August 10, 1929): 194. Laura Robicheaux also isolated this particular statement by Rogers and provided more context. Rogers not only argued that athletics might prevent women from attracting "the most worthy fathers for their children," he contended that women should concentrate on "provid[ing] the most healthful physiques for child bearing and build[ing] the most maternal emotional and social patterns." He continued, "Intense forms of physical and psychic conflicts, of which athletics provide the best example in modern life, and of which Olympic games provide the extreme type, tend to destroy girls' physical and psychic charm and adaptability for motherhood." See Laura Robicheaux, "An Analysis of Attitudes toward Women's Athletics in the U.S. in the Early Twentieth Century," *Canadian Journal of History of Sport and Physical Education* 6 (May 1975): 18.

45. Frederick Rand Rogers, "Competition for Girls," *American Physical Education Review* 34 (March 1929): 168–69. Alice Allene Sefton expressed similar sentiments in 1937, writing, "It is usually when they are exceeding their powers that women appear unlovely. When a woman sets her jaw in grim determination to win at any cost, or plays so long that lines of fatigue draw her face into contortions, and she loses control of her coordinations, then she sacrifices some of her beauty because she is violating principles of health. The game has gone beyond the limits of beneficial activity. That look of ghastly strain, that awkwardness and lack of equilibrium and that breathlessness should not be chalked against the sport itself, but should be controlled through careful guidance, frequent check-ups, and suitable environmental conditions." See Alice Allene Sefton, "Must Women in Sports Look Beautiful?," *Journal of Health and Physical Education* 8 (October 1937): 510.

46. Katherine Hale, "Fair Sex Has Become Prominent in Intramural Sports This Year," *Orange and White*, February 27, 1930, 7.

47. Gerber, "The Controlled Development of Collegiate Sport for Women," 2–4. Joan S. Hult has pointed out that Lee's sample contained many biases. Lee sent her questionnaires only to members of organizations that opposed varsity competition for women, people Hult believed were "likely to be predisposed to a nonvarsity model." Moreover, Hult pointed out that most of the institutions that did not respond to the 1930 survey actually had varsity teams on campus. See Hult, "The Governance of Athletics for Girls and Women," 71–72.

48. Adam R. Hornbuckle, "Women's Sports and Physical Education at the University of Tennessee: 1899–1939" (MA thesis, University of Tennessee, Knoxville, 1983). See pages 52–77 for a discussion of the development of varsity basketball at the University of Tennessee, and see 79 and 83 for the two quotes. The second quote

appeared in the University of Tennessee Student newspaper, the *Orange and White*, on April 8, 1926, page 1.

49. Hornbuckle, "Women's Sports and Physical Education at the University of Tennessee," 83–84.

50. Le'Ellen Kubow, "Once Upon a Time There Was This Stick . . . ," June 14, 1971 ("1:12," CU-67.1), Student Papers on University of California, Berkeley, Sports and Other Subjects Relating to Athletics, UCB.

51. "Resolutions of the Section on Women's Athletics of the American Physical Education Association," 53.

52. Wayman, "Women's Division of the National Amateur Athletic Federation," 5, 6 (quote on 5).

53. Anna Hiss, "Considering Centralization: Separate Administration of Women" ("Statistics, 1929–30," 3R236), University of Texas Physical Training for Women Records, CAH, UTXA, 2; Jodi Vandenberg-Daves, "The Manly Pursuit of a Partnership between the Sexes: The Debate over YMCA Programs for Women and Girls, 1914–1933," *Journal of American History* 78 (March 1992): 1334–35, 1339–41, 1344–46.

54. T. L. Belmont to H. Y. Benedict, February 27, 1930 ("Statistics, 1929–30," 3R236), University of Texas Physical Training for Women Records, CAH, UTXA.

55. Nancy Cole Dosch, "The Sacrifice of Maidens or Healthy Sportswomen? The Medical Debate over Women's Basketball," in *A Century of Women 's Basketball*, ed. Hult and Trekell, 126. For the best single study of medical views of women's athletic abilities and the importance of these views, see Patricia A. Vertinsky, *The Eternally Wounded Woman: Women, Doctors, and Exercise in the Late Nineteenth Century* (Urbana: University of Illinois Press, 1994).

56. Quote found in Dosch, "The Sacrifice of Maidens or Healthy Sportswomen?," 130. Original quote comes from Marjorie Bateman, "Health Aspects of Girls' Basketball," *Mind and Body* 42 (April 1935): 21.

57. Ethel Perrin, "Health Safeguards in Athletics for Girls and Women," *Research Quarterly* 3 (October 1932): 93–94.

58. Perrin, "Health Safeguards in Athletics for Girls and Women," 93–94. Educators worried about the emotional damage that athletics could cause as well as the physical damage. On top of encouraging unfeminine competitive desires, many feared that the pressure of playing highly competitive games was too much for the young women to bear.

59. "University of Texas Sports Association and Intramural Sports for Women," 1935 ("History of Clubs and U.T.S.A.," 3R244), University of Texas Physical Training for Women Records, CAH, UTXA.

60. "Constitution and By-Laws of the Women's Athletic Association of the University of Maryland, 1935– 1936," 2–7 ("Women's Athletic Association—Minutes, Awards, Constitution, Point System, 1933–37," ser. 1, box 6), Papers of Adele H. Stamp, SC, UML.

61. Laurie Jo Bissell, "Women's Athletic Association at University of California, Berkeley" ("Student Papers on University of California, Berkeley, Sports and Other Subjects Relating to Athletics," CU-283: 7), UCB; "Women's Athletic Association Bulletin," 1 (September 23, 1929): 3, ("W.A.A. Advisors Reports, Fall 1925–Spring 1930," CU-283: 7), Women's Athletic Association Records, 1921–1972, UCB.

62. "Women's Athletic Association Bulletin," 1 (September 23, 1929): 3.

63. See "Point System of Athletic Awards" ("Athletics-Awards, Point System of," box 1), Special Collections and Archives, Maryville College, Tennessee.

64. Gerber, "The Controlled Development of Collegiate Sport for Women," 9. Gerber noted that "few departments of physical education for women separated their three functions of teacher preparation, general physical education and extra-curricular physical recreation or sport into different staff responsibilities. The same people who ran the sport programs conducted the teacher education programs and this indoctrinated the teachers-to-be in the national philosophy. The result was a remarkable unanimity of opinion expressed in the literature and practices for several decades" (9). The example of the University of Texas illustrates the close coordination of activity and education programs. Early in the 1930s, one Texan explained how her university's different components worked together toward common goals: "surrounded by these very same facilities, by the organization of class work, and by the activities of the Women's Athletic Association and being a definite participant for three years, the University of Texas girl is given every opportunity to develop her love of activity, her vital forces, and her power as a leader." Even after 1933–34, when the University of Texas inaugurated a novel experiment that officially divided the women's intramurals and the University of Texas Sports Association (UTSA was the name given in 1932 to the Texas WAA), the programs remained symbiotic. Although each of the two programs enjoyed more autonomy than at almost all other institutions, they were by no means completely independent because of the continuing personnel overlap. Anna Hiss, the director of physical training for women, still served as the director of intramural sports and the faculty advisor of the USTA. Moreover, three additional members of the physical education faculty had seats on the intramurals committee, and the intramural council's secretary also functioned as the general secretary of the USTA. See "University of Texas Sports Association and Intramural Sports for Women," 1.

65. For an example of the traditional view of women's athletics, see the University of Texas, where the stated purpose of the women's intramural program was to have "a sport for every girl and every girl in a sport." The "aims" also included these sentiments: "to establish ideals based on participation rather than competition," "to see that sports are wisely chosen, wisely promoted, and wisely supervised," "to promote competition that stresses enjoyment of sport and the development of good sportsmanship and character rather than those types that emphasize the making and breaking of records and the winning of championships for the enjoyment of spectators or for the athletic reputation or commercial advantage of the institution and the organization," and "to promote interest in awards for athletic accomplishment that have little or no intrinsic value," among other things. See "University of Texas Sports Association and Intramural Sports for Women," 4–5.

66. Hornbuckle, "Women's Sports and Physical Education at the University of Tennessee," 84–86.

67. Ibid., 89–92, 94–100.

68. Nancy Brown, "A Comparison of the Number of Participants in the Women's Athletic Association before and after the Abolishment of the Physical Education Requirement," 3–4 ("U .C.W.A.A.," 3:10, CU-67.1), Student Papers on University of California, Berkeley, Sports and Other Subjects Relating to Athletics,

UCB. For the intended lack of competition between intramural programs and the regular WAA teams and sports, see Frederica Bernhard, "W.A.A. Intramural Sports, Fall, 1933" ("I.M. Managers Reports," CU-283:4), Women's Athletic Association Records, 1921–1972, UCB. In this report Bernhard noted, "The Board wishes to continue its policy of providing an opportunity for competition for a relatively small number of students, particularly those students who are not attending regular coaching practices of the various sports in W.A.A. It feels that an understanding of conditions here makes it quite clear that a large intramural organization cannot function in competition with so many other campus activities" (1).

69. "Women's Athletic Association Bulletin," 2 (February 24, 1930) in ("High School Sports Day Reports," CU-283: 6), Women's Athletic Association Records, 1921–1972, UCB; Louise S. Cobb, "Review of W.A.A., Fall, 1930" ("W.A.A. Advisor's Reports, Fall 1930–Spring 1935," CU-283, box 7), Women's Athletic Association Records, 1921–1972, UCB.

70. "Intramural Activities, Spring, 1931" ("I.M. Managers Reports," CU-283:4), Women's Athletic Association Records, 1921–1972, UCB.

71. Frederica Bernhard, "Intramural Organization, Fall, 1931," 1 ("I.M. Managers Reports," CU-283:4), Women's Athletic Association Records, 1921–1972, UCB.

72. Bernhard, "Intramural Organization, Fall, 1931," 2–3; Frederica Bernhard, "Intramural Organization, Spring, 1932" ("I.M. Managers Reports," CU-283:4), Women's Athletic Association Records, 1921–1972, UCB.

73. Frederica Bernhard, "W.A.A. Intramural Organization, Spring, 1933" ("I.M. Managers Reports," CU283:4), Women's Athletic Association Records, 1921–1972, UCB; Bernhard, "W.A.A. Intramural Sports, Fall, 1933."

74. Frederica Bernhard, "W.A.A. Intramural Sports, Fall and Spring 1936–37," 2 ("I.M. Managers Reports," CU-283:4), Women's Athletic Association Records, 1921–1972, UCB; Frederica Bernhard, "Intramural Sports Report, Fall, 1938" ("I.M. Managers Reports," CU-283:4), Women's Athletic Association Records, 1921–1972, UCB; Frederica Bernhard, "Intramural Sports Report, Spring, 1939," 6 ("I.M. Managers Reports," CU-283:4), Women's Athletic Association Records, 1921–1972, UCB.

75. *Reveille* 29 (1930): 215 and 217 (quote on 215).

76. *Reveille* 30 (1931): 211, 216, 217; *Reveille* 31 (1932): 195, 202.

77. *Reveille* 32 (1933): no page number given, see "Women's Basketball" section.

78. *Reveille* 32 (1934): 203.

79. Ibid.

80. Ibid., 203 and 206.

81. *Terrapin* (1936): 175. The UM yearbook changed its name in the 1935–36 school year from the *Reveille* to the *Terrapin*.

82. *Terrapin* (1936): 185; *Terrapin* (1937): 164–65.

83. *Terrapin* (1940): 148–49.

CHAPTER 5. "The Instinctive Urge to Compete"

1. The National Association of College Women, founded by Mary Church Terrell in 1910, condemned intercollegiate athletics in 1929 because of "all their undesirable physiological and sociological features." Terrell, quoted in Rita

Liberti, "'We Were Ladies, We Just Played Basketball Like Boys': African American Womanhood and Competitive Basketball at Bennett College, 1928–1942," *Journal of Sport History* 26 (1999): 575.

2. Cahn, *Coming on Strong*, 69–70 (quotations on 70). Liberti, "'We Were Ladies,'" 567–68.

3. Quoted in Liberti, "'We Were Ladies,'" 576.

4. Cahn, *Coming on Strong*, 70. For a larger discussion of how African American colleges and universities viewed men's athletics as a forum through which they might "engage white society in a broad-based dialogue about democratic principles and practices," see Patrick B. Miller, "To 'Bring the Race along Rapidly': Sport, Student Culture, and Educational Mission at Historically Black Colleges during the Interwar Years," *History of Education Quarterly* 35 (1995): 111.

5. Shaw, *What a Woman Ought to Be and to Do*, chap. 2 and 3, *passim* (quotation on 7).

6. Cahn, *Coming on Strong*, 66; Helen Schleman, "Experimental Play Days: Experimental Intercollegiate Competition for Women," *Journal of Health and Physical Education* 1 (February 1930): 8.

7. Ethel M. Bowers, "Play Days and Festivals," a section of a larger article entitled "News of Girls' and Women's Athletics, Conducted by the Women's Athletic Section, American Physical Education Association, and the Women's Division, N.A.A.F.," *American Physical Education Review* 34 (October 1929): 472.

8. Kubow, "Once Upon a Time There Was This Stick," 2–4; Marilyn Figone, "A History of Women's Crew at the University of California" (1:9, CU-67.1), Student Papers on University of California, Berkeley, Sports and Other Subjects Relating to Athletics, UCB, 5–6; Schleman, "Experimental Play Days," 8.

9. Margaret Connable to [University of California WAA] President, November 3, 1927 ("Triangular Sports Day," CU-283:5), Women's Athletic Association Records, 1921–1972, UCB; "Triangular Sports Day, 1929 [Program]" ("Triangular Sports Day," CU-283:5), Women's Athletic Association Records, 1921–1972, UCB; Louise S. Cobb, "Triangular Sports Day, December 1929" ("Triangular Sports Day," CU-283:5), Women's Athletic Association Records, 1921–1972, UCB.

10. Louise S. Cobb, "Review of W.A.A., Spring 1929" ("W.A.A. Advisors Reports, Fall 1925–Spring 1930," CU-283: 7), Women's Athletic Association Records, 1921–1972, UCB.

11. WAA Minutes, February 24, 1931, 126; March 10, 1931, 128; March 17, 1931, 129–30, (W.A.A. Minute Book, vol. 3, CU-283), Women's Athletic Association Records, 1921–1972, UCB. First quotation is from February 24 meeting. The guideline quotations are from the March 17 meeting.

12. WAA Minutes, October 11, 1932, vol. 3, 186–87.

13. WAA Minutes, September 12, 1932, vol. 3, 227.

14. WAA Minutes, October 30, 1934, vol. 4, 30; WAA Minutes, November 13, 1934, vol. 4, 37.

15. Louise S. Cobb, "The Women's Athletic Association, 1935–1936" ("W.A.A. Advisor's Reports, Fall 1935–Spring 1940," CU-283:7), Women's Athletic Association Records, 1921–1972, UCB.

16. "Triangular Sports Day Luncheon Committee Report, 1937" ("Triangle Sports Day," CU-283:5), Women's Athletic Association Records, 1921–1972, UCB;

"Minutes of the Triangular Conference, October 15, 1937" ("Triangle Sports Day," CU-283:5), Women's Athletic Association Records, 1921–1972, UCB; Louise S. Cobb, "W.A.A. Council Notes," September 21, 1937 ("W.A.A. Advisor's Reports, Fall 1935–Spring 1940," CU-283:7), Women's Athletic Association Records, 1921–1972, UCB.

17. "Report Submitted by Dorris Berry" ("Triangular Sports Day," CU-283:5), Women's Athletic Association Records, 1921–1972, UCB.

18. For a description of the plans for the 1938 TSD, see "Minutes of the Triangular Conference, April 23, 1938" ("Triangle Sports Day," CU-283:5), Women's Athletic Association Records, 1921–1972, UCB. To see Victorville University's invitation to an "intercollegiate Riding meet," see WAA Minutes, vol. 4, March 28, 1939. To read about an invitation from San Francisco State College to a Riflery Play Day, see Louise S. Cobb, "W.A.A. Council Notes, March 4, 1939" ("W.A.A. Advisor's Reports, Fall 1935–Spring 1940," CU-283:7), Women's Athletic Association Records, 1921–1972, UCB. To read the discussion about the dangers of having too many TSDs, see WAA Minutes, March 5, 1940, vol. 4, 251.

19. For Schleman's argument, see Schleman, "Experimental Play Days," 8.

20. Schleman, "Experimental Play Days," 8–10 (quotation on 10).

21. Elizabeth Halsey, "Play Day at the University of Michigan," *Journal of Health and Physical Education* 1 (February 1930): 12–13.

22. Cahn, *Coming on Strong*, 66; *Reveille* 34 (1934): 204; *Terrapin* (1936): 173.

23. *Terrapin* (1936): 190 and 191; *Terrapin* (1940): 148.

24. Cahn, *Coming on Strong*, 57; *Reveille* 29 (1930): 218. Page 215 of this same edition recognizes rifle as "Maryland's only intercollegiate sport." In the 1932–33 academic year, the University of Maryland women's rifle team won twenty-five out of twenty-seven matches. They competed against teams from all across the country. A partial listing of their opponents includes the University of California at Los Angeles, the University of California at Berkeley, the University of Wichita, South Dakota State, the University of Missouri, Columbia University, Northwestern University, Louisiana State College, the University of Georgia, the University of Michigan, Cornell University, the University of Vermont, Washington University, and Cornell University. For a complete listing, see the "Women's Rifle Team" section in the *Reveille* 32 (1933). While it appears obvious that the women's team did not travel for matches against these scattered teams, the yearbooks do not often refer to the matches as "telegraphic meets." Exceptions to this rule appear in the 1935 and 1936 editions. See The Terrapin (1935): 117, and the *Terrapin* (1936): 193. For information on the rarer, and therefore more noteworthy, face-to-face competitions with George Washington University and Beaver College, see the "Maryland Women in Sports" section in the *Terrapin* (1941).

25. *Reveille* 29 (1930): 218; *Reveille* 30 (1931): 220.

26. *Reveille* 31 (1932): 204; "Women's Rifle Team Section," *Reveille* 32 (1933).

27. *Terrapin* (1937): 167. This page identifies the members of the team who won varsity letters and the freshmen who earned numerals. It also explains that "the success of the team may be attributed to the patient and expert instruction of Sergeant George J. Uhrinak." This was Uhrinak' s first year, but his predecessors had also been male.

28. See *Reveille* 29 (1930): 219; *Reveille* 31 (1932): 205; *Reveille* 32 (1933): "Women's Rifle Team" section; and *Terrapin* (1938): "Women's Rifle Team" section.

Also see WAA Minutes, January 27, 1931, vol. 3, 119, Women's Athletic Association Records, 1921–1972, UCB; WAA Minutes, February 3, 1931, 121, and WAA Minutes, February 17, 1931, 124; Louise S. Cobb, "W.A.A. Council Notes," March 4, 1939 ("W.A.A. Advisor's Reports, Fall 1935–Spring 1940," CU-283:7), Women's Athletic Association Records, 1921–1972, UCB; WAA Minutes, October 1, 1940, vol. 5, 25.

29. Louise S. Cobb, "Notes From W.A.A. Council, February 4, 1936" ("W.A.A. Advisor's Reports, Fall 1935–Spring 1940," CU-283:7), Women's Athletic Association Records, 1921–1972, UCB.

30. Ibid.

31. Gladys E. Palmer to L. W. St. John, November 1, 1940, 1 ("Women's National Collegiate Athletic Association: 1940–41, 1949," 9/e–5a/8), Accession 84/94, Women's Athletics, TOSUA.

32. Ibid., 2.

33. Evans, *Born for Liberty,* 206–8. Evans discusses the importance to American women of a "closely linked network of women in the New Deal." These women were important not just for what they did but also for what they symbolized to American women and other "people on the margins" of society (ibid., 207).

34. Blanche M. Trilling, "The Significance of Physical Education in Modern Life," *Journal of Health and Physical Education* 9 (January 1938): 3.

35. See Adele H. Stamp to Albert C. Ritchie, January 24, 1929 ("Governor Albert C. Ritchie—Correspondence," ser. 1, box 4), Papers of Adele H. Stamp, SC, UML; "Secretary's Report for the Month of April, 1931" (League of Nations Association [MD Branch], 1931–1941, Official Correspondence, Other Papers, Minutes, Publications," ser. 2, box 7), Papers of Adele H. Stamp, SC, UML; Adele H. Stamp to J. Edgar Hoover, June 20, 1939 ("Prince George Country Federation of Women's Clubs, Letters [J. Edgar Hoover], 1937–1951, Meeting Announcements, News Clippings," ser. 2, box 9), Papers of Adele H. Stamp, SC, UML.

36. "Notes on Interview with Anna Hiss," 4–5 ("Notes on Interview with Anna Hiss," 3R246), Physical Training for Women Records, CAH, UTXA. For example, neither Hiss nor Stamp spoke out in favor of the OSU plan for a women's NCA.A and an intercollegiate golf tournament.

37. Mary Daniels, "The Historical Transition of Women's Sports at The Ohio State University, 1885–1975, and Its Impact on the National Women's Intercollegiate Setting during That Period" (PhD diss., Ohio State University, 1977), 92–107 (quotation on 125).

38. Gittings, "Why Cramp Competition?," 10.

39. Daniels, "The Historical Transition of Women's Sports at The Ohio State University," 136; "The Future" section of "Girls Athletics."

40. Daniels, "The Historical Transition of Women's Sports at the Ohio State University," 124.

41. Gittings "Why Cramp Competition?," 54.

42. Ibid., 11 (quotation on 12).

43. Ibid., 54.

44. Ibid. As mentioned in chapter 4, the YMCA/YWCA interaction of the 1920s demonstrates that this fear of creeping male organizational dominance was not paranoia. See Vandenberg-Daves, "The Manly Pursuit of a Partnership between the Sexes."

45. Grace. B. Daviess, "In Answer to 'Why Cramp Competition?,'" *Journal of Health and Physical Education* 2 (March 1931): 29.

46. Anne Hodgkins, "In Answer to 'Why Cramp Competition?,'" *Journal of Health and Physical Education* 2 (March 1931): 29.

47. Ibid.

48. Helen Jacobs, "Women's Tennis," *California Monthly* 24 (April 1930): 27.

49. Ibid., 27, 46 (quotations on 27).

50. Myrtle K . Miller, "The 1937 National Archery Meet," *Journal of Health and Physical Education* 8 (December 1937) 616–17, 636–37; Louise S. Cobb, "W.A.A. Council Notes," February 1, 1938 ("W.A.A. Advisor's Reports, Fall 1935–Spring 1940," CU-283:7), Women's Athletic Association Records, 1921–1972, UCB.

51. Cahn, *Coming on Strong,* 97.

52. Ibid., 97–98; Hult, "The Governance of Athletics for Girls and Women," 72.

53. Ibid.; LeKubow, "Once Upon a Time There Was This Stick," 2–4; Louise S. Cobb, "Notes from W.A.A. Council, January 21, 1930" ("W.A.A. Advisors Reports, Fall 1925–Spring 1930," CU-283:7), Women's Athletic Association Records, 1921–1972, UCB; WAA Minutes, January 28, 1930, 86 (W.A.A. Minute Book, vol. 3, CU-283), Women's Athletic Association Records, 1921–1972, UCB; Cahn, *Coming on Strong,* 97.

54. WAA Minutes, September 8, 1941, 144 (W.A.A. Minute Book, vol. 3, CU-283), Women's Athletic Association Records, 1921–1972, UCB.

55. For examples of other times the California WAA discussed hockey events, see WAA Minutes,

November 13, 1934 (vol. 4, 36) and November 5, 1935 (vol. 4, 73). See also the "Minutes of the Finance Committee Meeting," September 26, 1938 (2:7, CU-282), Associated Students Records, UCB.

56. Gladys Palmer, "Policies in Women's Athletics," *Journal of Health and Physical Education* 9 (November 1938): 567 and 187.

57. Ibid., 566.

58. Sumption, *Sports for Women,* 72, 97.

59. Palmer, "Policies in Women's Athletics," 567 (emphasis in original).

60. University of Texas director of women's physical education Anna Hiss had made a similar argument in early 1937 in her article "Girls' Basketball Leagues: What About Them—and Our Responsibilities?" Hiss called for trained physical educators to get involved in municipal and industrial leagues, assisting those outside the academy to coordinate and operate their tournaments by the correct standards. Hiss wrote, "Damage has been done by the conscientious objectors who are unwilling to get in and work with the 'questionable' groups. Would it not be wise to grasp every opportunity that comes our way, or even to seek opportunities of affiliation which would enable us to assist in these tournaments? Eventually we may be able to give something of real value to the leagues." See Anna Hiss, "Girls' Basketball Leagues: What About Them—and Our Responsibilities?," *Journal of Health and Physical Education* 8 (February 1937): 104.

61. Daniels, "The Historical Transition of Women's Sports at The Ohio State University," 136.

62. Gladys Palmer, "Concerning Competition," 1 ("Physical Education: Golf: Intercollegiate Tournament [Women]: 1941–1942," RG 9/e-1/17), Director of Athletics, TOSUA.

63. Palmer, "Concerning Competition," 3.

64. Ibid.

65. See R. Smith, "Women's Control of American College Sport," 116, footnote 31.

66. See "The Future" section of "Girls Athletics."

67. Palmer, "Concerning Competition"; R. Smith, "Women's Control of American College Sport," 110.

68. "Yost Speech," 1 ("Intercollegiate Golf Tournament: 1941," 9/e–5a/8), Accession 84/94, Women's Athletics, TOSUA; "Program for the Intercollegiate Golf Tournament for Women" ("Physical Education: Golf: Intercollegiate Tournament [Women]: 1941–1942," 9/e–1117), Director of Athletics, TOSUA.

69. Daniels, "The Historical Transition of Women's Sports at The Ohio State University," 144; Dorothy [Sumption] and Tony [Violet Boynton] to Gladys Palmer, April 2, 1941 ("Competition: Issues Concerning: 1941, 1951," 9/e–5a/8), Accession 84/94, Women's Athletics, TOSUA. Punctuation and capitalization mine.

70. Daniels, "The Historical Transition of Women's Sports at The Ohio State University," 145; Ruth H. Atwell to Gladys Palmer, April 24, 1941 ("Tournament Correspondence: 1941," 9/3–15/1/18), Women's Golf, TOSUA.

71. Daniels, "The Historical Transition of Women's Sports at The Ohio State University, 145." Daniels interviewed Yost in January 1975.

72. Both quotations come from "Yost Speech," 5.

73. All information and quotations are from "Yost's Notes" ("College Director's Convention: 1941," 9/e–5a/8), Accession 84/94, Women's Athletics, TOSUA. Ronald Smith refers to these pages as Gladys Palmer's "Diary, April 26–29." I disagree with this attribution for several reasons. First, the pages refer to Palmer as "Miss Palmer" and to Yost as "Yost." In fact, the author refers to only Palmer as a "Miss." It seems doubtful that an author would reserve a title only for herself in an informal journal of a conference. Secondly, in the section describing the Sunday afternoon meeting the author wrote, "Watson and Yost to tea where we were first ignored, then jumped on." The use of "we" implies that the author was either Yost or Geneva Watson. Later in the text, however, the author noted, "I don't think Geneva convinced her." Finally, in her dissertation, Mary Daniels consulted the same notes and interviewed Mary Yost extensively, presumably discussing the notes with her, and Daniels refers to the papers as the "personal notes of Mary Yost." See Daniels, "The Historical Transition of Women's Sports at The Ohio State University," 147.

74. The article notes that the paper was first presented at the April 1938 convention. See Palmer, "Policies in Women's Athletics." See Evelyn Bielefeld to Gladys Palmer, April 24, 1941, and Ruth Links to Mary Yost, May 13, 1941 ("Tournament: Correspondence: 1941," 9/e–15/1/18), Women's Golf, TOSUA.

75. Janet Owen was not new to debates about women's college athletics. In 1936 she had published an article entitled "Publicity—Your Right Hand Man" (*Journal of Health and Physical Education* 7 [October 1936]: 481–84, 520–22).

76. Janet Owen, "Sports among Women: National Collegiate Golf Tourney Is Opposed by Physical Education Directors," *New York Herald Tribune,* May 3, 1941 ("Physical Education: Golf: Intercollegiate Tournament [Women]: 1941–1942," 9/e–1/7), Director of Athletics, TOSUA. For a fuller discussion of American socialism and communism during the 1930s, as well as of the fears of these groups, see Ellen

Schrecker, *Many Are the Crimes: McCarthyism in America* (New York: Little, Brown, and Company, 1998).

77. For more on this topic, see chapter 3. Also, see again Yost, "The Place of Varsity Athletics in a Program of 'Athletics for All;'"; Sanders, "Builders of Character of Teachers of Activities?"; Stoddard, "The Relation of Physical Education to the Purposes of Democracy"; Oberteuffer, "Physical Education and the Democratic Ideal"; Hughes, "The Role of Intercollegiate Athletics in National Preparedness," Scott, "The Ramparts We Watch."

78. Daniels, "The Historical Transition of Women's Sports at The Ohio State University," 148–49 (quotation on 149). For a complete listing of schools represented, see ibid., 149–50. To view the entry forms themselves, see the folder "Tournament (1st): 1941: (2nd) 1946" (9/e–15/1/4), Women's Golf, TOSUA. Based on remarks and introductions from the opening banquet, the actual number of participants seems to have been thirty. The photograph of the 1941 contestants included in the 1946 entry form, however, included thirty golfers with one not included.

79. For examples of these letters see Katherine W. Montgomery to Gladys Palmer, undated ("Tournament: Correspondence: 1941," 9/e–15/1/18), Women's Golf, TOSUA; Elizabeth Halsey to Gladys Palmer, May 1, 1941 ("Competition: Issues Concerning: 1941, 1951," 9/e–5a/8), Women's Athletics, TOSUA. Halsey was the University of Michigan author of an earlier-cited article about play days.

80. "Yost Speech," 5. For examples of correspondence regarding the disapproving observers coming to Columbus, see Ruth H. Atwell to Gladys Palmer, June 20, 1941, and June 27, 1941 ("Tournament Correspondence: 1941," 9/e–15/1/18), Women's Golf, TOSUA. Atwell was the "jellyfish" from the Atlantic City convention and was also the chairman of the National Section of Women's Athletics of the American Association for Health, Physical Education, and Recreation. Also see the letter copied to Palmer from Elizabeth Kelley, president of the National Association of Directors of Teachers of Physical Education for College Women, to Helen Hazeltine, June 29, 1941 ("Tournament [1st]: 1941; [2nd] 1946," 9/e–15/1/4), Women's Golf, TOSUA.

81. "Remarks Made before the Tournament," 5 ("Physical Education: Golf: Intercollegiate Tournament [Women]: 1941–1942," 9/e–l/17), Director of Athletics, TOSUA.

82. "Yost Speech," 6, 2, and 8; "First Women's Intercollegiate Golf Tournament Held at The Ohio State University Golf Course, June 30 to July 3, 1941," 9 ("Intercollegiate Golf Tournament: 1941," 9/e–5a/8), Women's Athletics, TOSUA.

83. Information and quotations from "Yost Speech," 6.

84. For comments from participants on the event, see pages 4–5 of "Meeting Held at the Ohio State University Golf Course, Thursday, July 3, 1941, 2:00 P.M." ("Physical Education: Golf: Intercollegiate Tournament [Women]: 1941–1942," 9/e–l/17), Director of Athletics, TOSUA. Palmer's thoughts appear on 5–6, with the quotation from page 6.

85. "Yost Speech," 9.

86. Rader, *American Sports*, 220–21 (quote on 220).

87. Ibid., 287.

88. R. Smith, "Women's Control of American College Sport," 110–11; Hult, "Governance of Athletics for Girls and Women," 73–74.

CHAPTER 6. Commercialized Sport and Imagined Communities

1. Susman, *Culture as History*, 199–200.

2. Benedict Anderson, *Imagined Communities: Reflections on the Origins and Spread of Nationalism*, rev. ed. (New York: Verso, 1991), 4 and 5 (quotation on 5). Historian Daniel Boorstin identified the importance of colleges and universities to feelings of community in the earliest days of US higher education. In his chapter "Culture with Many Capitals: The Booster College," Boorstin argued, "The distinctively American college was neither public nor private, but a *community* institution." See Daniel J. Boostin, *The Americans: The National Experience* (New York: Random House, 1965), 152–61 (quotation on 160). Thomas Bender has discussed the nature of American communities in ways similar to Anderson. Bender argued, "Territorially based interaction represents only one pattern of community, a pattern that becomes less and less evident over the course of American history." Bender also wrote that "community . . . is best defined as a network of social relations marked by mutuality and emotional bonds." Again, this definition applies nicely to the bands of alumni, or just citizens, who root for a particular state university's athletic teams. See Thomas Bender, *Community and Social Change in America* (New Brunswick, NJ: Rutgers University Press, 1978), 6 and 7.

3. Anderson, *Imagined Communities*, 6–7 (quotations on 6).

4. Ibid., 7.

5. Chapter 3, "The Origins of National Consciousness," addresses most directly the importance of print capitalism to the formation of national identities. See especially pages 37–39, 44–46. Chapter 2, "Cultural Roots," explores the significance of the breakdown of traditional notions of time. Anderson, *Imagined Communities*.

6. Scholars of the American consumer culture usually argue that it appeared in its mature form during the 1920s, and they associate its emergence with a shift in societal valuations of an individual's "character" and personality. Susman has argued that United States underwent a gradual shift in emphasis from inner-directed "character" stressing morality to outer-directed "personality" emphasizing popularity and admiration. He reviewed more than two hundred sources and found that many words were directly associated with "character." According to Susman, these words included "*citizenship, duty, democracy, work, building, golden deeds, outdoor life, conquest, honor, reputation, morals, manners, integrity*, and above all, *manhood*" (emphasis his). Throughout the 1930s, athletic leaders offered most of these words as products of intercollegiate athletics. See Susman, *Culture as History*, 273–74.

7. *Sixty-Sixth Annual Report of the Board of Trustees of the Ohio State University to the Governor of Ohio, for the Year Ending June 30, 1936* (Columbus: Ohio State University, 1936), quotes from pages 1 and 60.

8. *Sixty-Fifth Annual Report of the Board of Trustees of the Ohio State University to the Governor of Ohio, for the Year Ending June 30, 1935*, 30.

9. Raymond A. Pearson to Deans, Directors and Heads of Administrative Departments, April 11, 1932 ("Publicity [1933]," ser. 7, box 31), Records of the President's Office, SC, UML.

10. Robert G. Sproul, "Report of the President of the University, December 31, 1932," in *Report of the President of the University of California, 1930–1932* (Berkeley: University of California, 1932), 9 and 10.

11. Robert G. Sproul, "Report of the President of the University," in *Report of the President of the University of California, 1938–1940* (Berkeley: University of California Press, 1941), 11. In 1932, University of Maryland president Raymond Pearson wrote, "It has been my conviction that the tangible values derived from the University of Maryland and its affiliated departments amount to several times as much annually as the funds expended to maintain the entire institution, and that the intangible values I have mentioned are in the nature of a net profit on the investment." See document beginning, "It is entirely proper that public funds expended by an Institution such as University of Maryland should be carefully considered by the people of the State" ("Publicity [1932–33]," ser. 7, box 31), Records of the President's Office, SC, UML.

12. Pollard, *History of the Ohio State University*, 293; Callcott, *History of the University of Maryland*, 319; Geary Eppley to Dr. Crothers, November 6, 1936 ("Geary Eppley, 1934–1936," ser. 2, box 4), Papers of Geary Eppley, SC, UML; C. Walter Cole to Faculty and Staff Members, May 1939 ("Alumni Day, 1939–1941," ser. 1, box 1), Papers of Geary Eppley, SC, UML.

13. "Minutes of Executive Session, April 12, 1938" (1:7," CU-282), Associated Student Records, UCB.

14. Sproul, "Report of the President of the University, December 31, 1932," 9. Thelin made this same point in the chapter called "Regional Pride and Institutional Prestige," writing, "Intercollegiate athletics joined agricultural extension services as a means by which the state university could extend real and symbolic affiliation to all citizens of the state or region." Thelin, *Games Colleges Play*, 70. At the University of Maryland, for example, in an explanation of the university's structure, the Department of Physical Education and Recreation was included in the same group as the Agricultural Experiment Station and the Extension Service. Moreover, the UM Board of Regents also served as the State Board of Agriculture. See "Efficiency and Economy," *Maryland Alumni News 8* (January 1937): 1.

15. Albert F. Woods, foreword to "New Athletic Field of the University of Maryland," 1920 ("New Buildings, June 1, 1937 through April 30, 1938 [1920–1938]," ser. 8, box N1), Records of the President's Office, SC, UML.

16. Savage, *American College Athletics*, 79.

17. "Keep Neyland," *Orange and White* (Knoxville), October 31, 1939.

18. L. A. Nichols to Arthur H. Breed, September 8, 1931 ("1931:329, A-E," CU-5, ser. 2), Office of the President Papers, UCB; J. F. MacKenzie to Agnes Robb, November 1, 1930 ("1930:283," CU-5, ser. 2), Office of the President Papers, UCB.

19. Charles H. Lupton to Geary Eppley, October 27, 1939 ("Football, 1937–39," ser. 2, box 2); and Geary Eppley to the President, November 16, 1936 ("Georgetown University, 1928–1938," ser. 2, box 2), both in Papers of Geary Eppley, SC, UML. In 1937, the University of Texas responded immediately to an inquiry from US congressman Lyndon Johnson's office about why he had not received his complimentary football pass. The ticket was in the mail the next day. See MB to WLMC, September 23, 1937 ("Intercollegiate Athletics, 1937–38," VF 5/E.A.), President's Office Records, 1907–1968, CAH, UTXA.

20. For quotations see J. C. G. to Robert G. Sproul, December 19, 1935 ("1935:390," CU-5, ser. 2), Office of the President Papers UCB. For more background information see folder "1935:390-Clippings" in the same location, especially, "Coast

Football Storm," *San Francisco News*, December 12, 1935. The letter also included this passage: "When Assemblyman Ray Williamson of San Francisco threatens to pull down the University of California by building up the state colleges at Fresno and San Jose and the Junior College at Sacramento, as a reprisal, we cannot go along with him. It is absurd to let this football issue decide our thinking about educational needs."

21. Sproul, "Report of the President of the University, December 31, 1932," 21; "University of Maryland Alumni Association Financial Statement for Fiscal Year June 1940 to June 1941" ("Alumni Day, 1939–1941," ser. 1, box 1), Papers of Geary Eppley, SC, UML.

22. See any volume of the *Maryland Alumni News* during the 1930s to see evidence of this point. See the *Ohio State University Monthly* 28 and 30 for the Ohio State evidence.

23. "Reader Comment," *California Monthly* 27 (September 1933): 125; "New Football Weekly," *California Monthly* 38 (June 1937): 21; *California Monthly* 41 (October 1938): 48.

24. George A. Pettitt, *Twenty-Eight Years in the Life of a University President* (Berkeley: University of California Press, 1966), 136.

25. "Football Registration," *Alcade* 18 (November 1929).

26. Advertisement, "The Tang of Football Is in the Air and the Thrill of College Days Is Once Again with US," *California Monthly* 23 (September 1929): 69; "Telegram to Be Used for Big Game Meetings," November 16, 1936 ("1936:330," CU-5, ser. 2), Office of the President Papers, UCB.

27. "The Tang of Football iIs in the Air and the Thrill of College Days Is Once Again with Us," 69.

28. "Big Game Rallies," *California Monthly* 27 (November 1931): 22.

29. "Football Movies," *Maryland Alumni News* 7 (January 1936): 1.

30. "Committee Report of Scouting and Use of Motion Pictures," 1937 (Intercollegiate Conference—Athletic Director's Correspondence, 1930–1938," 9/e–1/9), Director of Athletics, TOSUA.

31. E. Gordon Hammond to Geary Eppley, April 6, 1937 (Geary Eppley, 1937–1961," ser. 2, box 4), Papers of Geary Eppley, SC, UML.

32. Nathan W. Dougherty, "Control of Athletics in the University of Tennessee," July 20, 1940 (box 21, 12), Nathan Washington Dougherty Collection, SC, UTNK; University of Tennessee Board of Trustees Minutes, April 10, 1940, 3, UTNA; OSU Athletic Board Minutes, May 28, 1930, "The Report of the Athletic Board by the Faculty Committee on Athletics and Athletic Eligibility for the Year 1937–38 to the University Faculty," 62; OSU Athletic Board Minutes, March 1, 1939, 9.

33. University of Texas Athletic Council Minutes, January 10, 1937, 428; Dana X. Bible to H. Y. Benedict, March 17, 1937 (emphasis in original) ("Intercollegiate Athletics, 1936–37," VF 5/E.B), President's Office Records, 1907–1968, CAH, UTXA. Two years later, alumni of the University of Maryland offered to raise $10,000 a year to add to a football coach's regular salary if this would allow Maryland to hire the best coach available. The alumni wanted Maryland to "enter upon a major football program whereby they will be able to play on par with major teams in the adjoining states such as Pennsylvania, University of Virginia, North Carolina, and Duke." See Charles H. Lupton to Geary Eppley, October 27, 1939.

34. "Coach of Bears Spurns $20,000 to Buy Players," Associated Press, no date ("1931:456," CU-5, ser. 2), Office of the President Papers, UCB.

35. For more on the perceived promise and implementation of university-sponsored educational radio programs, see Joan Shelley Rubin, *The Making of Middlebrow Culture* (Chapel Hill: University of North Carolina Press, 1992), 270–76. In 1936, OSU president Rightmire wrote, "More directly than any other way, perhaps, the University brings to the people of Ohio its resources through radio. No agency of human communication has more powerfully gripped the minds of men, and none so swiftly and widely makes human contact possible." See *Sixty-Sixth Annual Report of the Board of Trustees of the Ohio State University to the Governor of Ohio, for the Year Ending June 30, 1936*, 39.

36. "Keep Neyland," October 31, 1939.

37. "Beating N.Y.U. Gains Vols Nation-Wide Fame," *Orange and White*, December 8, 1931. An article in December 1931 addressed many of these same points, noting, "It is becoming more obvious that practice games with easy opponents will not fill the stands. Schools that are anxious to hold their spectator interest will therefore have to be careful in building their schedules to include more teams that offer close and interesting rivalry." See "Is Football Waning?," *Journal of Health and Physical Education* 2 (December 1931): 22. As Andrew Doyle illustrated through his discussion of the University of Alabama's 1926 and 1927 trips to the Rose Bowl in California, a victory by a southern team against a prominent team from outside the region could galvanize the entire South. After Alabama shocked the University of Washington, beating its team 20–19, an Atlanta newspaper argued that an accurate headline should read, "The South 20, the West 19." See Andrew Doyle, "'Causes Won, Not Lost': College Football and the Modernization of the American South," *International Journal of the History of Sport* 11 (August 1994): 235.

38. Stadtman, *The University of California*, 266–67 (quoted on 268). For more on the sense of rivalry between northern and southern California and how this related to the UCB-UCLA relationship, see Pettitt, *Twenty-Eight Years in the Life of a University President*, 134–35.

39. Stadtman, *The University of California*, 268; S. W. Cunningham to Robert G. Sproul, March 15, 1932 ("1932:435," CU-5, ser. 2), Office of the President Papers, UCB. The perceived Berkeley preference for USC over UCLA was sure to rile the UCLA supporters. As Thelin pointed out, UCLA was locked into a fierce competition with USC for superiority in Los Angeles. Having UCB play USC, a school with lower academic standards at the time, when it would not face UCLA, a school with the exact same standards, made no sense to many Californians. See Thelin, *Games College Play*, 27.

40. "University of California vs. U.C.L.A. Football game, November 4, 1933" ("1933:833," CU-5, ser. 2), Office of the President Papers, UCB.

41. Robert G. Sproul's Prepared Remarks, November 4, 1933 ("1933:500," CU-5, ser. 2), Office of the President Papers, UCB.

42. Ibid.

43. S. W. Cunningham to Robert G. Sproul, March 15, 1932.

44. Howard J. Savage, John T. McGovern, and Harold W. Bentley, *Carnegie Foundation for the Advancement of Teaching: Current Developments in American College Sport*, Bulletin 26 (New York: Carnegie Foundation for the Advancement of Teaching), 1931.

45. A Mother to President University of California [no date] ("1931:79," CU-5, ser. 2), Office of President Papers, UCB.

46. "Tennessee Goes West," unattributed article in W. W. Coile to James D. Hoskins, December 30, 1939 ("Civil Works Administration [1933–1935]," AR–1, box 4), President's Papers, 1867–1954, SC, UTNK.

47. H. L. Ferguson to Gentlemen, October 25, 1931, and Robert G. Sproul to H. L. Ferguson, October 31, 1931 ("1931:41," CU-5, ser. 2), Office of the President Papers, UCB. In 1935, the University of Texas Athletic Council refused to accept a Lucky Strike advertisement for the football program's front cover. See University of Texas Athletic Council Minutes, May 24, 1935, 375.

48. Pollard, *Ohio State Athletics*, 285; University of Texas Athletic Council Minutes, March 19, 1931, 375, and November 16, 1932. Fielding Yost, the University of Michigan athletic director, wrote to Big Ten commissioner John Griffith to explain his university's band's actions. According to Yost, the university could not afford to send its band to Columbus for the game, and Buick came through with the money. In gratitude, the Michigan band formed "B U C K I" on the field and then, while playing "Thanks for the Memories," the band moved the "I" between the "U" and the "C." According to Yost, this formation lasted only five seconds. Yost also acknowledged that the band thanked Buick over the public address system, but he pointed out that he did not consider this an advertisement and that Ohio State had sold advertisements for the game programs and the broadcasts anyway. See copy of letter from Fielding H. Yost to John L. Griffith" December 9, 1938 ("Intercollegiate Conference—Athletic Director's Correspondence, 1938–1940," 9/e–1/9), Director of Athletics, TOSUA.

49. William A. Dynes to L. B. Broughton, October 17, 1935 ("Football, 1931–36," ser. 2, box 5), Papers of Geary Eppley, SC, UML.

50. G. F. Pollock to E. M. Livingston, October 14, 1935 ("Football 1931–36" ser. 2, box 5); and Geary Eppley to Sidney Mc Ferrin, January 13, 1938 ("Football, 1937–39," ser. 2, box 5), both in Papers of Geary Eppley, SC, UML.

51. For example, the University of Maryland athletic director made frequent visits to Maryland civic clubs. See Henry K. Pasma to Geary Eppley, October 12, 1937 ("Geary Eppley, 1937–1961," ser. 2, box 4), Papers of Geary Eppley, SC, UML.

52. Paul J. Kruesi to J. P. Hess, October 15, 1938 (Folder 12, AR–8, box 2), University of Tennessee Business Managers Papers, SC, UTNK.

53. For more about the meager revenue generated by the radio contracts, see chapter 2 (in this book) and Watterson, *College Football*, 182. Watterson referred to the broadcast contracts as a "small but helpful source of income" and pointed out that at many schools "the profits barely justified commercial radio. Nevertheless, the profit motive triumphed in most cases over arguments for preserving amateur athletics" (182). The Minutes of the Executive Committee of the Southern Conference, September 27–28, 1931 ("Southern Conference Minutes, 1930–31," ser. 2, box 14), Papers of Geary Eppley, SC, UML; James F. Yates to H. C. Byrd, February 3, 1932 ("Southern Conference, 1932, January–February," ser. 2, box 10), Papers of Geary Eppley, SC, UML; Minutes of the University of Texas Athletic Council, September 9, 1932, 312, and September 4, 1934, 35. For the most comprehensive study of the communications revolution in college sports, see Ronald A. Smith, *Play-by-Play: Radio, Television, and Big-Time College Sport* (Baltimore: The Johns Hopkins University Press, 2001).

54. James F. Yates to H. C. Byrd, February 3, 1932.

55. D.M.B., "Don't Stop Broadcasts," *California Monthly* 34 (March 1935): 6.

56. Mr. and Mrs. C. C. Crampton to Robert G. Sproul, November 25, 1935 ("1935:330," CU-5, ser. 2), UCB.

57. Sperber, *Shake Down the Thunder*, 461, 452–53, 393.

58. James F. Yates to H. C. Byrd, February 3, 1932.

59. W. Y. Boswell, House Resolution Number 2, December 2, 1931 ("Athletic Association [1900–1945], AR–1, box 3), President's Papers, 1867–1954, SC, UTNK.

60. Gilbert, *Neyland*, 125.

61. Minutes of Southern Conference Annual Meeting, December 13, 1935 ("Southern Conference, 1935," ser. 2, box 10), Papers of Geary Eppley, SC, UML.

62. J. E. Gurich to Robert G. Sproul, May 5, 1933 ("1933:500," CU-5, ser. 2), Office of the President Papers, UCB.

63. *California Monthly* 38 (April 1937): 21.

64. John McNamara, *University of Maryland Football Vault: The History of the Terrapins* (Atlanta, GA: Whitman Publishing, LLC, 2009).

Epilogue

1. James J. Duderstadt, *Intercollegiate Athletics and the American University* (Ann Arbor: University of Michigan Press, 2008), 11–12.

2. Murray Sperber, *Beer and Circus: How Big-Time College Sports Is Crippling Undergraduate Education* (New York: Henry Holt, 2000); James Shulman and William Bowen, *The Game of Life: College Sports and Educational Values* (Princeton: Princeton University Press, 2001).

3. Shulman and Bowen, *The Game of Life*, 269 and 271.

4. Knight Foundation Commission on Intercollegiate Athletics, *A Call to Action: Reconnecting College Sports and Higher Education*, 29, see http://www.knightcommission.org/images/pdfs/2001_knight_report.pdf, accessed October 4, 2014.

ESSAY ON SOURCES

While this brief essay will never be able to acknowledge all of the books and articles that have enabled me to write this book, my hope is that it will be useful to readers who want some guidance about where to look for some of the most important works on the variety of topics and themes that this book addresses. Put differently, in the language of my students, I want to use this space to give a "shout out" to all of the scholars who have paved the way for me and a "heads up" to those who want to follow me down some of the paths I have traveled. In no way, however, should readers consider this list exhaustive; it is intended, instead, to highlight the authors and works that were most influential on my thinking and writing.

My academic training is in modern US history, and I feel like I should begin with some of the most important general works on the Great Depression era. David Kennedy's *Freedom from Fear: The American People in Depression and War, 1929–1945* (Oxford University Press, 1999) remains one of the most readable and scholarly overviews of the Depression and World War II eras and is a fantastic place to start for readers wanting to get a general sense of the period. Warren Susman's *Culture as History: The Transformation of American Society in the Twentieth Century* (Pantheon, 1985) contains a number of incredibly thoughtful and insightful essays on American culture and life of the 1920s and 1930s. His questions about popular culture and the way the Depression affected the American middle class, as much as his answers, influenced the early scope of this project. While its topic is not as directly relevant as some of these other works, Benedict Anderson's *Imagined Communities: Reflections on the Origins and Spread of Nationalism* (Verso, 1991) was just as important in shaping my approach to this topic. Anderson's thoughts about how national feelings are formed and perpetuated helped me understand the ways that alumni and fan communities operated during the Depression.

Other classic texts on the political, social, and economic history of the Depression include Lizabeth Cohen's *Making a New Deal: Industrial Workers in Chicago, 1919–1939* (Cambridge University Press,

1990) and William Leuchtenburg's *Franklin D. Roosevelt and the New Deal, 1932–1940* (Harper and Row, 1963). Of course, it is hard to go wrong with Studs Terkel's *Hard Times: An Oral History of the Great Depression* (Random House, 1970) if one wants to read about the ways that the Depression affected the lives of all types of Americans. If you are looking for a fictional account of the growing inequality of the industrializing era, Upton Sinclair's *The Flivver King* offers a fascinating account of the diverging fortunes of Henry Ford's family and that of one of his workers. That one of the worker's sons ends up being a football star at the University of Michigan and benefits from the corruption associated with his status only makes the book more interesting and relevant. The fact that all of these books remain in print, with many of them recently appearing in updated editions, speaks to their legacy and importance.

Anyone writing about college sports owes a great debt to Ronald Smith, and I am no exception to this rule. Smith's *Sports and Freedom: The Rise of Big-Time College Athletics* (Oxford University Press, 1988) documents the rise of US intercollegiate athletics and destroys the myth of a pure, idyllic past of virtuous student athletes and pure amateurism. Readers interested in learning more about US intercollegiate athletics should probably start here. In addition to his many other works in the field, Smith's 2003 *Play-by-Play: Radio, Television, and Big-Time College Sport* (Johns Hopkins University Press) is the definitive account of the complicated rise of college sports-broadcasting agreements and networks.

For those more interested in college football, John Watterson has delivered the authoritative book that the field has long needed. His *College Football: History, Spectacle, Controversy* (Johns Hopkins University Press, 2002) is a fantastic read, and it should satisfy almost any reader's appetite for a work that details the rise and development of college football and that places it squarely in the broader context of US history. John Thelin's *Games Colleges Play: Scandal and Reform in Intercollegiate Athletics* (Johns Hopkins University Press, 1996) covers much of the same territory as Watterson's book, but Thelin has a more narrow focus on major scandals and controversies. If, for example, readers want more detail on the Carnegie report than is provided in this book, they would benefit from picking up Thelin's book.

More recently, Brian Ingrassia's *The Rise of Gridiron University: Higher Education's Uneasy Alliance with Big-Time Football* (University Press of Kansas, 2013) offers fascinating insights into the reasons football found a permanent place on American campuses in the late 1800s and early 1900s.

For works that examine the cultural meanings of college football, readers should immediately turn to the works of Michael Oriard. A former University of Notre Dame football player, Oriard has authored at least two books that should be required reading for serious students of US sports history. His *King Football: Sport and Spectacle in the Golden Age of Radio and Newsreels, Movies and Magazines, the Weekly and the Daily Press* (University of North Carolina Press, 2001) offers a close reading of popular press accounts to discern the ways that football achieved true cultural significance in American life, and his *Reading Football: How the Popular Press Created an American Spectacle* (University of North Carolina Press, 1993) is equally valuable to anyone interested in how college football became an important cultural phenomenon at the end of the nineteenth and the beginning of the twentieth centuries.

One of the best books about college football during this, or any period, is Robin Lester's narrative of the rise and fall of the University of Chicago's football team. While my book is a story of institutional commitment to big-time athletics, Lester's *Stagg's University: The Rise, Decline, and Fall of Big-Time Football at Chicago* (University of Illinois Press, 1995) does a masterful job documenting one prominent university's reasons for abandoning its spot in the big-time athletic hierarchy. Murray Sperber, on the other hand, utilizes an enormous amount of primary sources to document the University of Notre Dame's desire to use football to raise its national profile and to establish itself as a leading university. His *Shake Down the Thunder: The Creation of Notre Dame Football* (Holt, 1993) is one of the best-written examinations of how a university consciously used football as a recruiting, marketing, and economic engine.

For books that look closely at sports during specific and related historical eras, readers have several excellent, if quite different, options. For the era immediately before the 1930s, Raymond Schmidt's *Shaping College Football: The Transformation of an American Sport, 1919–1930*

(Syracuse University Press, 2007) documents the institutional commitments universities made to their athletic programs in the 1920s, while also detailing the emergence of several stars and newly prominent programs across the nation. Similarly, Kurt Kemper's *College Football and American Culture in the Cold War Era* (University of Illinois Press, 2009) continues the discussion of how many Americans viewed college athletics as political and promotional vehicles during the decades after the Depression.

Charles Alexander's *Breaking the Slump: Baseball in the Depression Era* (Columbia University Press, 2002) examines the economics of professional baseball during the 1930s, and it served as an inspiration for (and a confirmation of) my approach in this book. I just hope my success at analyzing financial trends and institutional responses comes close to approximating his. William Baker's biography of Jesse Owens, *Jesse Owens: An American Life* (University of Illinois Press, 1986), still stands as the best biography of the Ohio State University Depression-era great. If readers want a broader look at how athletics became overtly politicized during this period, then they have several options in front of them. David Large's *Nazi Games: The Olympics of 1936* (W. W. Norton, 2007) is one of the best.

If Watterson is the starting place for readers who want more on college football, then Susan Cahn's *Coming on Strong* (Harvard University Press, 1994) plays the same role for folks who are interested in learning more about the broader history of women's sports, both inside and outside of schools. It's simply the place to start for almost any topic related to modern American women's sport. For works with more specific foci, Joan Hult and Marianna Trekell's edited collection, *A Century of Women's Basketball: From Frailty to Final Four* (American Alliance for Health, Physical Education, Recreation, & Dance, 1991), is still quite useful, as are Susan Cayleff's *Babe: The Life and Legend of Babe Didrikson Zaharias* (University of Illinois Press, 1996) and Larry Engelmann's *The Goddess and the American Girl: The Story of Suzanne Lenglen and Helen Wills* (Oxford University Press, 1988). Ying Wushanley's *Playing Nice and Losing: The Struggle for Control of Women's Intercollegiate Athletics, 1960–2000* (Syracuse University Press, 2004) is an excellent resource for those who want to explore the development of women's college sports further.

I would be remiss if I didn't conclude this brief essay with a special thanks to the scholars who have devoted an enormous amount of time and effort to the largely thankless task of writing institutional histories. Books on the history of a single university are almost never destined to make someone's career or to win prestigious awards, but they are essential to people interested in the questions that have fascinated me. Each of the universities examined in this book is fortunate to have had, at some time in its history, a scholar who was willing to devote years to writing a history of the university or its athletic programs. My work would not have been possible without their efforts, and I want to conclude this brief essay by expressing my gratitude to them.

INDEX